DATE DUE

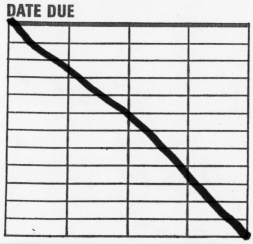

THE MAGNIFICENT CHARTER

BOOKS BY J. B. EDMOND

*The Magnificent Charter: The Origin and Role
of the Morrill Land-Grant Colleges and Universities*

Fundamentals of Horticulture
(with A. M. Musser and F. S. Andrews,
first and second editions; with T. L. Senn and F. S. Andrews,
third edition; with T. L. Senn, F. S. Andrews,
and R. G. Halfacre, fourth edition)

Sweet Potatoes: Production, Processing and Marketing
(with G. R. Ammerman)

THE MAGNIFICENT CHARTER

The Origin and Role of the Morrill
Land-Grant Colleges and Universities

J. B. Edmond
Professor Emeritus of Horticulture
Mississippi State University

An Exposition-University Book

Exposition Press   Hicksville, New York

Library of Congress Catalog Card Number: 78-59962

ISBN 0-682-49079-2 (Hardcover)
0-682-49081-4 (Paperback)

Printed in the United States of America

To all faculties past and present
and to all students past and present
of the Morrill land-grant colleges and universities

CONTENTS

TABLES AND FIGURES

TABLES

FIGURES

FOREWORD

Joseph Bailey Edmond was born in a cottage by the railroad tracks on October 11, 1894, in Yorkshire, England. In 1912 after eight years of formal school in England, he came to America with his father and moved to Saginaw, Michigan. His father pursued railroading the rest of his career and Joseph became interested in horticulture and has pursued this career throughout the rest of his lifetime.

During World War I he served in the 32nd Infantry division of the Michigan-Wisconsin National Guard in France. Following the war he enrolled in a college preparatory course at Michigan Agricultural College. In 1923, he received his B.S. degree from the original "Cow College"–Michigan State University. He enrolled in another land-grant college, Iowa State University, and obtained his Master of Science degree in 1924. Then he returned to Michigan State as an instructor in horticulture until 1929 when he transferred to the University of Maryland, another land-grant institution, where he obtained his Ph.D. degree in 1933.

"Dr. Joe," as he was known by the students, was on the horticulture staff at Mississippi A & M College from September 1931 to August 1935, at which time he moved to Clemson Agricultural College in South Carolina. In 1944, he served with the State Department in the New Hebrides as a part of the war effort. Following the war, Dr. Edmond worked for the Texas, Georgia, and Louisiana Agricultural Experiment Stations and taught horticulture at the Berry schools near Rome, Georgia, before returning to Mississippi State University and continuing his career in teaching at land-grant institutions.

Professor Emeritus Joseph Bailey Edmond has continued to live at Mississippi State University since his retirement in 1962. During his professional career he maintained that "sophomores" were his primary speciality. His deep interest in students is confirmed by his establishment of trust funds for the Joseph B. Edmond Student Awards Program of the Southern Region of the American Society for Horticultural Science. These contests are held annually and the cash awards have been perpetuated by trust funds.

Dr. Edmond's unique history as an immigrant to America has put him in an unusual position to appreciate the vast, cumulative benefits which have accrued to all Americans from the Morrill land-grant system, as it was established and maintained by the Morrill Land-Grant Act of 1862. Dr. Edmond has worked at more than a half a dozen land-grant institutions and has been especially interested in the tremendous impact of these institutions on the development of modern America.

J. P. OVERCASH
Professor of Fruit Science
Mississippi State University

PREFACE

The purpose of this little book is to provide an opportunity for the student to acquire a working knowledge and appreciation of the part the Morrill land-grant colleges and universities have played in the life and development of the United States and its people. This development started in 1855 when two states, Michigan and Pennsylvania, established within their respective borders an entirely new type of four-year college— a college for the education and training of young men in the great field of agriculture. Later, Maryland, in 1856, and Iowa, in 1858, also established a four-year college for the education and training of young men in the field of agriculture. Finally, the Congress in 1862 passed the first Morrill Act which not only provided for the education and training of young men and young women in agriculture but also for the training of young men and women in the mechanic arts. Further, the Morrill Act provided for the establishment of this new type of college in each of the respective states and territories. In general, these new colleges became known as Agricultural or Agricultural and Mechanical (A and M) Colleges.

In the beginning, the first presidents and the first faculties of each respective college found that there was no science of North American agriculture. Consequently, they initiated programs to develop this science. In general, the professors (1) held workshops or conferences with groups of farmers throughout the respective states and territories to determine the farmers' pertinent production problems, (2) conducted experiments at each college to obtain data for the solution of these problems, and (3) disseminated the results of these experiments to the farmers of their respective states and territories. In other words, the professors carried the colleges to the farmers right from the start. This method of operation was extremely beneficial to each of the two groups: the professors began to upbuild the science of North American agriculture, and the farmers began to realize that the Morrill land-grant colleges were available for the solution of their production problems. In this way, the Great Triad of American Agriculture, the so-called green revolution, was born: (1) the research phase—the use of research data in the education and training of students, (2) the resident teaching phase and the dissemination of the results of research data to farm people, and (3) the extension phase.

As a result, and in a relatively short time, the Agricultural and the Agricultural and Mechanical Colleges became an integral part in the life of the rural people.

Since the Great Triad in agriculture promoted the welfare of the farmer, the legislature of the various states and territories, as well as the Congress, appropriated funds for the development of research, resident teaching, and extension programs in all fields of constructive endeavor— in engineering, home economics, business and industry, education, applied science, veterinary medicine, liberal arts, and so forth. In other words, a Great Triad—research, resident teaching, and extension—has developed in all fields, and accordingly the Morrill land-grant colleges and universities extended their services to all fields. Further, a crowning achievement of these institutions is the development of continuous or continuation education—the opportunity for all of the people to enrich their lives by learning after their formal period of education. Thus, the Morrill land-grant colleges have never been "ivory towers". They have always been, and we hope they always will be, an integral part in the lives of all the people. Their relation to the growth and development of the people as a whole is a wonderful story, and the writer hopes the reader will enjoy reading the book as much as he has enjoyed putting this wonderful story together.

In conclusion, the author expresses thanks and appreciation to all colleagues who have assisted in any way in the preparation of the manuscript. In particular, he is indebted to Dr. J. P. Overcash, Professor of Fruit Science, Mississippi State University, for writing the foreword, to Mrs. Luceille Mitlin, Martha Irby, Mary Downey, and Roseanne Hinesley of the Library Staff of Mississippi State University for assistance in library research, to Dr. George Lewis and Mrs. Frances Coleman for use of the facilities of the Library of Mississippi State University, to Drs. C. C. Singletary and B. J. Stojanovic for providing office space in the Plant Science Building of Mississippi State University, to Mrs. Janice Malbon, Certified Professional Secretary, Starkville, Mississippi, for typing the manuscript, and to Dr. William L. Giles, President Emeritus, Mississippi State University, for his encouragement and his making me "feel at home."

April 15, 1978   J. B. EDMOND

THE MAGNIFICENT CHARTER

1

THE FIRST TAX-SUPPORTED
PEOPLES' COLLEGES

*Religion, morality, and knowledge being necessary for good
government and the happiness of mankind, schools and the means
of education shall forever be encouraged.*
—THE NORTHWEST ORDINANCE, 1787

THE STATUS OF EARLY
NORTH AMERICAN INDIAN AGRICULTURE

In common with other members of the human race the American
Indian obtained his food and clothing, either directly or indirectly,
from the green plant. Grasses in the wild sustained the American bison,
which supplied meat, clothing, and shelter; green aquatic plants sustained many kinds and varieties of fish; and green land plants in the
wild supplied food for fowl in the wild, turkeys, partridges, grouse,
and pigeons. Further, many native fruit and vegetable crops were
available: North American and Muscadine grapes, North American
plums, blackberries, huckleberries, strawberries, and cranberries, and
snap beans, lima beans, tepary beans, pumpkins, and squash. Of major
interest is corn. By the time of the 1492 discovery: (1) the Indians had
discovered and isolated many types of corn—flint, dent, sweet, and
pop; (2) they had learned how to grow, fertilize, and cultivate the
plants, and how to store and grind the kernels into a meal from which
to make their bread; and (3) they knew how to extend the culture of
this valuable crop-plant from its native home in Peru throughout the
United States and to the southern part of Canada.

THE STATUS OF COLONIAL AGRICULTURE

Essentially, colonial agriculture was a blend or mixture of British
and North American Indian agriculture. With the exception of the potato
and possibly the tomato, the British were unfamiliar with the kinds of
plants grown by the Indians, and the Indians in turn were unfamiliar
with the kinds grown by the British. For example, the British had no
knowledge of the culture of corn, the basic bread crop of the Indians,
and the Indians had no knowledge of the culture of wheat, the basic

3

bread crop of the British. Further, the English colonists had to accustom themselves to the relatively rigorous climate of North America, with its hot summers and cold winters, as compared with the milder climate of England, with its cool summers and mild winters. The colonists had to develop methods of clearing the land (the girdling of trees and planting of seed among the dead trees and stumps was not uncommon), and determine the adaptability of European methods to the North American climate. Of great significance was the colonial adaptation of Indian methods in the production and use of corn. In general, the Indians taught the colonists how to grow and fertilize the plant, and how to harvest, store, and grind the kernels for the making of meal. In fact, the baked meal called johnnycake soon became a popular article of diet among the early settlers.

THE STATUS OF HIGHER EDUCATION
DURING COLONIAL TIMES

During the colonial period institutions of higher learning were called colleges. In general, these institutions were modeled on or patterned after the single college of the English and Scottish universities. Examples are the several colleges of Oxford and Cambridge universities. With the exception of Kings' College, now known as Columbia University, and the College of Philadelphia, now called the University of Pennsylvania,[1] the colleges were denominational institutions and were founded by a specific religious sect. For example, the Puritans of Massachusetts founded Harvard College, the Congregationalists of Connecticut founded Yale College, and the Presbyterians of New Jersey founded Princeton College. In general, only nine institutions of higher learning were established during the colonial period and they were for men only.

For any given college the governing body consisted of a group of laymen, usually leaders of the congregation, called the Board of Trustees. These boards assumed both the legislative and executive phases in the running of the college. In other words, they appointed the president and faculty, approved the courses of study, and established rules and regulations for the conduct of the students. The president simply followed the directions of the Board, the faculty had no authority in running the college, and the students had no voice in the formation of rules and regulations for their conduct. The courses of study consisted of large doses of Latin, Greek, and moral philosophy, moderate doses of mathematics and religious subjects, and small doses of science.

---

[1]King's College and the College of Philadelphia were founded by the colonial governments of New York and Pennsylvania, respectively.

Tuition was high, and very few, if any, scholarships were available. In fact, only the wealthy could afford to send their young men to this type of institution.

TWO NEW IDEAS

The first settlers dreamed of a new kind of education. They wanted colleges that would meet the practical needs of *all* the citizens more directly than did the institutions that stressed classical studies and training only for the learned professions of law, human medicine, and the ministry. They wanted peoples' colleges that their sons *and daughters* could attend at minimum cost and that would put emphasis on research and instruction that might increase agricultural production, improve the conditions of life of *all* of the people, and support the young nation's growing industries. In other words, the people believed that children of the nonwealthy as well as the wealthy should have the opportunity to acquire a college education, and that agriculture and other nation-wide industries should be included in college courses and curricula.

THE PUBLIC DOMAIN AND THE LAND-GRANTS

The public domain refers to the area of land that belongs to the public and is administered and disposed of by the federal government. From 1781, when the Union was established, to 1867, when the territory of Alaska was formed, the United States acquired huge tracts of land, as follows: (1) the cession of land from 1781 to 1802 by Massachusetts, New York, Virginia, Connecticut, North Carolina, South Carolina, and Georgia, each of which had claims of land outside its original boundary to the federal government; (2) the Louisiana Purchase in 1803, the Florida Purchase in 1819; (3) the treaty with Great Britain in 1846; (4) the treaty with Mexico in 1848; (5) the Texas Proposal in 1850; (6) the Gadsden Purchase in 1853; and (7) the Alaska Purchase in 1867. This land area in the aggregate was enormous—a total of 1 billion, 442 million acres, and was known as the public domain.[2]

To promote settlement of the country and education of *all* of the people, Congress made three types of land-grants: (1) land-grants for the physiographic improvement of the land. Examples are the building of canals, highways, and certain railroads and the building of drainage ditches through swampy, potentially fertile areas; (2) land-grants to political and religious exiles, to explorers for the federal government,

---

[2]About one-fourth of the public domain still exists, but most of it comprises the mountains of the western states and is practically worthless for agricultural production.

and to veteran soldiers of the Revolution; and (3) land-grants for the education of all of the people. Of these educational grants, there were three types. The first type is known as section grants for the establishment and support of the first-to-eighth-grade schools. At first the sixteenth section of each township was set aside solely for the support of these schools. Later, as settlement proceeded westward to the semiarid and arid areas, this grant was increased to two sections and finally to four sections per township. If these designated sections were in private hands, the states were permitted to select other sections from the public domain. The usual shape of a township was a square six miles on each side, with a total area of thirty-six square miles. Each section had an area of 640 acres, or one square mile.

These section grants have had a profound effect on the development of the American system of education. They resulted in the development of the little one-room township schools throughout the country in which all the children of a township were given the opportunity to acquire a first-to-eighth-grade education. Horace Mann, a New England legislator, was the principal proponent of this system. In 1837, he stated that a free and comprehensive education is the birthright of each child. Accordingly, the people of the various states and territories, in agreement with this right, abolished child labor in the factories, and authorized the development of curricula for each of the eight grades.

The second type of grant is known as township grants. In 1836 the Congress authorized the granting of two townships: one for the establishment of a seminary of learning within a given territory and one other for the establishment of a first state university within any given state. In many cases the location of the seminary of learning became the location of the first state university. Examples are Louisiana State University, the University of Michigan, and the University of Wisconsin. In fact, a total of 46,080 acres was allotted to the endowment of each state university. For this reason, the first state universities may be considered as land-grant institutions.

The third type is known as the proportional or quantity grants for the establishment and support of colleges of agriculture and engineering and related subjects. Thirty thousand acres of the public domain were allotted for each member of Congress, in accordance with the census of 1860. For example, Rhode Island with its two senators and two representatives was entitled to 120,000 acres, Mississippi with its two senators and five representatives was entitled to 210,000 acres, and Pennsylvania with its two senators and twenty-four representatives was entitled to 780,000 acres. Because Representative and later Senator Justin S. Morrill of Vermont sponsored the legislation that awarded these grants, they are referred to as the Morrill land-grants, and the colleges that received the benefits of the Morrill land-grants are referred to in this book as the Morrill land-grant colleges and universities.

THE FIRST TAX-SUPPORTED PEOPLES' COLLEGES

To develop and determine the practicability of the two ideas set forth on page 5, the people of four states established peoples' colleges as follows: the Agricultural College of the State of Michigan, the Farmers' High School of Pennsylvania, the Maryland Agricultural College, and the Iowa Agricultural College and State Farm. There are at least three reasons why "agriculture" or "farmers" is a part of the official name: agriculture during colonial times, and during the first hundred years in the life of the nation, was by far the major occupation of the people; most of the people lived on farms and in small towns and in villages; and, most important, agriculture was a worthy subject for study in college.

THE AGRICULTURAL COLLEGE
OF THE STATE OF MICHIGAN—1855[3]

In the establishment of the Michigan institution, two important events occurred. The first was the State Constitutional Convention of 1850. As with similar organizations the work of the Convention was done by several committees. In particular, the Committee on Education was requested to "inquire into the expediency of providing for the establishment of an agricultural school and a model farm in connection therewith." As a result of their work, an excellent provision for the promotion of agriculture was included in the State Constitution. This provision, embodied as Article 3, Section 11, states: "The Legislature shall encourage the promotion of intellectual, scientific, and agricultural improvement and shall as soon as practicable, provide for the establishment of an agricultural school."

The second event occurred between 1850 and 1855 and consisted of a great debate throughout the state and within the Michigan State Agricultural Society on the location and the administration of the proposed school. Should the college be attached to and become an integral part of the University of Michigan at Ann Arbor? Or at the State Normal

---

[3]Between 1855 and 1964, the Michigan Institution has had six official names: Agricultural College of the State of Michigan, 1855; State Agricultural College, 1861; Michigan Agricultural College, 1862; Michigan State College of Agriculture and Applied Science, 1925; Michigan State University of Agriculture and Applied Science, 1955; and Michigan State University, 1964.

School at Ypsilanti? Or should it be established in a place in isolation from any other higher educational institution? Finally, in December, 1854, the State Agricultural Society passed the following resolution: "Resolved that the agricultural college shall be separate from any other institution." It presented a memorial to the legislature "praying for an appropriation sufficient to purchase a body of land suitable for an experimental farm and erection of suitable buildings for an agricultural school placing it on a basis of its own, separate from other institutions of learning and for the endowment of the same in such manner as shall place it upon an equality with the best colleges of the state."

Events in 1855 proceeded rapidly. A bill for the establishment of the college with an endowment of twenty-two sections of land[4] was introduced in the legislature on February 3; it passed both houses on February 9; and the bill was signed by Governor Kinsely S. Bingham on February 12, which is considered the founding date of the college.

A legislative committee, after inspecting ten proposed sites, selected a 676-acre tract three miles east of the village of Lansing. The Board of Education (trustees) authorized the erection of three buildings: College Hall with offices, classrooms, library, and laboratories; Saints Rest with rooms and dining halls for housing the students; and a brick barn for housing the farm animals. The Board appointed Dr. J. R. Williams, a graduate of Harvard, as president of the institution; approved a curriculum consisting of subjects within botany, chemistry, mathematics, history, and English; and established rules and regulations for the conduct of the students. The college formally opened with dedication services in the Chapel on May 13, 1857, began instruction with an enrollment of sixty-three young men on the following day, and graduated seven of these young men with the degree of bachelor of science in agriculture in May, 1861.

President Williams, in the major address of the dedication exercises, set the tone of the institution and stressed the need to develop the "whole man": "First, we will begin with the farmer himself. It has been aptly said that the only part of European agriculture that has not been improved is the man who tills the soil. Now there is where we ought to begin. Morally, mentally, and physically he must be a man before he can be a farmer. He should be able to execute the duties of highly respected stations with self-reliance and intelligence. He should be qualified to keep his accounts, survey his land, and speak and write his native tongue with ease and vigor. He must learn to subordinate himself with his animal and vegetable life around him to those inex-

---

[4]The twenty-two sections were part of an original grant from the federal government.

orable laws, moral and physical, the violation of which meets with swift retribution. A great advantage of such colleges as this is that the farmer will learn to observe, learn to think, and learn to learn."[5]

THE FARMERS' HIGH SCHOOL
OF PENNSYLVANIA—1855

As with Michigan Agricultural College, the Farmers' High School of Pennsylvania was established by the people through their representatives in the state legislature and under the sponsorship of the Pennsylvania State Agricultural Society. The chairman of the Society at its second annual meeting (1853) appointed a committee to inquire into the expediency of establishing an agricultural school. This committee in turn recommended that a general convention be held to consider this proposal. This proposal was met with acclaim and enthusiasm and resulted in the establishment of a charter of incorporation. However, this charter required a Board of Trustees consisting of a representative from each of the fifty agricultural societies within the state. This large number proved to be unwieldly for the successful transaction of business. As a result the legislature approved a second charter, which required a total of thirteen men instead of the original fifty. Governor James Pollack signed the charter of incorporation on February 22, 1855. Thus, the first two tax-supported peoples' colleges were established at practically the same time.

However, unlike the situation in Michigan, and in common with the original thirteen states, no public land for a land-grant was available in Pennsylvania for the endowment of the college. In general, funds became available by acts of the state legislature, and through the generosity of agricultural societies of the State of Pennsylvania and private individuals. Between 1855 and 1861 the state legislature made two appropriations: one for $50,000 in 1857 and one other for $49,900 in 1861. The State Agricultural Society gave $10,000; the legacy of Mr. Elliott Cresson, a public-spirited citizen of Philadelphia, gave $5,000; five men of the original Board of Trustees gave $2,500 each, and the citizens of Center County donated $1,000. In addition, General James Irwin, a member of the original Board of Trustees, donated two hundred acres of his farm in Center County for the establishment of an experimental farm in connection with the school. This undoubtedly explains why the Peoples' College of Pennsylvania was established in Center County.

As at the Michigan College, the Board of Trustees assumed respon-

---

[5]This in the author's opinion is a remarkable statement.

sibility for both the legislative and the executive functions of the school. In general, they determined the beginning and the end of the school year, appointed the president and members of the faculty, outlined the courses of study, developed the rules and regulations for the conduct of the students, and determined the entrance requirements and the number of students entitled to enter from each of the several counties. In addition, the Board authorized the erection of a building for the housing of the students and the conducting of classes. This building, known as "Old Main," still functions as an integral part of the University. They also appointed Dr. Evan Pugh as president of the college.

Dr. Pugh was the son of a Pennsylvania farmer-blacksmith. He attended the Manual Labor Academy at Whitestown, New York, earned the Ph.D. at the University of Göttingen, Germany, with a major in chemistry, and spent two years at the Rothamstead Agricultural Experiment Station of Great Britain, the oldest agricultural experiment station in the world. In 1862, he was elected a fellow of the Royal Philosophic Society and a fellow of the American Philosophic Society. Other members of the faculty included J. S. Whiten, professor of natural science and botany; R. C. Allison, professor of mathematics and history; and David Wilson, professor of English and English literature.

As at the Michigan college, classes for any given year began in the early spring and closed in the early fall with the vacation period during the winter. At the beginning, all courses were of college grade, and a four-year curriculum was established comprising English, mathematics, philosophy, and science. The Farmers' High School opened its doors on February 16, 1859, with an enrollment of a hundred and nine students and graduated fourteen students with the bachelor of science in agriculture degree in 1861. One year later the legislature changed the official name of the institution to the Agricultural College of Pennsylvania, and in 1874 to Pennsylvania State College—the first agricultural college to acquire the name State College.

MARYLAND AGRICULTURAL COLLEGE—1856

A unique case is the formation of Maryland Agricultural College. In sharp contrast to the Michigan, Pennsylvania, and Iowa institutions, Maryland Agricultural College was founded by planters more or less as a business corporation rather than by the taxpayers as a whole. Some of these planters were members of the Maryland State Agricultural Society, and in society affairs Mr. C. B. Calvert was their leader. Mr. Calvert descended from the Lords Baltimore and was a son of a wealthy planter. He graduated from the University of Virginia at the age of nineteen and returned to Riverdale, about six miles northeast of Washington, D.C., to manage his father's estate, which included a 2,200-acre hay and dairy farm. For many years he was president of the Maryland State Agricultural Society, a leader in the U.S. Agricultural Society, and a promoter in the creation of the U.S. Department of Agriculture. In 1851, when the Maryland State Agricultural Society was discussing problems pertaining to the funding of the proposed college, Calvert suggested the sale of stock certificates that would have a total value of $50,000. In 1856 a large delegation of the Society appeared before the General Assembly, the state legislature, with a petition to approve the sale of the stock, provided the General Assembly appropriate $6,000 annually to help defray the expenses of the proposed college. In 1856 a bill granting this request was passed by the State House of Representatives by a vote of 40 to 4, by the State Senate by a vote of 20 to 2, and signed by Governor T. W. Ligon on March 6. Thus, March 6, 1856, may be considered the founding date of the institution.

In January, 1858, the shareholders met to elect a Board of Trustees with C. B. Calvert as president and N. B. Worthington, editor of the *American Farmer*, as secretary. The Board, in turn, assumed responsibility for both the legislative and executive functions in the management of the college. A committee on location, after visiting several proposed sites, selected a 420-acre tract of the Calvert Riverdale plantation. Other committees arranged for the renovation of the Rossborough Inn and the barns and for the building of homes for the faculty and for a five-story classroom, laboratory, and office building. The Board also appointed the president and members of the faculty as follows: Benjamin Hullowell, president and professor of philosophy, engineering, and history; G. C. Schaeffer, M.D., professor of agriculture, chemistry, geology, and mineralogy; H. D. Gough, professor of mathematics, astronomy, and engineering; and B. Lorino, professor of languages. On October 6, 1858, the college opened with an enrollment of thirty-four students.

In a series of meetings the members of the Board were not in agreement on the purpose of the college. Should the college be given over to the education of young men of the poor as well as those of the rich? Or should the institution be given over to the education of the rich only? The former would require no or very little tuition and an opportunity for the students to work their way through, and the latter would permit the assessment of large fees. The prospectus or outlook for a source of funds seems to have been the deciding factor, since the amount of money from sale of the stock and the small annual state appropriation would have been insufficient to defray the expenses of the college, let alone supply funds for growth. As a result, the advocates of free tuition and manual labor were decisively defeated and the Board set the annual fees for each student at $260 a year. Thus, at one stroke the founders rejected their earlier democratic ideals, and turned the little college into an institution for the sons of the wealthy. In addition, the Civil War had a drastic effect on student enrollment. Because of enlistments, only seventeen students remained on campus for the 1860-1861 session. In fact, the Maryland Agricultural College was practically inactive during the last two years of the war. In 1865 with the Morrill endowment in operation the state legislature assumed responsibility for the funding of the college and in this way Maryland Agricultural College became a tax-supported institution, and the first land-grant college of the State of Maryland.

IOWA AGRICULTURAL COLLEGE
AND STATE FARM—1858[6]

As with the Agricultural College of the State of Michigan, the Farmers' High School of Pennsylvania, the Iowa Agricultural College and State Farm was established by the people of Iowa through their representatives in the state legislature. As with the other two states, the editors of farm magazines and the leaders of the Iowa State Agricultural Society agitated for equal opportunity for all of the people to acquire a college education. For example, the *Iowa Farmer and Horticulturist* published a plan for an agricultural school that included the following features: (1) a farm for the conducting of experiments to test and expand scientific knowledge in agriculture, (2) an instructural program for all sciences underlying agriculture, and (3) a modern farm to demonstrate the best practices. In 1856 the Iowa State Agricultural Society at its third annual fair in Des Moines endorsed a measure for the establishment of an agricultural school. In 1857 this measure passed the House by a vote of 39 to 22, but amendments of the Senate that the House disapproved could not be reconciled before the end of the session. In 1858 the debate in the General Assembly centered on the question of whether the opportunity to acquire a college education should be limited to children of the wealthy or extended to children of the poor as well as the wealthy. Mr. P. F. Gue, a former president of the State Agricultural Society and a member of the House, made an eloquent plea for equal opportunity for all of the people: "Why should land-grants and money endowments be given to enable the wealthy to choose the so-called learned professions to get all the inestimable

---

[6]In the past there has been disagreement as to whether Michigan Agricultural College or Iowa Agricultural College was the first land-grant college. In the author's opinion, both institutions are entitled to the term "first," since the records show that the legislature of the State of Michigan awarded twenty-two sections of land for the establishment of the Michigan institution, and the legislature of the State of Iowa was the first to qualify for the Morrill Endowment. On this basis, Michigan Agricultural College may be considered the first land-grant institution, and Iowa Agricultural College the first Morrill land-grant institution.

benefits of a university education, while the sons and daughters of the mechanics, the farmers and all grades of workers are deprived by means of scant income from participating in the benefits of a higher education." The measure, as finally passed, reads: "A bill for an act to provide for the establishment of a state college and farm with a board of trustees which shall be connected with the entire agricultural enterprises of the state." The bill passed the House by a vote of 49 to 5, and the Senate by a vote of 24 to 5, and it was signed by Governor Lowe on March 22, 1858, which may be considered the founding date of the Iowa State Agricultural College and State Farm.

The legislature authorized that the proceeds from the sale of five sections of land (3,200 acres) from a previous land-grant shall be added to the college fund, and that the Board of Trustees shall consist of eleven men derived from nominations of the County Agricultural Societies and apportioned by the judicial districts, with the governor of the state and the president of the State Agricultural Society as ex-officio members, and the president of the college as chairman. The Board of Trustees in turn through appropriate committees selected the site of the college, determined the entrance requirements, and established the professorships and courses of instruction. From offers of each of six counties the Board selected a 648-acre tract of prairie land in the northwest part of Story County, the present location. Tuition is to be *"forever free to students of the state over fourteen years of age and who have been residents of the state at least six months prior to their admission.* Applicants must be of good moral character, be able to read and write the English language with ease and correctness and also to pass a satisfactory examination in the fundamental rules of arithmetic."

The Board in 1868 selected Dr. Adonjah S. Welch to be president of the institution. Dr. Welch was born on a farm near East Hampton, Connecticut, the eldest child of a widowed mother. He graduated from the University of Michigan with a B.A. in 1846, an M.A. in 1852, and a L.L.D. in 1878. Between 1852 and 1865 Dr. Welch served as principal of the new state normal school at Ypsilanti, Michigan, now East Michigan University, organized the first township school in the state, and served on the Board of Education (Trustees) of Michigan Agricultural College. Between 1865 and 1868 he was engaged in the production of lumber and fruit near Jacksonville, Florida.

The Board of Trustees also established four professorships and subjects to be taught under each: (1) physics, natural history, chemistry, geology, mineralogy, meteorology; (2) mathematics, arithmetic, geometry, trigonometry, conic sections, astronomy, surveying, civil engineering, bookkeeping; (3) zoology, entomology, ornithology, ichthyology, animal anatomy, veterinary art; and (4) botany, flower growing, horticulture, forestry, vegetable anatomy. As at the other three colleges, any given school year began in the spring, and ended in the fall, with the vacation period in the winter. During this period many students taught in the township schools. The first students consisted of sixty-nine men and nine women. Thus, Iowa State University has the distinction of being the first of the Morrill land-grant colleges to matriculate and graduate women.

REFERENCES

Beal, William J. 1915. *History of Michigan Agricultural College,* pp. 27-38. Michigan Agricultural College, East Lansing, MI.

> The author was an outstanding botanist during the latter part of the nineteenth century. He presents an interesting account of conditions at the college during the first fifty years of its existence.

Dunaway, Wayland F. 1946. *History of Pennsylvania State College,* chapter 1. Lancaster Press, Inc. Lancaster, PA.

> The development of the new idea that all fields of human activity are worthy of study in college.

Calcott, George H. 1965. *A History of the University of Maryland,* chapter 6. Maryland Historical Society, Baltimore, MD.

> An explanation of the need to keep the farmer a first-class citizen and to promote agriculture to the status of a profession.

Clawson, Marion. 1968. *The Land System of the United States,* chapters 5 and 7. University of Nebraska Press, Lincoln, NB.

> A concise and enlightened discussion on the origin and disposal of the public domain.

Ross, Earle D. 1942. *A History of Iowa State,* chapter 1. The Iowa State College Press, Ames, IA.

> The vision of a new education for a new society and the need to combine science with practice.

Sneider, Vern. 1969. "The Big Guinea Hen Search," *Ford Times,* February.

> The author discovers the geometric pattern of the farmland of the Northwest Territory and sets forth reasons why the roads are one mile apart and why villages and small cities were established ten to twelve miles apart.

2

THE MAGNIFICENT CHARTER EMERGES

Progress occurs when courageous, skillful leaders seize the opportunity to change things for the better.

—Harry S Truman

THE NATURE OF THE CHARTER
AND PROVISIONS FOR ACCEPTANCE

The term "magnificent charter" refers to the Morrill Land-Grant College Act of 1862. The title of the act reads: "An Act donating public lands to the several states and territories which may provide colleges for the benefit of agriculture and the mechanic arts." The Act contains five sections, as follows: Section 1 states the amount of land of the public domain that shall be allotted to each state, *"that there be granted to the several states . . . an amount of public land a quantity equal to 30,000 acres for each senator and representative in Congress under the census of 1860."*

Section 2 pertains to the need for the use of land script. In 1862, with the exception of the states of Illinois, Michigan, and Wisconsin, all of the states immediately east of the Mississippi had no public lands, and all of the states immediately west of the Mississippi had lesser quantities of public land than those farther away. For the states that had no or only small quantities of public land the Congress authorized the use of land script, or land-procurement certificates. In general, immediately after any given state had qualified to receive its script, the governor appointed a commission to advertise and receive bids for the sale of the script. For the most part, the bidders were private individuals or land companies that handled large blocks of script. For example, the state of Ohio received land script for 630,000 acres. This script was sold to thirty-six individuals, but three of these persons bought script for 576,000 acres. *"The Secretary of the Interior is hereby directed to issue to each state . . . land script to the amount in acres for the deficiency of its distributive share; such script to be sold by said states and the proceeds thereof applied to the purposes and uses described in this Act and for no other proper purpose whatever."*

Section 3 requires that each state shall bear the expenses incurred in taking over and selling the land for the endowment of its college: "All expenses incurred in the management and dispersion of the monies which may be received therefrom shall be paid by the states to which they belong or to the treasury of such states so that the entire proceeds of the sale of said land shall be applied without any diminution whatever to the purposes stated."

Section 4 contains two distinct provisions: (1) the conditions by which the money is invested, and (2) the prime object of the Act: "All monies derived from the sale of the lands shall be invested in stocks of the United States, or of the states, or some other safe stocks yielding not less than five percent per annum upon the par value of said stocks and that the monies so invested shall constitute a permanent fund the capital of which shall remain forever undiminished." *"Each state may take and claim the benefits of the Act to the endowment, support and maintenance of at least one college, where the leading object shall be, without excluding other scientific and classical studies, and including military tactics, to teach such branches of learning as are related to agriculture and the mechanic arts in such a manner as the legislatures of the states may respectively prescribe in order to promote the liberal and practical education of the industrial classes in the several pursuits and professions in life."*

Section 5 presents the conditions for acceptance by the people of each state, and permits the purchase of a farm for experimental purposes. "If any portion of the funds invested . . . shall by any act be diminished or lost it shall be replaced by the state to which it belongs. A sum not exceeding ten percent of the amount received by any state may be expended for the purpose of lands for sites or experimental farms whenever authorized by the respective legislatures of said states. . . . No portion of the endowment nor the interest thereon shall be applied, directly or indirectly whatsoever, to the purchase, erection, preservation or repair of any building or buildings. . . . Each state shall make an annual report regarding the progress of the college, recording any improvement or experiments made with their costs and results, and other such matters, including state, industrial, and economical statistics as may be supposed useful, one copy of which shall be transmitted by mail free, by each and to all other colleges which may be endowed under the provisions of this Act, and one copy to the Secretary of the Interior." (This copy now goes to the Secretary of Agriculture.)

In general, this requirement had a far-reaching and beneficial effect. It bound the land-grant colleges to each other and to the federal government, and encouraged the exchange of ideas for improvement among the several institutions. "Finally, no state shall be entitled to the benefits of this Act unless it shall express its acceptance thereof, by its Legislature, within two years from the date of its approval by the President." Later, the Congress extended this period to four years.

ANALYSIS AND INTERPRETATION OF THE EDUCATIONAL FEATURES OF THE ACT

Pertinent phrases of the Act and their meaning are presented as follows: the endowment, support, and maintenance of at least *one college. What is a college?* Certainly, a college is not a trade school or a vocational school or an apprentice school or even a farm school. In general, these schools are training establishments. They train students for efficiency in a specific task, whereas colleges train students not only for efficiency in specific tasks but also for effective citizenship in a democracy. In other words, trade schools and the like develop only the vocational aspects of the individual, whereas colleges develop all aspects.

The leading object shall be to teach such branches of learning as are related to *agriculture and the mechanic arts.* What is the meaning of the term "agriculture"? Is it synonymous with the term "farming"? Actually, agriculture is more than farming. It includes not only the production of agricultural products but also the processing, transporting, merchandising, and the consumption of agricultural products. In other words, "agriculture" is a generic term and includes many industries and many phases of human activity. What is the meaning of the term "mechanic arts"? As contrasted with the terms "fine arts" or "liberal arts," "mechanic arts" refers to the industrial activities of the people. Examples are the designing and making of machines, the designing and erecting of buildings, and the development and maintenance of transportation systems. As with agriculture, the term "mechanic arts"[1] is generic in nature and includes many industries and covers a wide range of human enterprises.

In order *to promote the liberal and classical education of the industrial classes.* What constitutes the industrial classes? Do these classes consist of laborers only, the laborers on the farm or laborers in the factories? As with the term "agriculture and mechanic arts," the term "industrial classes" is generic in nature and includes all people who combine the work of their brains with that of their hands in all productive endeavors. Thus, on this basis the term "industrial classes" includes practically everybody.

---

[1]As explained in chapter 7, mechanic arts developed into the various phases of engineering.

Without excluding other scientific and classical studies. What does this phrase mean? It means that the founding fathers wanted these land-grant institutions to be colleges in the truest and broadest sense. In other words, they wanted to educate young men and young women for places of leadership in the young republic and more specifically for places of leadership in their respective communities. As is well known, leadership is necessary in all forms of constructive endeavor.

In such manner as the legislature of the various states may prescribe. What are the implications of this phrase? Note that each state was free to develop the curricula of its land-grant institution according to its own needs and requirements. Further, the Act placed no restrictions on the location of each institution or on the ways and means by which each institution shall be conducted, such as the employment of the faculty, the admittance of women, the amount of tuition, and the rules and regulations pertaining to the conduct of the students. Undoubtedly, the Congress wanted the legislatures of the various states to assume certain responsibilities in the operation and development of their colleges. Thus, by following the procedure of the Act the federal government and the state governments became active partners in the growth and development of the land-grant college system. As shown in subsequent chapters, this is an excellent example of the federal government and state governments working together at their best.

And including military tactics. Why was instruction in military science included? As is well known, the nation was in the midst of the Civil War when the Morrill Act was passed. The Northern forces found themselves with a lack of effective officers—educated men trained in military science. Thus, the founding fathers believed that instruction in military science at the land-grant colleges would assist greatly in the development of a corps of reserve officers adequately educated and trained for leadership in the armed forces of the future. This provision has served the nation quite well.

In the several pursuits and professions in life. What are the implications of this phrase? Note that both pursuits and professions are indicated. In general, "pursuits" refer to any constructive occupation, whereas "profession" refers to vocations that require an effective education. In this way, the Act encouraged the education of students in all fields of human endeavor. In other words, the objectives of the Morrill Act are not limited to the teaching and investigations in agriculture and the mechanic arts only, but include teaching and investigations in all constructive fields. As shown in subsequent chapters, the inclusion of this phrase in the Charter greatly increased the opportunities for service not only to people in agriculture and in engineering, but to people engaged in all other constructive fields.

LEADERS IN THE MOVEMENT

As with all other national movements in a democracy certain persons became leaders in promoting the two new ideas: (1) that agriculture is worthy of study in college, and (2) that children of both the wealthy and the nonwealthy should have equal opportunity to acquire a college education. As a result, they became leaders in the movement. A brief description on the part played by five leaders or founding fathers follows.

SIMON DEWITT. Simon DeWitt was born in Ulster County, New York, and graduated from Queens College,[2] New Jersey, in 1776. During the Revolution he served as Chief Quartermaster of the Continental Army, and after the War he became quite active in the promotion of agricultural education in New York, particularly as a member of the New York Society for the Promotion of Agriculture, Arts and Manufactures. He served as its second vice-president, first vice-president, and president and presented a paper on a method for developing new varieties of potatoes and preserving the sweetness of butter. In 1779 DeWitt advocated the establishment of a school in the business of husbandry with instruction reinforced by experimentation. In 1819 he presented a paper before the Legislature of the State of New York entitled, "A Consideration on the Necessity of Establishing an Agricultural College and Having More of the Children of the Wealthy Educated for the Profession of Farming." Although no immediate action resulted from this proposal, it was remarkably prophetic and undoubtedly helped to promote public opinion in the movement that resulted in the passage of the Morrill Land-Grant Act of 1862.

ALDEN PARTRIDGE. Alden Partridge was born at Norwick, Vermont, in 1785, and educated at Dartmouth College and the United States Military Academy. He founded the American Literary and Scientific and Military Academy, which later became Norwich University. In this institution courses were offered in chemistry, botany, and geology and in practical engineering and agriculture. Norwich is only twelve miles from Strafford, the home of Justin S. Morrill, and, according to True,[3] a historian of agricultural education, "Partridge and Morrill became friends and exchanged ideas regarding the role of the federal government in promoting the higher education of the people." In fact, Partridge prepared a petition that was read in the House of Representatives of the federal government on January 21, 1841. In this petition

---

[2]Queens College later became the State University of New Jersey.
[3]Alfred C. True. 1969. *A History of Agricultural Education in the United States, 1785-1925.* Arno Press and New York Times, New York, NY.

the various states were to receive funds from the sale of land of the public domain in proportion to the number of representatives in Congress, and they were to establish schools to provide instruction in basic science, in certain classical subjects and in engineering, agriculture, manufactures, and commerce.

THOMAS G. CLEMSON. Thomas G. Clemson was born in Philadelphia, Pennsylvania, in 1807, and graduated from the Royal Mint of Paris in 1831. Clemson distinguished himself as a mining engineer, as a diplomat, and as a promoter of scientific agriculture. From 1852 to 1861 he conducted experiments with manures and fertilizers on his hundred-acre farm in Prince George's County, Maryland; wrote numerous articles in farm magazines; assisted in the establishment of Maryland Agricultural College; supported the passage of the Morrill Act of 1859; and served as the first superintendent of agricultural affairs in the Department of Interior. From 1862 to 1888 Clemson served as president of the Pendleton (South Carolina) Farmers' Society, as a member of the South Carolina Agriculture and Mechanical Society, and as a writer of articles in support of agricultural education. However, Clemson is best known for his part in the establishment of Clemson Agricultural College. He and Mrs. Clemson (née Anna Marie Calhoun) willed the Fort Hill Farm, consisting of 814 acres that formerly belonged to J. C. Calhoun, to the State of South Carolina for the establishment of Clemson Agricultural College, now known as Clemson University.

JONATHAN B. TURNER. Jonathan B. Turner was born at Templeton in Massachusetts and educated for the ministry at Yale University. In 1833 he migrated to Jacksonville, Illinois, and for two decades served as professor of rhetoric and belles lettres at Illinois College, a small denominational institution at Jacksonville. Turner belonged to and was quite active in many organizations: the Illinois State Historical Society, the Illinois State Agricultural Society, the Illinois State Horticultural Society, and the Illinois Industrial League. In fact, it seems that the League was formed specifically to promote educational opportunities for the farming and working classes. At its fourth meeting, the League authorized the preparation of a pamphlet that embodied Turner's plan to require the federal government to make grants of land for the higher educational needs of the common people. This pamphlet was widely distributed throughout the United States and in general it received favorable comments from the editors of many news magazines and journals: the *New York Tribune,* the *St. Louis Valley Farmer,* the *Cultivator,* the *Horticulturist,* and the *Prairie Farmer.* Thus, by 1854 the plan of Turner and his co-workers was made known not only to the farm leaders throughout the country but to members of the Senate and the House of the United States Congress.

JUSTIN S. MORRILL. Justin S. Morrill was born at Strafford, Vermont, in 1810, the son of a blacksmith-farmer, the owner and operator of a blacksmith shop and small farm. Morrill attended grade school and for a short time two academies that correspond to our present-day high schools. From 1834 to 1848 he was a businessman, first as a clerk in a mercantile store and later as a partner in the successful operation of four stores. He retired from business in 1848. From 1852 to 1888 Morrill was a representative of the people, first as a delegate of the Whig Party in the national convention of 1852, and then as a representative and finally as a senator of the U.S. Congress. In 1856 he introduced a resolution in the House that the Committee on Public Lands look into the feasibility of establishing one or more national agricultural schools in the country. From 1856 to 1857 Morrill was an official delegate from the state of Vermont at the meeting of the U.S. Agricultural Society held in Washington, D.C. At this meeting, Turner's plan was presented and discussed. Hence, Morrill in all probability became familiar with the Illinois Plan.

In 1857 he introduced the so-called first land-grant bill, the allotting of 20,000 acres for each senator and representative in Congress and 60,000 acres to each of the territories. Although this bill was favorably reported by the Committee on Public Lands and passed by both the Senate and the House, it was vetoed by President Buchanan in 1859. Despite this veto Morrill and his supporters remained resolute. Events rapidly changed in their favor. In 1860 the Illinois State Agricultural and Horticultural Society memorialized Congress to grant to each state a definite amount of land for the establishment of an industrial university. Also in 1860 Turner asked Abraham Lincoln and Stephen A. Douglas in their respective campaigns for the presidency to support the land-grant college bill. Lincoln is said to have replied, "If I am elected I will support your bill for state universities." And Douglas is supposed to have said, "If I am elected, I will sign your bill."

In 1861, with the secession of the Southern states, opposition of the Southern delegates to the first bill no longer existed. Thus, the way was clear for the passage of the so-called second bill. It was approved by the Senate by a vote of 32-7, by the House by a vote of 90-25, and signed by President Lincoln on July 2, 1862. As compared with the first bill, the second bill omitted the land allotment to the territories, increased the land allotment from 20,000 to 30,000 acres for each senator and representative, and required instruction in military science and tactics.

As with other great movements, the leaders were not without their supporters. In general, they had the support of the officers and members of the Patrons of Husbandry, otherwise known as the State Granges, the officers and members of numerous agricultural societies, and the editors of farm journals and magazines. More specifically, they had the active support of Dr. J. R. Williams, President of the Agricultural College of the State of Michigan; Dr. Avan Pugh, President of Farmers' High School of Pennsylvania; and Mr. Freeman G. Carey, President of the Farmers' College of Ohio, a private institution, and Senator Ben Wade of Ohio, who steered the bill in its passage through the Senate. Because all of these men were active in behalf of the people, the passage of the bill came about by popular demand of the people as a whole.

LOCATION AND CLASSIFICATION OF
THE WHITE MORRILL LAND-GRANT COLLEGES

As previously stated, the Morrill Act placed no restriction on the location of the Morrill land-grant colleges. In other words, the people of the various states through their respective legislatures were at liberty to locate the institution at any place they so desired. As shown in table 2-1 the people of some states located their white Morrill land-grant institutions with and as an integral part of the first state university, while the people of other states established their white Morrill land-grant colleges at a place other than that of the first state university. As these institutions have grown and developed throughout the years, five more or less distinct groups have existed. These are set forth in table 2-1. Note that fourteen states established their respective Morrill land-grant college as an integral part of the first state university; seventeen established their respective college at a place other than that of the first state university; fifteen had no first state university in 1862, and promoted the development of the Morrill land-grant college to become the first state university; two originated as industrial universities; and three attached their respective land-grant college to the first state university and later established the college at a separate place.

The Pre-Emption and Homestead Acts. The Pre-Emption and Homestead Acts provided an opportunity for the poor worker in the factory and the poor immigrant from the "Old Countries" to own and manage his own farm. Specifically, the Pre-Emption Act, passed in 1841, permitted a homesteader to obtain title to his land after he had occupied the land for at least six months and had paid $1.25 per acre for it. The Homestead Act[4] permitted the settler to obtain a standard allotment of land—160 acres from 1862 to 1908, 320 acres between 1909 and 1911, and 640 acres in 1912 and subsequent years—free of charge,

---

[4]The Congress passed and President Lincoln signed into law the Homestead Act of 1862. He stated, "I am in favor of settling the wild lands into small parcels so that every poor man may have a home." The Congress repealed the Act in 1976.

provided that he was the head of a family or at least twenty-one years of age, that he was a citizen of the United States or if not he had declared his intention of becoming a citizen, and that he live on and cultivate some of the land for a period of five years.[5] The possibility of

Table 2-1.

LOCATION OF THE WHITE MORRILL
LAND-GRANT COLLEGES AND UNIVERSITIES

As an Integral Part of the First State University

Arizona, California, Georgia, Idaho, Louisiana, Minnesota, Missouri, New Jersey, Nevada, New York, Puerto Rico,* Tennessee, Wisconsin, Wyoming

As a Separate Institution

Alabama, Colorado, Indiana, Iowa, Kansas, Michigan, Montana, North Dakota, New Mexico, Oklahoma, Oregon, Pennsylvania, South Dakota, Texas, Utah, Virginia, Washington

*As an Agricultural or Agricultural and Mechanical College
That Developed into the First State University*

Alaska, Connecticut, Delaware, Florida, Hawaii, Kentucky, Maine, Maryland, Massachusetts, Nebraska, New Hampshire, New Mexico, Ohio, Rhode Island, West Virginia

As Industrial Universities

Illinois, Arkansas

*As an Integral Part of the First State University
Later Established as a Separate Institution*

Mississippi, North Carolina, South Carolina

*The Congress extended the benefits of the Morrill Acts to the territories as well as to the states.

owning a farm was beyond the wildest dreams of the poor factory worker and the poor immigrant. Thousands upon thousands of families took advantage of this opportunity. According to Clawson, "A total of 285 million acres of the public domain was disposed of as homesteads." Thus, the Pre-Emption and Homestead Acts helped to establish in a relatively short time a large number of independently operated family

[5]Later the period was reduced to three years.

farms—a characteristic feature of the American system of productive agriculture.[6]

REFERENCES

Clawson, Marion. 1968. *The Land System of the United States,* chapter 7. University of Nebraska Press, Lincoln, NB.

    The two opposing arguments on the disposal of the public domain, should any given area be sold to a relatively small number of individuals or to a large number? In the former case settlement and improvement of the land would proceed at a slow rate, but, in the latter, settlement and improvement would proceed rapidly; the struggle between the settlers and the land speculators, and the effect of the Pre-Emption and Homestead Acts and their successors in the development of family farms.

Lockmiller, David A. 1939. *History of North Carolina State College,* pp. 241-44. Edwards and Broughton, Raleigh, NC.

    The Morrill Land-Grant Act of 1862 as it appears in the *Statutes at Large of the United States,* XII, 503-505.

Nevins, Allan. 1962. *The Origins of the Land-Grant Colleges and State Universities.* Civil War Centennial Commission, Washington, DC.

    A discussion of changes in three directions: from higher education for the few to higher education for the many, from the classics of Rome and Greece to science and its practical application, and from a closed to an open system of education.

True, Alfred C. 1969. *A History of Agricultural Education in the United States, 1785-1925,* part 3, pp. 95-119. Arno Press and New York Times, New York, NY.

    Principal Topics: The origin and intent of the Morrill Land-Grant Act of 1862, the use of the land script, and the work and accomplishments of the land-grant colleges from 1862 to 1872.

---

[6]The modern conception of a family farm is not based on size, but rather on economic and management considerations. The adult members of a given family control the capital expenditures and make the day-to-day decisions in the management of the farm. On this basis a family farm may vary in size from ten acres (e.g., a market garden farm near a city) to 10,000 acres (e.g., a wheat farm in western Washington).

3

THE CRITICAL YEARS

For gold is tried in the fire, and acceptable men in the fire of adversity.

—ECCLESIASTICUS 2:5 (*circa 180* B.C.)

THE STATUS OF AGRICULTURE—1862-1890

Prior to 1861 the Southern states believed they had the right to secede from the union of states known as the United States of America. On the other hand, the Northern states objected to this so-called right. As a result, the tragic and unfortunate fratricidal war of 1861 to 1865 took place.[1]

How did agriculture fare in the North and in the South during this trying period? In the North as in all wars thousands of workers left the farms to join the armed forces. At the same time the demand for food increased and farmers began to make extensive use of horse-drawn machines, reapers, mowers, cultivators, rakes, and seed-drills. Since only a small portion of Pennsylvania was invaded and since only the southern part of Ohio and Indiana was raided, by far the majority of farms in the North remained intact, undisturbed, and productive.

In the South thousands of workers left the farms to join the armed forces also, but the slaves remained to raise the crops. Further, the contest between the Federal and Confederate forces in northern Virginia, in Tennessee, in northern and central Mississippi, and in northern Alabama, combined with the raids from Atlanta to Savannah, from Savannah to Columbia, and from Columbia to Raleigh, destroyed thousands of plantations and disrupted the work of the slaves. As a result, and in sharp contrast to the situation in the North, the plantation system was disrupted and impoverished.

How did agriculture fare immediately after the War? In the North, with the Congressional delegates of the South absent from Washington, the Congress passed the Homestead Act. This, combined with the large grants of land to certain railroads, notably the Union Pacific, the

---

[1]Allan Nevins and Henry Steele Commager. 1956. *A Pocket History of the United States*, chapter 2. New York. The authors called the conflict of 1861 to 1865 "The Brothers' War."

Central Pacific, and the Northern Pacific, opened immense tracts of the public domain to the development of family farms. Thousands upon thousands took advantage of this golden opportunity: owners and renters of farms in the East, workers in industrial factories in the East, and more particularly the poor immigrants and their families from the "Old Countries." To these immigrants while they were in the "Old Country" the owning of a farm was far beyond their reach and aspirations.

In the South the situation militated against the reestablishment of the plantation system. Important factors were the low market price of cotton, the unadaptability of the Negro to a system of working for wages, the excessive taxes imposed by the Reconstruction governments, and more particularly the lack of research data as the foundation for the establishment of new industries. As a result, thousands of plantation owners were forced to sell their plantations either in their entirety or in part, and large areas of land became idle. Because of this, together with grants of land to certain railways in Alabama, Mississippi, Louisiana, and Arkansas, large areas of land became available for sale to the public. With fertile land selling from $3 to $5 per acre, thousands of farm families enlarged their holdings, and thousands of families of the landless nonwealthy classes became owners of relatively small family farms. According to the U.S. Department of Agriculture, farms in the South averaged 335 acres in 1860 and 153 acres in 1880. Further, the number of farms increased. For example, in South Carolina there were 33,000 farms in 1860 and 94,000 farms in 1880. Thus, on the positive side, the effect of the Civil War was to increase the number of family farms—a system that has been advantageous not only for the development of the individuals on the same farm but also for the benefit of the nation as a whole.

THE STRUGGLE OF MORRILL LAND-GRANT COLLEGES FOR EXISTENCE

From 1862 to about 1890 the Morrill land-grant colleges had a hard time. Money was scarce. The Northern states had accumulated a huge debt in prosecution of the War, and the Southern states were broke. Further, certain legislators of both sections were reluctant to appropriate funds for the advancement of the two new ideas: (1) that children of the nonwealthy as well as children of the wealthy are entitled to the opportunity to acquire a college education, and (2) that agriculture, the basic and only essential industry, is entitled to the attention of the best minds. In the struggle for existence many factors were involved, and most of these are either directly or indirectly concerned with the acceptance of the Morrill Endowment. They are placed in one of two groups: factors pertaining to all of the Morrill land-grant colleges, and factors specific to certain institutions only.

FACTORS PERTAINING TO ALL COLLEGES

Competition for the Morrill Endowment

From February, 1862, to about 1870 the Morrill land-grant colleges were not secure in their exclusive right to the income from the Morrill Endowment. This was particularly the case for Pennsylvania, Ohio, New York, Iowa, and several other states. In 1865 the legislature of Pennsylvania entertained a bill to divide the income from the Morrill Endowment into five parts, with equal shares going to the University of Lewisville, Pennsylvania College at Gettysburg, Western University at Pittsburgh, the Polytechnic College at Philadelphia, and the Agricultural College at State College. The trustees of the agricultural college countered with a memorandum to the effect that the division of the income would force the agricultural college to close and that the liberal arts colleges listed in the bill did not conform either in letter or in spirit to the requirements of the Morrill Act. Finally, the legislature passed an act that made the Agricultural College of Pennsylvania the sole beneficiary of the Morrill Endowment.

The legislature of Ohio accepted the Morrill Endowment in 1864 and established the Ohio Agricultural and Mechanical College in 1870. Between 1864 and 1870 the legislature received memorials for the establishment of professorships of agriculture at several liberal arts institutions: Miami University, Ohio University, Wooster College, and Mount Julian College. During this period also and for four consecutive years the State Board of Agriculture with the backing of farmers organizations sent resolutions to the legislature in favor of awarding the Endowment to one institution. Finally, in 1870 the legislature passed a bill in favor of the newly established Ohio Agricultural and Mechanical College.

The turn of events in New York State is unique and very interesting. The state accepted its land-grant in 1863, and for the next two years the activities of two men finally culminated in the establishment of the land-grant college as an integral part of Cornell University. At first Charles Cook, a member of the State Assembly, argued that the Endowment should go to Peoples' College, a private institution, and Ezra Cornell, also a member of the State Assembly, joined with others in circulating a petition that the bounty should go to Ovid Agricultural College, also a private institution. To avoid any deadlock Judge Folger

of Geneva introduced a resolution that would have given half of the
Endowment to Peoples' College and the other half to Ovid Agricultural
College, and Ezra Cornell proposed that the trustees of each institution
develop a fund from the purchase of the land script and locate land
of the public domain to which each college was entitled. At the same
time, each of the twenty colleges of the state stood ready to demand
through its representatives in the legislature its share of the Morrill
Endowment. Finally, Ezra Cornell, with the encouragement of his friend,
Andrew D. White, also a member of the State Assembly, conceived
the idea of buying the land script himself and donating a major part
of his property to the state for the establishment of a well-rounded
university with its land-grant college at Ithaca.[2] A grateful legislature
accepted the donation in 1865 and immediately passed an act that
named the university with its land-grant college in honor of the donor—
hence the name Cornell University. Thus, because of strong leadership
in the Assembly and the wealth of the donor, the land-grant college of
New York was located and placed on a firm financial foundation in a
relatively short time.

As previously stated, the legislature of Iowa established the Iowa
Agricultural College and Farm in 1858 and accepted the Morrill Endowment in 1862. In 1864 the state representative from Floyd County,
the seat of the first state university, introduced a bill to divide the
federal bounty, receipts from the sale of 240,000 acres, between the
university at Iowa City and the agricultural college at Ames, noting
that "to develop a new college within the time set by the Morrill Act
would necessitate a greater expense than the state was prepared to
make." Judge Francis Springer, a trustee of the university, submitted a
memorandum to the legislature relative to attaching the land-grant
college to the university. However, Suel Foster, a pioneer farmer and
leader, and Benjamin Gue, a senator in the legislature, opposed these
efforts. In fact, the rivalry for the Morrill Endowment was so keen that
a debate took place in the Iowa House of Representatives. Former
Governor Kirkland led the forces for the university, while Senator Gue
and Representative Maxwell led the forces for the newly established
agricultural college. The proponents for the newly established agricultural college won the debate, since the legislature in 1864 voted
to assign the Morrill Endowment to the agricultural college. Here again

---

[2]New York received land script for 989,920 acres. This acreage was located in
the pine lands of northern Wisconsin. When the State Comptroller had sold 76,000
acres (for $64,000), Mr. Cornell bought the remainder of the acreage in the name
of the University and held it until 1882. By this time the pine land had increased
in value from 84 cents per acre to about $5 per acre.

the land-grant college was permanently located in a relatively short time.

Competition for the Morrill Endowment also occurred between places in Louisiana, Minnesota, and Missouri and between literary colleges in Maine, Illinois, Oregon, and Virginia.

Attitude of the Administration, Faculty, and Students of Classical Colleges

Between 1872 and 1875 there was a pronounced reaction toward any further endowment of the Morrill land-grant colleges. The most heated opposition came from the sectarian and privately endowed institutions. For example, in 1872, James McCosh, president of Princeton, stated that the land-grant colleges were not meeting the objectives of the Morrill Act since very few students were taking agriculture and that additional grants would be a waste and an abuse. Further, he maintained that receipts from the sale of public land could be more advantageously used for the development of high schools and graduate schools. Charles W. Elliott, president of Harvard, opposed the use of federal grants for both high schools and graduate schools. He believed that the grants would interfere with the development of a race of self-reliant and independent freeborn men. The presidents of the Morrill land-grant colleges countered this argument by pointing out that, since the Morrill land-grant charter was quite broad, the primary objective of the colleges was the development of leaders in an industrial democracy and that the number of graduates who would practice farming was irrelevant. This controversy even entered the halls of Congress. In 1874 the House of Representatives authorized the formation of a committee to determine whether the Morrill land-grant colleges were meeting the requirements as set forth in the Morrill Act. After investigating the situation for one year, the committee found that the colleges had complied with the letter and spirit of the law. In fact, they congratulated the presidents and faculties of the several Morrill land-grant institutions for the progress they had made despite various adverse circumstances.

Lack of a Science of American Agriculture

Agriculture is based on the activities of the crop-plant, and the science of agriculture is based on the science of crop-plants and crop-animals. In crop-plants the basic or fundamental processes are photosynthesis, respiration, and water absorption-transpiration. By 1862, because of the basic work in the discovery of photosynthesis by Ingenhouz, 1773, Priestley, 1774, Senebier, 1782, de Saussure, 1804, and Mayer,

1845,[3] the relation of the sun and chlorophyll to photosynthesis and the growth and yield of crop-plants began to be appreciated. However, the exact role of the other two processes, respiration and water absorption-transpiration, in relation to yield remained to be discovered.

Further, prior to 1840 most people accepted the Aristotelian theory that plants obtained their nourishment from the soil in the form of humus. Liebig, a prominent agricultural scientist, showed that the roots do not absorb humus or any other complex organic compound but that they absorb the ions of relatively simple *inorganic* substances such as the nitrate ion, the phosphate ion, the potassium ion, and the calcium ion.

In crop-animals the fundamental process is respiration. By 1862 animal scientists knew that free oxygen is absorbed and that carbon dioxide and water are given off in respiration, but they had very little knowledge on the effect of various kinds of feed on the rate of the process and on the production of beef and pork, the production of milk, and the production of eggs. Moreover, many basic sciences underlying agriculture were either in the embryonic stage or had not been initiated. For example, sciences in the embryonic stages were those pertaining to the anatomy and physiology of crop-plants and crop-animals, and sciences that had not been started were those pertaining to genetics and plant and animal breeding, the biochemistry of crop-plants and crop-animals, design and statistics for experimental work in agriculture, and the processing and marketing of plant and animal products. Thus, the fundamental knowledge available to the teacher of agriculture was quite limited. He knew that plants absorb carbon dioxide through the leaves or green stems and that in the presence of sunlight this substance combines with water in the formation of sugars and related compounds. He also knew that the roots absorbed water and mineral substances dissolved in the water, but he had no basic information on the relation of photosynthesis and water absorption-transpiration to the growth and development of crops and on the effects of various environmental factors on each of these fundamental processes.

Fortunately, the founding fathers of the land-grant colleges in their wisdom provided funds for the purchase of at least one farm at each college, and one of the first tasks of the professors of agriculture consisted in putting the farms in order for the conducting of experiments: the upbuilding of the soil of the rundown farms of the East, the development of contours and terraces on the badly eroded soils of the Southeast, and the breaking of the prairie or clearing of the forest

---

[3]Ingenhouz, Senebier, and de Saussure respectively discovered that light, carbon dioxide, and water are needed in photosynthesis; de Saussure discovered that oxygen is given off, and Mayer formulated the energy relations of this basic biochemical reaction.

of the raw farms in the Midwest. Despite these adverse conditions the teachers of agriculture took off their coats and went to work with a will.

Financial Difficulties

As stated in chapter 2, the Morrill Act imposed restrictions not only on the use of the money of the original endowment but also on the use of the income from the endowment. As stated in Section 4, Subsection 1, of the Morrill Act, "not more than 10 percent of the amount received by any state shall be expended for the purchase of land or experimental farms," and, in Section 4, Subsection 2, "no portion of said fund or any interest therefrom shall be applied directly or indirectly under any pretense whatever to the purchase, erection, preservation, or repair of any laboratory or building." Thus, the money from the Morrill Endowment was restricted to the purchase of a farm for experimental work and to paying salaries of the president and the faculty and to buying supplies and equipment for the classroom and laboratory. The reason for these restrictions was that the federal government wanted each state to have a definite part in the building and development of its land-grant college(s). In other words, the federal government through the Morrill Act provided funds for the initiation or birth of each college, and the states provided funds for the erection of the various buildings and laboratories.

Unfortunately for the land-grant colleges, business and commerce throughout the country was in a depressed state during the latter part of the nineteenth century. As a result, money was scarce and the state legislatures were inclined to retrench rather than appropriate funds for new and untried projects. For example, the legislature of Massachusetts in 1870 expected its college, the Massachusetts Agricultural College, to be self-supporting from the income of the Morrill Endowment, student fees, and the sale of products from the farm. However, in the absence of any state appropriation, the college was $32,000 in debt by 1879. The legislature appropriated $32,000 to discharge this debt, and at the same time it made the trustees of the College personally responsible for any debt incurred in excess of income. To avoid any indebtedness the trustees sold all the livestock except the herd of Ayrshires, abolished one professorship, reduced the salaries of the remaining professors, and withheld the salary of the president.

In 1878 the legislature of the state of Pennsylvania appropriated $80,000 to pay for the mortgage of Old Main, the first college building, and failed to make another appropriation until 1887—a period of nine years. Many other examples could be cited. As shown in table 3-1, the income from the Morrill Endowment was relatively low. This was particularly true in the case of the so-called land script states. How did the land-grant colleges get away from this period of stunted growth? As in the agitation for and passage of the Morrill Act of 1862, the people, through their representatives in the state legislatures and the Congress, and the presidents of the colleges urged the federal government to further endow the land-grant institutions. This endowment is embodied in the Morrill Act of 1890 with its Nelson Amendment of 1907 and is discussed more fully in chapter 5.

Table 3-1.

ACREAGE, PRICES, AND INCOME RECEIVED BY CERTAIN STATES
WITH AND WITHOUT ANY PUBLIC DOMAIN.*

State	*States with Public Domain* Allotment (1,000 acres)	Price/Acre	Annual Income ($1,000)
CA	150	5.00	37.5
IA	240	2.39	28.6
KS	90	4.30	19.4
MI	240	3.25	39.0
MN	120	5.62	33.7
WI	240	1.25	15.0

States without Public Domain

CT	180	0.75	6.8
IL	480	0.70	16.8
ME	210	0.56	5.9
MA	360	0.66	11.9
NC	270	0.46	6.2
RI	120	0.42	2.5

*From Alfred C. True, 1969, *A History of Agricultural Education in the United states, 1785-1925.* U.S. Department of Agriculture Miscellaneous Publication 36, Washington, DC.

FACTORS SPECIFIC TO CERTAIN INSTITUTIONS

The Land-grant College Attached to a Privately Endowed Institution

As previously stated, most states in the East were money-poor. In fact, the legislatures of most states had hardly enough money for current expenses, let alone funds for the promotion for the two new ideas in education. To avoid making large appropriations and to take advantage of existing educational faculties three states attached their respective Morrill land-grant colleges to a privately endowed institution: Connecticut to Yale College in 1862, Rhode Island to Brown University in 1863, and New Hampshire to Dartmouth College in 1866. Unfortunately, the land-grant college failed to prosper at each of these institutions. In general, the presidents and faculties favored the classical type of education rather than the science-with-practice type, and they discouraged rather than encouraged the prospective student of agriculture and mechanic arts by making him take a stiff entrance examination and by insisting that he take many courses in the classics, a few courses in science, and hardly any courses in applied science.

For example, the department of agriculture at Yale College graduated only seven students in twenty-four years while the department of agriculture at Storrs Agricultural College graduated thirty-four students in four years. The president of Brown University stated that the "classic curricula required a patina that the exponents of utility are unable to match," and the president of Dartmouth in a commencement address stated "that for the most part the agricultural courses fitted students for highway surveyors, selectmen, and perhaps members of the legislature." In other words, Yale, Brown, and Dartmouth were primarily classical institutions and they were unsympathetic to the new philosophy of education that was emerging at the time. Further, none of these institutions had bought a farm and none had allowed the land-grant college to develop into a public service institution.

This attitude toward the Morrill land-grant college aroused the ire, wrath, and indignation of the State Grange and the State Agricultural Society(ies) of each state, and these societies in turn petitioned the state legislature to establish the land-grant college at a new location. Accordingly, in 1893 the college at Yale was attached to Storrs Agricultural College, which later became Connecticut Agricultural College and finally the University of Connecticut; the college at Brown was established near the village of Kingston as the Rhode Island Agricultural College and finally as the University of Rhode Island; and the college at Dartmouth was established near the village of Durham as the New Hampshire Agricultural College and finally as the University of New Hampshire. Unfortunately, about thirty years had been wasted, but fortunately the three land-grant institutions were now free to grow and begin their services to all of the people.

The Land-Grant College Attached to a Denominational College

Two states, Kentucky and Oregon, attached their respective land-grant college to a denominational institution. The situation in Kentucky was unique. In 1863 the legislature qualified for its Morrill Endowment, and the president of the State Agricultural Society reported that only one institution, Transylvania University at Lexington, was interested in having the college located on its campus. In 1865 the legislature passed an act that consolidated Transylvania University with Kentucky University, a denominational school largely supported by the Church of Christ, and in the same year the legislature joined the A and M College of Kentucky to Kentucky University. Thus, three institutions were brought together in one campus and as one university: the A and M College of Kentucky, Transylvania University, and Kentucky University. It was officially known as Kentucky University.

The Church of Christ prospered at Lexington. By August, 1869, the congregation had outgrown the seating capacity of the parent church on Main Street, and in April, 1870, they purchased a second church, one that had formerly belonged to the Presbyterian Church on the corner of Second and Broadway, under the stipulation that the second congregation would be governed by the board of elders of the first congregation. Unfortunately, dissension soon occurred between members of each of the two churches. Unfortunately, too, certain members of the Board of Curators (Trustees) and faculty belonged to one church while other members of the Board of Curators and the faculty belonged to the other. Understandably, the legislature was reluctant to appropriate money while this squabble was going on. The poor agricultural and mechanical college remained an innocent victim. At the same time, its enrollment dropped and its prestige decreased.

Finally, the legislature in 1878 detached the A and M College from Kentucky University and established the college in isolation from Kentucky University at a new location. The city of Lexington donated its fifty-two-acre fairgrounds and park, and the counties of Lexington and Fayette gave $60,000 for the construction of buildings and land for the experimental farm. Thus, at long last, after a period of thirteen years, the Kentucky A and M College was free to grow and start its period of service to all of the people.

In 1868, the legislature of the state of Oregon attached its Morrill land-grant college to Corvallis College at Corvallis, a denominational institution supported by the Methodist Episcopal Church South. Corvallis College started as a private academy in 1858, and by 1868 it offered two types of curricula: the classical leading to the bachelor of arts, and the scientific leading to the bachelor of science. However, with the attachment of the land-grant college the legislature changed the name from Corvallis College to Oregon Agricultural College. Between 1868 and 1884 there was a conflict of interest between the faculty of the schools established by Corvallis College and that of the schools established by the Morrill Act. To remove this disagreement and discord, the state of Oregon assumed complete control in 1885, and changed the name of the school to Oregon Agricultural College.

The Land-Grant College Attached to the First State University

At the beginning three states attached their respective Morrill land-grant college to their first state university: Mississippi to the University of Mississippi in 1871; North Carolina to the University of North Carolina in 1875; and South Carolina to the University of South Carolina in 1880. Here again the departments of agriculture and mechanic arts failed to prosper at each institution. Because of the unfriendly attitude of the faculty and the student body of the classical schools and colleges of these universities, enrollment in agriculture and mechanic arts was exceedingly low. Within a period of six years at no time were there more than twelve students taking agriculture at the University of Mississippi, and not one student had graduated in agriculture at the University of North Carolina or at the University of South Carolina. Further, the land-grant college at the University of South Carolina was particularly handicapped because of the mismanagement of the funds from the Morrill Endowment. In 1869 the legislature sold the land script for $191,800 and this sum was invested in state bonds. Unfortunately, the income was hypothecated to New York to pay other obligations. The students in general science, agriculture, and chemistry took identical programs. They were required to take two years in French and German and one year each of English, history, mathematics, and political economy.

As a result of the mismanagement of the land-grant college fund by North Carolina and South Carolina and the negative attitude of faculty and students toward the land-grant college at each of the three universities, farm leaders conducted wide and vigorous campaigns to separate the land-grant college from the state university. Active groups included the State Grange of Mississippi, the State Agricultural Society and the Wautaga Club of North Carolina, and the Tillman Movement in South Carolina. In general, these campaigns were successful. Accordingly, the land-grant college of Mississippi was separated from the University of Mississippi and established just east of the village of Starkville as Mississippi A and M College, now Mississippi State University; that of North Carolina was separated from the University at Chapel Hill and established just west of the village of Raleigh as North Carolina A and M College, now North Carolina State University; and that of South Carolina was separated from the University at Columbia and established at Fort Hill, the home of Thomas G. Clemson, as Clemson Agricultural College, now Clemson University.

The Classics vs. Science with Practice at the Same Institution

According to Dunaway, a seventeen-year period from 1871 to 1888 is considered the classical era in the history of Pennsylvania State University. During this period there was a consistent trend away from the idea of the industrial college, with a corresponding drift toward a curriculum resembling that of the classical college. This trend was imperceptible at first, but it became more evident with each succeeding year. Naturally, this trend led to disruption and dissatisfaction rather than harmony among the students, faculty, and trustees. In fact, distinct lines of cleavage developed between the faculty and the trustees. Finally, two legislative committees, one in 1879 and the other in 1880, investigated the situation and found that no instruction had been given in engineering or in mechanic arts. This led to the development of a curriculum in engineering and to reorganization of the curriculum in agriculture and in related sciences more in line with the requirements set forth by the Morrill Act.

Summary

Despite the difficulties of the early period, the agriculture and mechanical colleges were gradually accepted as an integral part of the life of the nation. In fact, by 1890 competition for the Morrill Endowment had ceased, each college had become permanently located, the professors of agriculture had started to conduct experiments on the farmer's production problems and to carry the results of their research to the farmers, and the people in general through their representatives in the federal and state legislative bodies had voiced their approval by endowing each of the three main phases of agriculture: research, teaching, and extension. These phases are discussed in chapters 4, 5, and 6, respectively.

REFERENCES

Fleming, Walter L. 1936. *Louisiana State University, 1860-1896*, chapter 12. Louisiana University Press, Baton Rouge, LA.
    The struggle for existence of a university during the so-called Reconstruction period, 1869-1873.
Hollis, Daniel W. 1956. *University of South Carolina*, vol. 2. chapter 7. University of South Carolina Press, Columbia, SC.
    The struggle of a tax-supported first state university with a group of denominational colleges, and with a movement to separate its Morrill land-grant college.

Hopkins, James F. 1951. *The University of Kentucky, Origins and Early Years,* chapter 5. The University of Kentucky Press, Lexington, KY.

The futility of combining two educational institutions: one designed to serve all of the people and one other designed to serve the religious phase of a particular sect only.

Stemmons, Walter. 1931. *Connecticut Agricultural College—A History,* chapter 3, "The Yale-Storrs Controversy." Storrs, CT, 1931.

An interesting account of the difficulties in attaching a school for instruction in agriculture and mechanic arts to a classical institution.

4

THE RESEARCH DIMENSION

Excellence in research is the foundation of excellence in teaching and excellence in extension.

The research dimension refers to the discovery of new knowledge in all fields of constructive endeavor. As previously stated, when the Morrill land-grant colleges were established, most of the people were engaged in the subsistence type of agriculture and in the closely related field of mechanic arts. Since the Morrill Act required the teaching of agriculture and mechanic arts, and since there was no science of American agriculture or American mechanic arts, it was imperative that the Morrill land-grant colleges begin to conduct research in these fields. This chapter deals primarily with the origin, growth, and development of agricultural, home economics, and engineering experiment stations in the United States.

RESEARCH IN AGRICULTURE

Research in agriculture is essentially a method for the discovery of useful information for the benefit of the farmer and the consumer. From the standpoint of the farmer the application of this information may increase the marketable yield per crop-plant or per crop-animal or per unit area or decrease the cost of production or do both. In either case, profits are increased. In other words, a prime function of experimental work in agriculture is to put money in "the farmer's pocketbook." In this way, the farmer receives an adequate return from his investment, maintains an acceptable standard of living, provides for the education of his children, and enjoys, with other citizens, the blessings of this great land—the United States of America. Further, from the standpoint of the consumer the application of the new information enables the farmer to place any given product on the market at reasonable cost to the consumer.

Reasons for Tax-Supported Agricultural Experiment Stations

In general, nonfarm industries, the industrial corporations, such as General Motors and other automobile makers, operate as large, well-coordinated units; that is, the rate of production and the rate of selling cars are coordinated. If the consumer demand is brisk, the rate of production can be correspondingly brisk. If, however, the consumer demand is low the rate of production can be correspondingly low. In either case, price structures are maintained and profits are sufficiently high for the employment of scientists for the solution of problems in the production and selling of automobiles. In sharp contrast to industrial corporations, the agricultural industry is composed for the most part of relatively small units, the so-called family farms. The gross profits from each unit are relatively low, much too low to employ high-salaried scientists and buy expensive equipment for the maintenance of research laboratories for the solution of its problems. Further, the products of the family farm are essential; that is, they feed and clothe the human race just as they fed and clothed the people of the past. In other words, agricultural experiment stations benefit everyone, and for this reason they are supported by public funds (taxes) and are considered public service institutions. In the United States there are two groups: (1) the state stations supported by state and federal funds, and (2) the federal stations supported by federal funds only.

THE STATE STATIONS

The First State Stations

As stated in chapter 3, when the Morrill land-grant colleges were established there was no body of research information that could be applied to the solution of the farmers' problems. Fortunately, for the farmers, the teachers, and the students, the Morrill Endowment provided funds for the purchase of a farm, and without exception all of the colleges took advantage of this farsighted provision. In fact, so great was the need for experimental information that all of the professors of agriculture and their students[1] started to put the farms in condition for the conducting of experiments immediately after the first classes convened, and many states established agricultural experiment stations within a short time after the colleges were established. Connecticut and California established the first and second stations in 1875, and North Carolina established the third station in 1877. Other states followed in rapid succession: Massachusetts in 1878, New York (Cornell) in 1879, New Jersey in 1880, New York, Ohio, and Tennessee in 1882, Alabama in 1883, Louisiana in 1884, and Kentucky in 1885. Altogether fourteen states were operating tax-supported agricultural experiment stations, most of them on meager funds, before the nationwide system of agricultural experiment stations was established in 1887.

---

[1]At that time the students were required to work a certain no. of hours each week.

A Model Farm vs. a Farm for Investigations. Between 1855 and 1863 the president and faculty of Michigan Agricultural College believed that the farm should be operated as a model farm rather than as a laboratory for the conducting of investigations. For example, the farm superintendent in 1863 stated, "The people of the State look to us for [the operation of] a model farm . . . and I am not going to fool away my time on experiments." Fortunately, a new president disagreed with the superintendent, since the operation of the college farm as a model would prevent the farm from being used as a laboratory for the conducting of experiments and as a laboratory for the instruction of students.

Condition of the College Farms for Scientific Investigations. In general, the college farm at the several colleges was either part of the primeval forest or prairie or in poor condition for the conducting of experiments. For example, the "farm" at Michigan State[2] was not a farm but part of the original forest. Of the original 677 acres all but ten acres sustained a dense growth of trees—oak, maple, ash, and other hardwoods. In general, the students assisted in felling the trees, splitting oak logs to suitable lengths for subsequent rail fences on the farm, sawing and splitting logs of oak and other kinds for the furnaces of the first two buildings, and plowing and preparing the soil between the stumps for the planting of seed of wheat, corn, legumes, and vegetables. Later, when the stumps had decayed sufficiently to permit their easy removal, the students removed them by using teams of oxen. Then, if artificial draining was necessary, they laid tile lines and finally they leveled the land mainly to fill the holes made by removing the stumps. Of the original 667 acres in trees 200 acres were ready for the production of crops in 1859—two years after the work started. When one considers the tools available at the time, this was a remarkable achievement.[3]

The farm at New Brunswick, New Jersey, the home of Rutgers University, comprised an unbroken block of 98.4 acres.[4] In general, this area was in a badly rundown condition. The soil was extremely low in fertility, yields of wheat averaged only six bushels per acre, stumps of the original trees existed on thirty acres, some spots were poorly drained, and the fences were down and broken. Consequently, the first job of the professor of agriculture and the students was to increase the fertility of the soil, remove all of the old stumps, lay lines of drain tile

---

[2]Madison Kuhn. 1955. *Michigan State. The First 100 Years.* Michigan State University Press, East Lansing, MI.

[3]The tools were quite primitive compared with the tools and equipment of modern times. Examples are manually handled plows, shovels, mattocks, hoes, sickles, scythes, and cradle scythes.

[4]*The First Annual Report of the New Jersey Agricultural Experiment Station,* 1880.

where necessary, and build new fences. Of these operations, increasing the fertility of the soil was found to take considerable time. In fact, according to the historian of the State University of New Jersey, a period of ten years was required to put the soil in a state of fertility sufficiently high for the conducting of experimental work.

The first experiments consisted of comparing manures and commercial fertilizers, testing varieties of major crops, and determining the behavior of new crops. At first the professor of agriculture and the administration believed that the yield of the experimental plots would pay for the cost of experimentation. In common with the first experiments of many other experiment stations, they found that this was not the case. The historian states: "Finally, it was accepted that extensive experimental work and profits from the experimental plots were incompatible."

The first farm at Mississippi State consisted of 350 acres known as the "Bell Tract." At the time the college acquired this tract it had been continuously cropped for a long period and finally abandoned for crop production. As a result, the slopes were badly eroded, and the bottoms and ditches were covered with trees and brush. Mr. F. A. Gulley, the professor of agriculture, in his report of the first year's work pointed out that "three-fourths of the land had been thrown out as not being worth longer cultivation, the major part of it being cut up by gullies, the bottoms grown up with trees and brush, and the whole of it devoid of either fences or buildings." Consequently, as at other colleges, the first job of the professors and the students was to fell the trees, grub out the stumps, and clean out the brush and the drainage ditches.[5] Later the college acquired another tract, the so-called North Farm, consisting of about 494 acres. In general, this farm was in much better shape for the conducting of experiments than the former 350-acre tract.

The first experiments consisted of testing varieties of apples, grapes, cotton, corn, and adapted vegetables, determining the most efficient forage crops and grasses, and comparing methods for the upbuilding of soils low in fertility. As in other states the yields of the experimental plots were expected to defray the cost of the experiments.

The first farm of the University of Nebraska consisted of two sections of saline land. However, this farm was found to be poorly adapted to crop production and a second farm was secured. In general, this farm consisting of 320 acres[6] was in a poor state of cultivation, excessively weedy, with grassy, untrimmed hedgerows, and broken-down fences. Consequently, the first job of the teachers and the students was

---

[5]As discussed in chapter 14, during the early period in the life of the colleges, all physically able male students were required to put in a certain amount of physical work on the experimental farms.

[6]From *Nebraska Agricultural Experiment Station Circular* **26**, 1925.

to get rid of the weeds, clean out the grass from and trim the hedges, and repair fences and buildings.

Experiments were started in 1873 on the testing of different kinds of sugar beet seed from Europe, and in 1875 with 23 kinds of small grains and clover, 38 varieties of potatoes, six kinds of wheat, 10 kinds of field and sweet corn, 14 kinds of beans, and 10 kinds of peas. As at other colleges, yields from the experimental plots were expected to defray the costs of experimentation.

Discovery of the Principle of Comparability. The early experiments were crude and superficial. In particular, the principle of comparability between any two treatments remained to be discovered and appreciated. Dr. Manley Miles, professor of agriculture at Michigan Agricultural College, seems to have been one of the first to recognize the need for comparability between any two treatments. He states, "Large portions of experiments made thus far have been of no value for the reason that too much is attempted. For example, a person wishing to test the value of different sizes of seed-pieces in potato production, plants his small potatoes in rows two feet apart and his large potatoes in rows three feet apart. Here, size of seed-piece and distance between rows, is a double variation. There was no condition the same and no chance to compare such experiments and a very large proportion of experiments have been vitiated in this way. It arises from attempting to determine two things at once; that is, the effect of variation in size of the seed and the effect of variation of spacing between the rows. You have two elements (factors), and you may try experiments as long as you please without any valuable results. It would be better to try one experiment and settle the matter in regard to size having all of the conditions precisely the same and then take as a separate experiment one in which the different distances of the rows are the object of the investigation." As a result, Dr. Miles recommended that experiments should be set up to determine the effects of one factor at a time rather than the effect of two or more factors at the same time or in the same experiment. Since that time agricultural scientists have developed experimental designs and techniques by which the principle of comparability is maintained with several factors in the same experiment. Further, with this type of design, the interaction or quantitative relation between any two variables in the experiment can be determined.

Origin and Development of the Nationwide System of State Stations

The reason for the establishment and maintenance of a nationwide system of agricultural experiment stations is to provide one of the blessings of America: the making available to all of the people a wide variety of high-quality food at reasonable cost. How did this far-reaching and beneficial system come about? In 1882 the presidents and professors of agriculture of the Morrill land-grant colleges in convention assembled formed an organization called the Association of Land-Grant Colleges and Experiment Stations. In 1885 delegates from this Association met with Mr. N. J. Coleman, the Federal Commissioner of Agriculture, to discuss the desirability of urging Congress to establish an agricultural experiment station within each of the several states and territories. The resolution reads as follows: "Resolved, that the condition and progress of American agriculture require national aid for investigation and experimentation in the several states and territories and that, therefore, this Convention approves the principles and general provisions of what is known as the Cullen Bill of the last Congress (1884), and urges the next Congress to the passage of this or similar act." The act became known as the Hatch Act.

The Hatch Act—Its Objectives and Provisions. The Congress passed the Hatch Act in 1887.[7] It was sponsored in the Congress by Representative W. H. Hatch of Missouri and by Senator J. Z. George of Mississippi, both leaders in the promotion of the science of American agriculture. Pertinent statements regarding the objectives, provisions, and funding of the Act follow. Section 1 reads: "To promote scientific investigation and experiments respecting the principles and applications of agricultural science, there shall be established, under the direction of the college or colleges or agricultural department or colleges in each state or territory, a department to be known and designated as an agricultural experiment station."

Section 2 states: "It shall be the object and duty of said experiment stations to conduct original researches or experiments on the physiology of plants and animals; the diseases to which they are severally subject with the remedies of the same; the chemical composition of plants at their different stages of growth; the comparative advantages of rotative cropping as pursued under a varying series of crops; the capacity of new plants or trees for acclimation; the analysis of soils and water; the chemical composition of manures, natural or artificial, with experiments designed to test their comparative effects on crops of different kinds; the adaptation and value of grasses and forage plants; the composition and digestibility of the different kinds of food for domestic animals, scientific and economic questions involved in production of butter and cheese; and such other researches or experiments bearing directly on the agricultural industry of the United States as may in each case be

---

[7]*Statutes at Large of the United States,* XXIV, 440-42. In accordance with the custom of naming the sponsor in the Senate and House respectively, this Act should more properly have been called the Hatch-George Act.

deemed as advisable, having due regard to the various conditions and needs of the respective States and Territories."

Section 5 states: "That out of the first annual appropriations so received by any station an amount not exceeding one-fifth may be expended in the erection, enlargement or repair of a building or buildings necessary for carrying on the work of such stations; and thereafter an amount not exceeding five percent of such annual appropriations may be so expended." Thus, the major part of the funds was restricted to the conducting of original research over a wide range of agricultural subjects, and only a small part was to be used for the erection and maintenance of buildings.

Other Federal Acts. Since the passage of the Hatch Act, other acts have provided federal funds for research in the nationwide system of state agricultural experiment stations. The name, date, and purpose of each act are presented in table 4-1.

Table 4-1.

U.S. FEDERAL ACTS GRANTING FUNDS FOR RESEARCH AT THE STATE AGRICULTURAL RESEARCH STATIONS°

Name of Act and Year Established	Field of Research
Hatch (1887)	Production problems of crop-plants and crop-animals
Adams (1906)	Basic research on production in all fields
Purnell (1925)	Production and marketing of agricultural products, home economics, and rural sociology
Bankhead-Jones (1935)	Genetic and environmental studies of crop-plants and crop-animals
Research and Marketing (1946)	Development of improved methods in production, processing, and marketing of agricultural products
New Hatch (1955)	Consolidation of previous five acts

°From U.S. Department of Agriculture Miscellaneous Publication 904, 1962, Washington, DC.

Administration of the funds. As previously stated, the funds are used to solve the problems of the farmer. In the solution of these problems, the project method is used. In general, this method consists in clearly defining (1) the nature of the problem, (2) the modus operandi for obtaining the data, (3) the method of analyzing the data, and (4) the period of the experiment. If, by the end of this period, the data are incomplete the project may be continued in its original

form or revised to meet any unforeseen situation. In the projects supported by federal funds both state and federal officers are involved. The federal officers are members of the Office of Experiment Stations of the U.S. Department of Agriculture, and the state officers are the directors of each respective experiment station and the leaders of the research projects.

The function of the members of the Office of Experiment Stations is annually to examine the records of expenditures to determine whether the funds have been used according to the various acts and to consult with the leaders of the projects to determine the progress each project is making. The function of the director is to administer the funds according to the provisions embodied in the various acts, and the function of the project leaders is to obtain the all-important experimental data. In general, these leaders operate in much the same manner as Dr. Norman E. Borlaug, a graduate of the land-grant college of the University of Minnesota and the winner of the Nobel Peace Prize for 1971; that is, they supervise *in situ* all phases in the growing of the experimental plants and animals, in taking the all-important experimental data, and in preparing the data for publication.

Fortunately for the solution of these projects the state and federal officers have many things in common: (1) they are graduates of the land-grant college system of the United States, (2) they attend regional and national meetings of their particular professions, (3) they belong to the same professional societies, and (4) they have the same outlook toward their fellowmen. In general, these characteristics in common have promoted harmony in their working relations with each other. Neither one has sought to dominate the other, and a spirit of helpfulness and cooperation has prevailed throughout. In this way duplication of projects in adjacent states has been reduced to a minimum, and, more importantly, experimental designs and techniques have become more or less uniform and standardized. This in turn has greatly increased efficiency in research and in the solution of the farmers' production, processing, and marketing problems. It is an instance of the state and federal governments working together at their best. In fact, this relation of the state and federal officials has been highly rewarding and could serve as a model for joint effort on the part of the state and federal governments in projects within fields other than agriculture and home economics.

The Modern State Agricultural Experiment Station System

As previously stated, when the Morrill land-grant colleges were established the professor of agriculture, with the assistance of his students, conducted experiments on the college farm. The professors soon discovered that the results obtained on the station farm did not always apply to all farms within the state. Subsequent tests showed that this situation was largely due to differences in the soils within any given state. For example, the soils of Georgia, South Carolina, North Carolina, and Virginia consist of two main types: the residual, fine-textured, poorly drained soils of the Piedmont, and the sedimentary, coarse-textured, well-drained soils of the Coastal Plain. The differences between these soils are so great that different systems of soil management are required. As a second example, the soils of Indiana, Michigan, and New York are of two main types: mineral soils derived from glacial till and muck or peat soils derived mostly from decomposed organic matter. Here again, these soils vary widely in texture, water-holding capacity, fertility, drainage, and slope, so that different systems of management are required. Many other examples could be cited.

Thus, because the same crop grown on different soils is likely to require different methods of maintaining fertility and different systems of soil management, a comparatively large number of branch or sub-experiment stations have developed. For example, Washington has five branch stations, Wisconsin has nine, and Nebraska has six. In general, the station at the land-grant college is the main or headquarters station, since it contains the offices of the director and the project leaders, and the other stations are known as branch stations or research centers. The location of the main and branch stations or research centers for the states of California, Michigan, and Mississippi are presented in figures 4.1, 4.2, and 4.3. Note that most of the branch stations or research centers are given over to the solution of problems of a specific industry, or of several industries within a specific environment.

THE FEDERAL STATIONS

Functions of the U.S. Department of Agriculture

In general, the functions of the U.S. Department of Agriculture are fourfold: (1) conducting research to solve the problems of the farmer and the homemaker, (2) disseminating the results of research in usable form to all of the people, (3) assisting the farmer and others to conserve the soil and other natural resources, and (4) maintaining quarantine lines to prevent the spread of serious pests and enforcing other regulatory measures. In general, the research program of the Department is national or regional in scope, whereas that of any given state is local in scope. Of these two types, research on problems that are national or regional in scope is particularly fitting to the function and nature of the Department. Thus, federal agricultural experiment stations are an integral part of the U.S. Department of Agriculture.

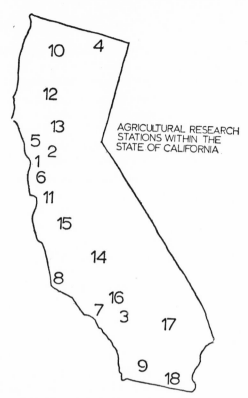

AGRICULTURAL RESEARCH
STATIONS WITHIN THE
STATE OF CALIFORNIA

FIGURE 4.1. *Agricultural research centers and field stations within the state of California. 1. University Station—Berkeley: Research on crops grown in the Santa Clara and adjacent valleys. 2. University Station—Davis: Research on crops and livestock grown in the Sacramento Valley. 3. University Station—Riverside: Research on all phases of subtropical horticulture with emphasis on citrus. 4. Tulelake Field Station: Investigations on field, forage, and vegetable crops with particular attention to production problems of potatoes. 5. Hopland Range Station: The improvement of the range and the management of sheep. 6. Deciduous Fruit Station: Research on diseases of deciduous fruit grown in the Santa Clara Valley. 7. Antaloupe Valley Field Station: Research on problems of field and vegetable crops grown in the Antaloupe Valley. 8. South Coast Field Station: Investigation of production problems of fruit, vegetable, and ornamental crops grown in the area. 9. Imperial Valley Field Station: Research with crops and livestock produced in the Imperial Valley. 10. Wolfskill Horticultural Station: Investigations on deciduous fruits grown in northern California. 11. Vegetable Crops Department Station: Research on production and marketing problems of vegetable crops grown in the Salinas Valley. 12. The Napa Experimental Vineyard: Investigation on the production of grapes. 13. U.S. Department of Agriculture Rice Station: Problems on the production of rice with a limited amount of research on alternate crops. 14. The U.S. San Joaquin Experiment Range: Research on problems pertaining to livestock on the range. 15. The U.S. Fruit Investigations Laboratory: Research with peaches and grapes and other fruits grown in the Fresno district. 16. The U.S. Cotton Field Station: Investigations on the production of cotton grown in the lower San Joaquin Valley. 17. The U.S. Date Garden: Problems on the production and management of dates. 18. The U.S. South West Field Station: Investigations on soils and crops of the Imperial Valley.*

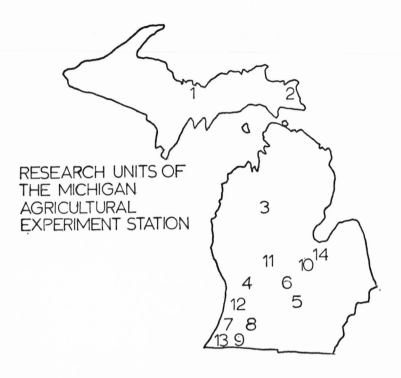

RESEARCH UNITS OF
THE MICHIGAN
AGRICULTURAL
EXPERIMENT STATION

FIGURE 4.2. *Agricultural and forestry research units within the state of Michigan. 1. Upper Peninsula Experiment Station, Chatham, established 1907: Beef, dairy, soils, and crops. 2. Dunbar Forest Experiment Station, Sault Sainte Marie, established 1925: Forest management. 3. Lake City Experiment Station, Lake City, established 1928: Breeding, feeding, and management of beef cattle; fish pond production studies. 4. Graham Horticultural Experiment Station, Grand Rapids, established 1919: Varieties, orchard soil management, spray methods. 5. Headquarters Station, 101 Agriculture Hall, East Lansing, established 1888: Research work in all phases of Michigan agriculture and related fields. 6. Muck Experiment Farm, Laingsburg; plots established 1941: Crop production practices on muck and peat soils. 7. South Haven Experiment Station, South Haven, established 1890: Breeding peaches, blueberries, apricots; small fruit management. 8. W. K. Kellogg Farm and Bird Sanctuary, Hickory Corners, and W. K. Kellogg Forest, Augusta, established 1928: Forest management, wildlife studies, mink production, and dairy nutrition. 9. Fred Russ Forest, Cassopolis, established 1942: Hardwood forest management. 10. Ferden Farm, Chesaning; plots established 1928: Soil management, with special emphasis on sugar beets (Land Leased). 11. Montcalm Experimental Farm, Entrican, established 1966: Research on crops for processing, with special emphasis on potatoes. (Land Leased). 12. Sodus Horticultural Experiment Station, Sodus, established 1954: Production of small fruit and vegetable crops. (Land Leased). 13. Trevor Nichols Experimental Farm, Fennville, established 1967: Studies related to fruit crop production with emphasis on pesticides research. 14. Saginaw Valley Beet and Bean Research Farm, Saginaw, established 1971: Studies related to production of sugar beets and dry edible beans in rotation programs.*

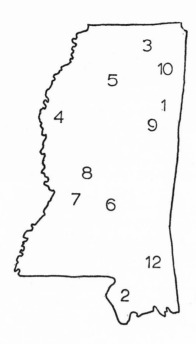

AGRICULTURE AND FORESTRY RESEARCH
UNITS OF MISSISSIPPI STATE UNIVERSITY

FIGURE 4.3. *Agricultural and forestry research units within the state of Mississippi.*
1. *Headquarters Agriculture and Forestry Research Center, Mississippi State, established 1888: Research in all phases of Mississippi agriculture, forestry, home economics, and related fields. 2. South Mississippi Research Center, Poplarville, established 1900: Research in all phases of agriculture of south Mississippi with emphasis on tung. 3. North Mississippi Research Center, Holly Springs, established 1902: Research on agriculture problems of the Hill Section of North Mississippi. 4. Delta Research Center, Stoneville, established 1904: Research on all phases of the agriculture and forestry of the Mississippi Delta. 5. Pontotoc Ridge-Flatwood Research Center, Pontotoc, established 1960: Research on agriculture problems characteristic of the Pontotoc-Flatwoods area. 6. Truck Crops Research Center, Crystal Springs, established 1938: Research on problems confronting growers in producing vegetables for fresh market and for processing. 7. Coastal Plain Research Center, Newton, established 1946: Research on problems of the agriculture and forestry industries of the Upper Coastal Plain. 8. Brown Loam Research Center, Oakley, established 1948: Research on problems of the Brown Loam area with emphasis on production of cattle. 9. Blackland Research Center, Brooksville, established 1946: Research on problems of crops grown in the Blackland area with emphasis on beef cattle and sheep. 10. Northeast Mississippi Research Center, Tupelo, established 1946: Research on crops grown in northeast Mississippi with emphasis on dairy production. 11. Forestry Research Center, Bothwell, established 1971: Intensive culture of pine forests and studies of tree improvement through genetics (Land Leased). 12. Horticulture Research Center, Beaumont, established 1971: Research on the economic production of vegetable crops, with emphasis on leafy vegetables.*

The Origin, Change in Location, and Growth of the Headquarters Station. As with the state experiment stations, only one federal station was established at first. This station began in 1862, with nine employees housed in the basement of the Patent Office Building in Washington, D.C. They conducted experiments mostly on plant propagation in the gardens and greenhouses between present-day Madison Avenue and Adams Drive and between Fourth and Sixth Streets, Northwest. Sometime later the Department acquired an area between Independence and Constitution Avenues for the conducting of experiments. With the continual demand and need for research, the Department in 1900 acquired the Arlington Farm, a 400-acre tract[8] on the Virginia side of the Potomac opposite Washington, for investigations in plant science. In 1910 the Department acquired a 475-acre tract fifteen miles northeast of Washington for investigations in animal science. Finally, in 1941 the experimental work on plant science at the Arlington Farm was transferred to the greatly enlarged experimental farm and laboratories at Beltsville, Maryland, which resulted in the formation of the present-day U.S. Department of Agriculture National Agricultural Research Center.

The Modern Nationwide System of Federal Stations

The modern federal system of agricultural experiment stations consists of the Headquarters Station—the National Agricultural Research Center at Beltsville, Maryland—the North, South, East, and West Utilization Laboratories, and a series of specific-purpose laboratories. The location and purpose of each of the laboratories are shown in table 4-2. Note the wide range of problems under investigation.

In general, the research workers at the Beltsville Station investigate problems that are national or international in scope, while those at the utilization and specific-purpose laboratories investigate problems that are regional or local in scope. In addition to the workers at federal stations, there are federal workers at the state stations. These workers may investigate problems singly, or, more frequently, they work as members of research teams consisting of both federal and state workers. For example, in 1939 Congress appropriated a modest sum of money for a cooperative and coordinated research program with sweet potatoes. The research team consisted of five federal workers and nine state workers and included five horticulturists, three plant physiologists, two biochemists, two plant pathologists, and one geneticist and plant breeder. Within a period of six years they had found answers to six cultural problems, and within a period of twenty years they had

---

[8]The Pentagon now occupies this tract.

Table 4-2.

NAME, LOCATION, AND PURPOSE OF U.S. DEPARTMENT
OF AGRICULTURE RESEARCH LABORATORIES*

Utilization Laboratory	*Location*	*Purpose* *(To develop new uses* *for crops shown)*
Northern	Peoria, IL	Cereal grains, soy beans
Southern	New Orleans, LA	Cotton, cotton seed, tung, peanuts
Eastern	Windmon, PA	Fruits, vegetables, tobacco
Western	Albany, CA	Wheat, wool, fruits and vegetables, rice

Special or *Specific Laboratory*	*Location*	*Purpose*
Cotton Ginning	Stoneville, MS	Study problems on cotton fiber
Cotton Boll Weevil	Mississippi State, MS	Eradicate the boll weevil
National Seed Storage	Fort Collins, CO	Preserve superior germ plasm
Vegetable Breeding	Charleston, SC	Develop superior varieties
Forest Products	Madison, WI	Investigate problems in use of wood
Salinity	Riverside, CA	Control salinity in soils
National Arboretum	District of Columbia	Study ornamental trees and shrubs
National Animal Disease	Ames, IA	Develop methods of control of infectious diseases
Dairy Breeding Research Center	University Park, PA	Study the breeding value of bulls and the storage of sperm
Plum Island Animal Disease Center	Plum Island, NY	Study the control of foreign diseases
European Parasite	France	Multiply insect predators

*From U.S. Department of Agriculture Yearbook for 1962.

developed a total of thirty-six new varieties.[9] This is just one instance
of teamwork at its best between state and federal workers and between
members of related disciplines, in this instance the sciences of plant

---

[9]From *Twenty Years of Cooperative Sweet Potato Research, 1939-1959.* Department of Horticulture, Louisiana State University, Baton Rouge, LA.

physiology, plant biochemistry, plant genetics, plant pathology, and horticulture, all of the members working together harmoniously for the success of the program as a whole.

THE SITUATION AT A TYPICAL MORRILL
LAND-GRANT UNIVERSITY

The campuses of most of the Morrill land-grant colleges, and in some instances the campuses of the branch stations, contain both state- and federally-supported laboratories for agricultural research. This placing of both state- and federally-supported scientists on the same campus is particularly advantageous in that it provides for quick and effective communication between individuals. Thus, whenever one worker wishes to consult with another worker in a related field all he has to do is pick up the phone or walk in a matter of minutes to the office of the other. No distinction exists as to whether one is a state or a federal worker. The main thing is the solution of the problem at hand.

Accomplishments

The accomplishments of the scientists of the agricultural experiment stations may be placed in three closely related categories:
1. The scientists have shown that the methods of science can solve problems in the production, processing, and marketing of agricultural products. In general, methods in science require the quantitative measure of performance. Examples are weight of product or plant per unit area, or weight of milk or butterfat per cow over a definite period of time. These quantitative measures, although crude at first, have become highly refined, so much so that a science of quantitative measurement in agriculture has developed. This science is known as the science of agricultural statistics and experimental field plot design. These refinements have instilled confidence in the investigators in the interpretation of their results, and in making recommendations to the farmers.
2. The scientists in the publication of their results have developed the scientific literature of agriculture. In other words, the experimental results constitute the science of each of the many fields of agriculture: agronomy, animal science, dairy science, entomology, horticulture, plant pathology and weed science, veterinary science, agricultural engineering, agricultural economics, and so forth. Since problems in production, processing, and marketing have increased with the years, the literature in any given field has accordingly increased, and the individual investigators must spend considerable time in order to keep up with the literature in his own and related fields.
3. The scientists right from the beginning felt that their function

did not end with the publication of their results but that they should show the farmer how to use the results. Invariably the application of the research makes farming more profitable; that is, it puts more money in the farmer's pocketbook. This philosophy or attitude on the part of the agricultural scientist toward his fellowman is doubtless the reason why the agricultural experiment stations have received public acclaim throughout the years. In the last analysis they bring happiness to mankind. As Einstein said in an address to the student body of the California Institute of Technology: "Concern for man himself and his fate must always form the chief interest of all technical endeavors . . . in order that the creations of our minds shall be a pleasure and not a curse to mankind."

RESEARCH IN HOME ECONOMICS

The reasons for the development of research in home economics are similar to those for the development of research in agriculture. At first there was no science of home economics, no set of abiding facts and principles that could be applied to the solution of any given situation. As a result, the research workers and teachers taught empirical home economics with emphasis on the "how" rather than the "why." In addition, the workers made contact with farmers' wives in order to determine the pertinent problems. This was particularly the case in the Midwest, where farm women auxiliary programs were conducted with those of the Farmers' Institutes. Iowa State College established the first kitchen for experimental purposes in 1877, and the University of Illinois employed the first full-time research worker in 1908. Examples of projects during this early period are the testing of popular and uncommon recipes on consumer acceptability, a study of different yeasts in the making of bread, and the determination of the role of pectins in the making of jelly. However, only a relatively small number of colleges were conducting investigations in home economics, and these were made in isolation and without coordination.

The Nationwide Research Program

The need to develop and support a nationwide research program in this subject was brought about by the food crises of World War I[10] and the discovery that certain vitamins were deficient in the diet of large segments of the population. Consequently, Congress, with the

---

[10] A slogan of World War I was "Food will Win the War," and the federal government requested all home economists to develop and disseminate information on the conservation of food.

consent of the people, provided funds by means of the Purnell Act for research in home economics at all of the Morrill land-grant colleges. In general, these research projects are of three types: (1) on foods and human nutrition, (2) on clothing and household and money management in the home, and (3) on social relations among members of the same family, and among families of the same community. Thus, with the establishment of a nationwide system of investigations in home economics, the scientific literature in this field increased rapidly, with a corresponding increase in teaching the "why," the law or principle underlying a process or practice, rather than the "how," the steps in performance of a process or practice.

RESEARCH IN ENGINEERING

In general, research in engineering consists of the investigation of problems within the broad field of engineering—civil, mechanical, mining, chemical, electrical, aerospace, or any other type of nonbiological engineering. This research may be beneficial to a large segment of society or it may be beneficial to a relatively small group only. Examples of the former are studies on the use of sunlight in providing heat for the home, or studies of insulating materials in the transfer of heat. Examples of the latter are studies on the comparative performance of engines operated by diesel fuel, steam, or gasoline. Thus, in contrast with research in agriculture, which benefits all of the people, research in engineering may be beneficial to a large segment of the population or to a relatively small or special group only. In other words, research in agriculture is open in nature, because the results on a particular problem are available to all of the farmers and consumers affected by that problem, whereas research in engineering is somewhat closed and monopolistic in nature. The results on any given problem are not always available to manufacturers affected by that problem.

The Obligation of the First Morrill Act

As stated in chapter 2, the Morrill Act required the teaching of such branches of learning as are related to agriculture and *the mechanic arts*. Consequently, the first Board of Trustees, the first presidents, and the first faculties at the various colleges felt that research in engineering was necessary in order to upbuild the science and teaching of engineering in its various fields. As a result, the Morrill land-grant colleges established research programs in engineering as far as their faculties and facilities permitted. Illinois established the first station in 1903, and other Morrill land-grant colleges followed in quick succession: Iowa State and Wisconsin in 1904, Pennsylvania State in 1908, Missouri in 1909, Kansas State in 1910, Ohio State in 1913, and Purdue in 1917. In fact, of the fifty-four Morrill land-grant colleges and universities forty-six had officially established an engineering experiment station by 1946.

Source of Funds and Modus Operandi

In sharp contrast to the agricultural experiment stations, intrastate rivalry has existed between the Morrill land-grant colleges and the first state universities. When the Morrill land-grant colleges applied for funds the first state universities opposed the measure, and when the first state universities applied for funds, the Morrill land-grant colleges opposed the measure. But each type of university found that it could obtain funds for research by the contract method. In general, for any given problem a contract or memorandum of agreement is drawn up by the experiment station on the one hand and the contracting agency on the other hand. Both public and private agencies honor this type of contract. Examples of public agencies are the National Science Foundation, National Aeronautical and Space Administration, U.S. Air Force, Office of Naval Research, National Oceanographic and Atmospheric Administration, National Marine Fisheries Service, U.S. Office of Transportation, and the departments of highways of the several states. Examples of private corporations are General Motors, General Electric, Hughes Aircraft Company, Bechtel Corporation, and the light and power companies of the several states. Examples of research projects conducted during the early period (1862 to 1940) are listed as follows. Note the wide range of subjects that were investigated.

synthesis and evaluation of convex-concave gear tooth surfaces
studies on refuse collection and sanitary landfill deposition
stabilization of Illinois soils
performance of lubricating oils in automotive engines
design and operation of cooling towers
studies on high frequency electric insulation
disposal of waste from creameries, beet-sugar factories,
    and paper mills
studies on the transfer of heat through building and insulating
    materials
studies on the physical and reinforcement properties of bamboo
development and operation of air-conditioning systems
tests of reinforced concrete beams
acoustics of auditoriums
alumination of farm and town houses
effectiveness of stated-speed-slow signs
impact tests of nickel-cromium steel
some effects of soil, water, and climate on the construction, life,
    and maintenance of highways

effect of quality and intensity of light on visual performance
boiler water troubles and treatments
truck operating costs

Examples of research projects during the modern period as follows.
Here again note the wide range of topics that were investigated.

some causes of paint peeling
air infiltration through weather-stripped and nonweather-stripped
   windows
studies on esturine pollution problems
data analysis and correlation with digital computers
high-quality water for rural homes
development of synthetic oxide pigments
thermal conductivity of emulsions and suspensions
effect of drying on the freezing-thawing durability of concrete
space enclosure systems, the variability of packing cell design
systems analysis of the economic utilization of warm water discharged
   from power generating stations
a study of new safety systems designed for nuclear power reactors
studies of the use of coal as a fuel for diesel engines
parking practices on college campuses of the United States
effect of heat treatment of garbage on survival of disease organisms

Accomplishments

In common with the research programs of the agricultural and home
economics experiment stations, the research programs of the engineering
experiment stations have promoted the welfare of the people in many
ways. In particular, they have developed new knowledge in each of
the great fields of engineering. This new knowledge in turn has been
invaluable in the education and training of young men and women
during their undergraduate years, and in their continuing education
after graduation. In this way, the engineering experiment stations have
promoted the efficiency of the numerous engineering enterprises throughout the United States and the remainder of the world.

RESEARCH PUBLICATIONS OF THE AGRICULTURE, HOME ECONOMICS, AND ENGINEERING EXPERIMENT STATIONS

Research publications of the experiment stations consist essentially
in the presentation and interpretation of the results of experimental
data. In general, the data on any given problem represent the frontier
of knowledge of that problem—the twilight zone between the known
and the unknown. Further, the running of experiments based on the

methods of science is exploratory in nature. For these reasons, the data are extremely valuable and should be immediately applied to the problem in question or stored for application to problems in the future. The presentation, interpretation, and storage of data are usually done by means of the printed word in the form of research publications. In general, these are of four types: (1) technical or research bulletins, (2) bulletins, (3) circulars and research reports, and (4) statistical bulletins. In general, technical or research publications contain new data on basic or fundamental problems that may or may not have immediate application and are of interest mainly to scientists working in the same or related fields. Bulletins present and interpret data that have immediate application over a relatively wide field. Circulars and research reports present and interpret data that can be applied to a specific problem or to a relatively narrow field. Finally, statistical bulletins of the U.S. Department of Agriculture are essentially inventory in nature; that is, they list and catalog the agricultural resources of the nation. Examples are the number of fruit trees, the production of agronomic, horticultural, and forest products for any given year, and the number of beef and dairy animals, hogs, sheep, and horses or mules over a definite period of time.

REFERENCES

Eddy, Edward D. 1956. *Colleges of Our Land and Times: The Land-Grant Idea in American Education.* Westport, CT, Greenwood Press, chapter 6, pp. 166-74.
     A former vice-president and provost of the University of New Hampshire presents an understandable statement of the research in agriculture, home economics, and engineering at the Morrill land-grant colleges and universities from 1915 to 1937.
Mumford, F. B. 1940. *The Land-Grant College Movement.* Missouri Agricultural Experiment Station Bulletin 419, Columbia, MO.
     The author, a former dean of the College of Agriculture of the University of Missouri, discusses the unique place of the Morrill land-grant college in human affairs. Principal topics are the development and spirit of the Morrill land-grant colleges and universities, and the origin and development of the agricultural experiment stations and the agricultural extension services.
Rossiter, Margaret W. 1975. *The Emergence of Agricultural Science.* Yale University Press, New Haven, CT.
     The author discusses the emergence of agricultural science in the United States, particularly in relation to the analysis of soils, the sources of nitrogen, and the role of essential elements in crop-plant metabolism.
True, Alfred C. 1937. *A History of Agricultural Experimentation and Research in the United States.* U.S. Department of Agriculture Miscellaneous Publication 251, Washington, DC.
     A detailed review of agricultural research in all of its phases from the colonial period to about 1925.

5

THE RESIDENT TEACHING
DIMENSION

*We do not learn for the sake of learning; only through its use does
knowledge bear fruit of benefit to man.*
—WALTER REUTHER, *Past President,*
American Society for Horticultural
Science

THE FUNCTION OF RESIDENT TEACHING

In general, agriculture comprises a galaxy of several distinct but
closely related fields. The fields of crop production—agronomy, horticulture, and soils; the fields of animal production—animal husbandry,
dairy husbandry, and poultry husbandry; the fields of agricultural and
biological engineering; and the fields of agricultural economics. These
fields are interrelated in that all of them are based on the activities of
the crop-plant, and they are distinct in that each field is concerned with
the production, processing, and marketing of distinct products for human
consumption and/or enjoyment. Further, each field is comparatively
wide and requires the development and training of leaders within any
one of its component parts. This development of leaders is the prime
function of the resident teaching dimension. Important steps in the
development of leadership in students are (1) inculcating the students
in the fundamentals underlying their respective field of interest, (2)
teaching them how to apply the fundamentals to the solution of practical problems, and (3) providing them with opportunities to learn
how to teach others.

In like manner, engineering is also a galaxy of fields—the fields of
mechanical, civil, electrical, chemical, petroleum, and aerospace engineering. Each field is comparatively wide and requires the development
and training of leaders within any one of its component parts. Here
again, steps in the development and training of leaders are quite similar
to those used within any one of the fields of agriculture. In fact, this
process is very similar for the development of students in all fields
embraced by the Morrill land-grant colleges and universities. In general,
these include the fields of agriculture, engineering, home economics,
business and industry, applied science, education, and veterinary and
human medicine.

RESIDENT TEACHING IN AGRICULTURE

The Early Period (1855-1907)

Status of Basic Reactions and Processes. Scientific agriculture is based on the energy relations of crop-plants and crop-animals. These in turn are centered on the rates of photosynthesis and on the rates of respiration, and water-absorption-transpiration in crop-plants, and on the rates of respiration and metabolism in crop-animals. During this early period the effect of both genetic and environmental factors on the rate of each of the three basic processes in crop-plants and the rate of the two basic reactions in crop-animals were not fully understood. In other words, and as pointed out in chapter 3, there was practically no science of American agriculture in 1855. Consequently, the professors of agriculture set about creating this science. In general, and as discussed in chapter 3, for any given state, they (1) visited and/or corresponded with the most progressive farmers to determine the most pertinent problems, (2) established experiments to provide data for the solution of any given problem, (3) invited growers in the vicinity of the college to observe the results of any given experiment, (4) published the results of the experiments in local newspapers and farm journals for the benefit of all the people, and (5) presented the results of experimental work in class for the benefit of the students. For any given industry within the wide field of agriculture, the experiments for the most part consisted in testing crop-plant varieties and breeds of farm animals, in evaluating crop-plant and crop-animal practices, and in developing new and more efficient practices. In this way, the science of American agriculture was born. In the meantime, the professors taught empirical agriculture—a method based on practices of the most progressive farmers. Thus, during this early period the teaching of empirical agriculture was dominant, with emphasis on the "how" of any given practice rather than on the "why."

Narrow vs. Broad Curricula in Developing Students. During the early period, the Board of Trustees of three institutions, Michigan Agricultural College, the Ohio Agricultural and Mechanical College, and Illinois Industrial University, were not fully agreed on the breadth of training for the students. Should the curricula be relatively narrow and limited to subjects that develop the technical aspects of the students only, or should the curricula be relatively wide, and include subjects that lead to the development of the "whole man"?

For example, the faculty of the Agricultural College of the State of Michigan in 1855 established a four-year course leading toward the development of the "whole man." As stated in chapter 1, Dr. J. L.

Williams, the president, said, "First, we would begin with the farmer himself. Morally, physically, and intellectually he must be a man before he can be a farmer. Besides he is also a citizen. He should be able to execute the responsibilities of citizenship with self-reliance and intelligence." However, in 1854, because of hard times (the state treasury was empty), and the philosophy of the state superintendent of public instruction (he favored training in the technical and practical aspects of agriculture only), the governing board reduced the courses of instruction from four years to two years by eliminating such courses as English literature, ethics, mathematics, history, and moral philosophy. Since the two-year course was published in many state newspapers and farm magazines, the people in general had opportunity to express their opinion on the subject. Understandably, most of the students, most of the editors, and most of the leaders in agriculture preferred the four-year course. Accordingly, since sentiment throughout the state had crystallized in favor of the broad curriculum, the legislature in 1851 passed a law that specified that "the agricultural course should embrace not less than four years" and that the curriculum should develop the "whole man." Thus, courses in the English language, English literature, ethics, government, history, mathematics, and philosophy were reinstated.

From 1870 to 1872 the Board of Trustees of the Ohio Agricultural and Mechanical College was split wide open on whether to establish a so-called narrow or wide curriculum. The exponents of the narrow curriculum believed that emphasis should be put on the practical aspects of agriculture only; that is, the courses should be set up to develop efficient farmers and mechanics. On the other hand, the exponents of the wide curriculum believed that all phases in the life of the farmer and mechanic should be considered; that is, the course should not only develop efficiency in his chosen field but also inculcate in him the responsibilities of first-class citizenship. On a vote of whether to adopt the narrow or broad curriculum, six favored the narrow and seven favored the broad. Thus, the Board established a curriculum designed to develop the "whole man."

The Illinois Industrial University opened its doors in 1868. At that time there were differences of opinion on the interpretation of the Morrill Act. In general, there were the so-called narrow-gaugers and the broad-gaugers. The narrow-gaugers wanted to exclude from the curriculum all subjects that were not directly connected with the field of agriculture and mechanic arts, such as studies in history, English, literature, and foreign languages. In sharp contrast the broad-gaugers wanted to include not only courses directly concerned with the fields of agriculture or mechanics but courses in the classics. In other words, should the curriculum aim to develop the technical side of the student only, or should it develop both the technical and the cultural side?

Dr. J. M. Gregory, the first president, by virtue of his education and experience, settled this question in favor of the broad-gaugers. He stated, "One-half of the public value of a body of educated agriculturists and machinists would be lost, if they lack the literary culture which will enable them to communicate through the press or by public speech their knowledge and discoveries."

Formation of the American Association of Agricultural Teachers. In 1870, the teachers of agriculture of the Morrill land-grant colleges in the states of the Midwest and the Northeast arranged through correspondence to get together for a meeting in Chicago. The purpose of this meeting was to exchange ideas and experiences and to discuss pertinent problems. An important feature of this and subsequent meetings was a discussion on the place of the compulsory labor requirement on the part of the students. For the most part, two types of labor projects had developed: (1) ordinary housekeeping chores such as sweeping floors, cleaning stables, digging ditches, and taking care of lawns, shrubs, and trees; and (2) assisting the teachers in the preparation of material for use in class. In general, the teachers agreed that projects of the former type had very little, if any, effect on the development of the students but that projects of the latter type, if properly conducted and coordinated with the classroom work, could have a beneficial effect.

In fact, the teachers agreed that the real object of student labor was to inculcate the students in the principles within their particular fields. As a result, the teachers eliminated the housekeeping chores but retained projects directly related to the student's sphere of interest. For example, students in dairy husbandry worked on curricula-related projects within the field of dairying, and students in agronomy or horticulture worked on curricula-related projects within the respective fields of agronomy and horticulture. In this way, and as discussed in chapter 14, the labor requirement gradually changed to the laboratory requirement of specific courses not only within the field of agriculture but also within the related fields of chemistry, physics, botany, and zoology.

The Intermediate Period (1907-1940)

Status of Basic Reactions and Processes. During the intermediate period the effects of both genetic and environmental factors on the basic biochemical reactions and biophysical processes in crop-plants and crop-animals received considerable attention. With crop-plants the effect of major genetic and environmental factors on the rates of photosynthesis, respiration, and water absorption-transpiration and their relation to the all-important marketable yield became well understood. With crop-animals, the effect of many major factors pertaining to breeds, feed, and environment on the rates of respiration and metabolism and their relation to the marketable yield, e.g., milk and its products, beef, bacon, and eggs, was also investigated and elucidated. As a result, the scientific literature of major crop-plants and crop-animals markedly increased. In other words, the many fields within the wide and expansive field of agriculture attained the status and prestige of an applied science. Thus, during this intermediate period, the teaching of scientific agriculture gradually displaced the teaching of empirical agriculture, with more emphasis on the "why" of any given practice rather than on the "how."

The Morrill Act of 1890 and its Nelson Amendment of 1907. The purpose of the Morrill Act of 1890, the so-called second Morrill Act, was to provide "for a more complete endowment and support of all of the Morrill land-grant colleges." It carried an initial appropriation of $1,500 to each state or territory and provided an annual increase of $1,000 for ten years, after which the appropriation would be $25,000. As with the Morrill Act of 1862 the funds could not be "spent for the purchase, erection, preservation or repair of any building or buildings." In fact, the Congress specifically restricted the use of the funds "to instruction in agriculture, the mechanic arts, the English language, the various branches of mathematics [and to], physical, natural and economic science with special reference to their applications in the industries of life, and to the facilities for such instruction."

The Nelson Amendment of 1907 also provided funds for an enlarged endowment and support of all of the Morrill land-grant colleges. It carried an initial appropriation of $5,000 to each state or territory and an annual increase of this sum by $5,000 for four years, after which the annual appropriation would be $25,000. The Amendment also included the following provisions: "The colleges may use a portion of this money for the preparation of instructors for teaching the elements of agriculture and mechanic arts in the grade and high schools." According to True[1] by 1910 forty-six of the land-grant colleges had developed training courses for the teaching of agriculture in high schools, and in more than half of these land-grant colleges the courses covered a period of three to four years.

The Modern Period (1940-1975)

Status of Basic Reactions and Processes. With the continued investment in agricultural research on the part of the people, as manifested by the growth and development of the state and federal agricultural experiment stations, and as briefly described in chapter 4, the scientific

---

[1]Alfred C. True. 1937. *A History of Agricultural Education in the United States.* U.S. Department of Agriculture Miscellaneous Publication 251, Washington, DC.

literature of the many fields of agriculture correspondingly increased. In fact, the rate of increase of knowledge was geometrical rather than arithmetical. With the major crop-plants, the effect of the principal environmental factors and practices on the rates of photosynthesis and respiration and water absorption-transpiration were well understood, and investigations were started on the relation of phytohormones and growth regulators to crop-plant behavior. With crop-animals, the relation of major environmental factors on the rates of respiration and metabolism was also well understood, and investigations were started in the effects of natural and synthetic hormones on animal behavior. As a result, and in sharp contrast to the early and intermediate periods, the teaching dimension during the modern period was almost entirely on a scientific basis, with emphasis almost entirely on the "why."

THE BLACK MORRILL LAND-GRANT COLLEGES

The black Morrill land-grant colleges are located in the Southeastern quadrant of the United States—one in each of the sixteen states presented in Table 5-1. Their development is divided into two periods: the early and the modern.

Table 5-1.
THE BLACK MORRILL LAND-GRANT COLLEGES AND UNIVERSITIES*

Established Before 1890

Lincoln University (Missouri) 1866, Alcorn A and M University (Mississippi) 1871, Virginia State College 1872, Arkansas A, M and N College 1875, Alabama A and M College 1875, Kentucky State University 1877, Prairie View A and M College (Texas) 1879, Southern University (Louisiana) 1880, Florida A and M University 1887, University of Maryland-Princess Ann 1887.

Established Between 1890 and 1913

Fort Valley State College (Georgia) 1890, Delaware State College 1891, North Carolina A and Technical College 1894, South Carolina State College 1896, Langston University (Oklahoma) 1897, Tennessee A and Ind. University 1913.

*From E. D. Eddy, Jr., 1957, *Colleges of Our Land and Time.* Harper and Bros., New York, NY.

The Early Period (1866-1940)

During the early period the black land-grant colleges encountered problems different from those of the corresponding white institutions.

In the first place, the educational level of the students was exceedingly low. For example, in 1914 a total of 5,998 students were enrolled in the sixteen colleges.[2] Of these 5,998 students, 3,367 were studying subjects at the grade school level, 2,618 were studying subjects at the high school level, and only 12 were ready for study of subjects at the college level. In the second place, no funds were available for research in any field. Consequently, the stimulation and satisfaction in acquiring new knowledge with its subsequent beneficial effect on resident teaching and extension were lacking. Thus, the program of the black land-grant colleges was confined largely to upgrading the educational level of the students and to training the students in the manual arts: for the young men training in the care of autos, farm tractors, and farm machinery, in carpentry, and in masonry; for the young women training in cooking and sewing and other phases of household management.

The Modern Period (1940-1970)

During the modern period the legislature of each respective state markedly increased the funds for resident teaching and extension work, and they appropriated funds for research in agriculture and home economics for each of the sixteen institutions. In addition, the black and white colleges of each state joined hands to coordinate their respective programs. This coordination has greatly strengthened the work of the black land-grant colleges. They are now engaged in each of the three great dimensions: research, resident teaching, and extension. Further, they belong with the white land-grant colleges and universities to the prestigious and highly respected Association of Land-Grant Colleges and Universities.

THE EFFECT OF FUNDS PROVIDED BY THE MORRILL ACT OF 1890 AND ITS NELSON AMENDMENT

In general, the funds provided by the Morrill Act of 1890 and its Amendment had a markedly beneficial effect on the resident teaching dimension of all of the Morrill land-grant colleges. In particular, they provided (1) for the expansion of the Department of Agriculture at each college into a School of Agriculture with its six traditional departments: agronomy soils, horticulture, animal husbandry, dairy husbandry, poultry husbandry, and agricultural economics; and for greatly strengthening the four supporting sciences: physics, chemistry, botany, and zoology; (2) for the expansion of the Department of Mechanic Arts at

---

[2]E. D. Eddy, Jr. 1957. *Colleges of Our Land and Time.* Harper and Bros., New York, NY.

each college into a School of Engineering with its four traditional departments: mechanical, civil, electrical, and chemical, and for strengthening the supporting sciences of advanced mathematics, physics, and chemistry; (3) for strengthening the teaching of English throughout the colleges as a whole; (4) for the establishment and support of certain black land-grant colleges and support of others; and (5) for increasing the salaries of the teachers in many of the colleges and in preventing decreases in others. More particularly, the use of these funds marked a transition of the teaching dimension from a period of doubt and uncertainty to a period of growth and development, with the subsequent extension of service to the people.

METHODS OF RESIDENT INSTRUCTION
DURING THE MODERN PERIOD

In any teaching situation, the chief components are the teacher and the students. In general, the teacher is an authority within a highly specialized field or subject, and he is likely to be a "hybrid," with the research and the resident teaching dimensions combined in one person. In this way, the teacher is familiar with the results of research within a highly specific field, and with the production and marketing problems within that field. Further, the student appreciates the opportunity to learn from a successful investigator. The principal methods in this research-teacher-student relationship are the lecture, the recitation, the seminar, and the research paper. Each method has advantages and disadvantages.

The Lecture

In the lecture method the principal objective is to provide an opportunity for the student to acquire basic knowledge within a highly specific field, and to learn how to apply this knowledge to the solution of practical problems within that field. In general, the teacher expounds or lectures, always keeping in mind the needs and requirements of the students. Naturally, for the freshman and sophomore levels the teacher emphasizes basic laws or concepts and their application to specific practices and problems. He uses various teaching methods—tables, graphs, slides, and filmstrips. At the same time, the teacher assists the student to take effective and meaningful notes—notes that will help the student to develop his working knowledge, to prepare him for examinations, and to assist him in his work after graduation. The main advantage of this method is that the teacher can cover a relatively large area of the subject in a short time. Its main disadvantage is that the active interest of the student is likely to be lost.

The Recitation

In the recitation method the principal objective is to provide an opportunity for further inculcation in the fundamentals, and more particularly to enable the student to take an active part in class. In general, the teacher assigns a particular topic, for example, a chapter in a text or a research paper for discussion in class, and asks questions primarily to determine whether any given student has mastered the assignment. Here again, the teacher is the authority. Quite often the topic for discussion consists of data from his own research program or that of an associate or group of associates. Thus, the main advantage of this method is that the teacher becomes familiar with the specific needs and requirements of the individual student. Its main disadvantage is that it is adapted to small classes only.

The Seminar

In the seminar method the primary objective is to provide an opportunity for the upperclassmen or graduate students to become teachers. In this method, the student is the active component while the teacher remains in the background. The method is based on the principle that one learns a subject by teaching the subject. In general, the method consists of reporting the results of research within the student's field of interest, by placing experimental data on the blackboard, and by discussing the data and making practical applications. The research may have been done by the student, by the teacher, or by an associate of the teacher. The main advantage of this method is that the student acquires competence and ability to interpret research results, and an ability to speak before an audience, in this case, his fellow classmates.

The Research Paper

In the three previous methods the students acquire ability to interpret data obtained by someone else. In the research paper the students collect, organize, and present their own data. In other words, the development of the research paper involves three overlapping sequential stages: (1) the selection of the problem and the preparation of an outline, which includes reasons for doing the work and the modus operandi for procuring the experimental data; (2) the recording of the data as the experiment progresses and the analyzing and the organizing of the data in summary form when the experiment has been completed; and (3) the preparation of the research paper, which includes a statement of the problem, a review of pertinent literature, the materials and methods used in securing the data, a discussion of the results, and a summary and conclusion. Naturally, all of these steps are performed with the counsel, advice, and guidance of the student's major professor.

The paper is now ready for dissemination to others. The student usually does this by presenting the paper at a seminar held at his own institution or in competition with the papers of other students at a regional or national meeting representing the student's field of interest. Examples of organizations that have student sections are the American Society for Horticultural Science, the American Dairy Association, and the American Society of Agricultural Engineers. To encourage student participation in these societies of his chosen field the society offers awards, usually for the first three outstanding papers. These awards usually consist of cash and a plaque or certificate. In general, most of the papers are excellent. From the standpoint of quality, they are on a par with those prepared and presented by the professors themselves. In this way, the students acquire competence and the ability to solve problems and to become familiar with the methods of science, with its potentialities and its limitations.

OUTSTANDING DEVELOPMENTS OF THE MODERN PERIOD

Outstanding developments of the modern period are (1) the honors program or college, (2) the revision of curricula, and (3) the use of professional counselors.

The Honors Program or College

In essence, the honors program consists of a group of superior students. In general, the program provides opportunities for the student to take advanced work in his chosen field, to exchange ideas with other superior students and with the faculty, and more particularly to conduct research and develop understandable research papers. For the most part, the program is under the guidance of a director, an honors committee or faculty, and an honors council consisting of groups of students enrolled in the program. High scholarship is required throughout, with the student having an average grade of B when he enters the program and maintaining an average grade of B while he is a member of the program. Although the modus operandi varies with the land-grant university, the objectives are the same—the development of scholars, since high scholarship is essential for the development of effective research, resident teaching, and extension programs throughout the country and the rest of the world.

Revision of Curricula

As previously stated, the quality of the resident teaching dimension depends on the quality of the research dimension. With the continuous discovery of new knowledge, the teaching dimension has always been dynamic—never static. This new knowledge coincided with the development of new departments within each school and with the development of new courses within each department. As a result, a rapid proliferation of courses took place, particularly during the intermediate period. This rapid proliferation led to considerable duplication of content of related courses. Although some repetition is necessary in teaching, frequent repetition is wasteful of the students' and teachers' time and the taxpayers' money. Consequently, the faculties of the land-grant colleges and universities reversed the trend toward duplication, and initiated studies toward effective consolidation of subject matter. For example, in 1964 the college of agriculture at Michigan State eliminated 94 courses (26 percent) and increased the proportion of 4- and 5-hour credit courses, the college of engineering reduced its credit-hour requirements for graduation from 212 to 180 (term basis), and the college of home economics made similar reductions. In 1969, the faculty of Mississippi State, in a university-wide study of curricula, reduced the number of hours required for graduation from 144 to 128 (semester basis). Thus, with the development of new knowledge in any given field, continuous revision of curricula in that field will always be necessary.

Counseling of Students

The counseling of students has always been an integral part of the resident teaching dimension of the land-grant colleges and universities. During the early and intermediate periods this was usually done by the student's major professor. There were definite reasons for this: The major professor had a working knowledge of employment opportunities in the student's field of interest, and of the student's academic performance within this and related fields. In other words, the prospective employer would send inquiries to the professor, and the professor in turn would inform the prospective employer about the qualifications of any student who might be interested. In fact, the prospective employer usually relied wholly on the professor in regard to the student's qualifications. In general, the weakness of this system was that very little attention was given over to the needs of the freshmen. However, this weakness was corrected during the fourth and fifth decades of the twentieth century when a definite number of freshmen within any given college were assigned to a teacher of that college. In general, the professor gave lectures on the origin and role of the college or university, the development of the school and department of the student's major field, and conducted tests on vocational interest and career opportunities.

During the modern period, two types of counseling services became available: (1) career counseling and (2) professional counseling. In career counseling, the students are assisted in making self-appraisals of vocational interest and in interpreting test data toward making a wise vocational choice. In professional counseling the students are assisted to overcome problems pertaining to their growth and development. The staff consists of persons trained in clinical psychology, counseling psychology, and guidance.

REFERENCES

Beal, William J. 1915. *History of the Michigan Agricultural College,* chapter 11. The Agricultural College, East Lansing, MI.

    Teachers of a pioneer land-grant college summarize their respective methods of instruction in chemistry, zoology, botany, veterinary medicine, mechanical engineering, drawing, and shop.

Eddy, E. D., Jr. 1957. *Colleges of Our Land and Time,* chapter 8, "The Negro Land-Grant Colleges." Harper and Bros., New York, NY.

    A sympathetic account of the problems of the black Morrill land-grant colleges during their early period.

Moores, R. G. 1970. *Fields of Rich Toil: The Development of the University of Illinois College of Agriculture,* chapter 3, "The Defeat of the Narrow-Gaugers." University of Illinois Press, Urbana, IL, Chicago, IL, and London, England.

    The controversy between the faculty who favored the broad, liberal education and those who favored the narrow, with the ultimate victory of the broad-gauged group.

True, Alfred C. 1969. *A History of Agricultural Education in the United States,* pp. 272-75. Arno Press and New York Times, New York, NY.

    A detailed account of the reasons for the passage of the Morrill Act of 1890.

6

THE EXTENSION DIMENSION

Many shall run to and fro and knowledge shall be increased.
—DANIEL 3:3

Diffusion of knowledge is the only guardian of true liberty.
—JAMES MADISON

The extension dimension refers to the application of the results of research in all fields of constructive endeavor. Thus, extension work is a form of teaching—a type of education. However, extension differs from resident teaching or instruction in the classroom and/or laboratory in that its philosophy is centered more on the "how" rather than on the "why" of any given reaction, process, or practice. In addition, there are no admission requirements, no prerequisites, no oral or written examinations, no grades, and no college credits. In other words, extension work simply provides opportunities for the individual to increase his efficiency and/or to improve his way of life.

THE GROWTH AND DEVELOPMENT OF EXTENSION WORK IN AGRICULTURE AND HOME ECONOMICS

As previously stated, extension work in agriculture and home economics is based on the results of research. Since these results have been obtained by the scientific method, they are sound, reliable, and relatively accurate, and if they are properly applied they produce excellent results. This is shown by the data in table 7-2 on page 102. Note the increase in the farmer's efficiency throughout the years as determined by the ratio in number of farm workers to the number of nonfarm workers in the United States. Note that as the farmer's efficiency increases the number of workers required for farm work decreases, and the number of workers available for nonfarm enterprises correspondingly increases. This is a matter of considerable importance. Although the production of abundant high-quality foods and fibers at reasonable cost is basic to human life and existence, the production of goods other than foods and fibers is necessary for the development of the so-called abundant and constructive life.

70

THE EARLY PERIOD (1862-1910)

The early period extends from the time the Morrill land-grant colleges were established to the work of Dr. Seaman A. Knapp at the beginning of the twentieth century. During this period several rather distinct but closely related methods developed to extend the results of research to the farmer and the farmer's family. These are briefly discussed as follows.

Personal Conferences and Correspondence

As stated in chapter 2, the Morrill Act provided for the purchase of a farm at each land-grant college, and the professor of agriculture started to conduct experiments as soon as the farm was in satisfactory condition for experimental work. However, before the professors could start their experiments they had to acquire a working knowledge of the farmer's pertinent problems. To acquire this knowledge, they visited the progressive farmers in the vicinity of the colleges and solicited inquiries in newspapers, farm journals, and magazines. In this way the personal conference and correspondence type of extension developed. In general, the professors spent considerable time in answering inquiries and writing articles for newspapers and farm magazines, since all of the letters and articles were written in longhand and secretarial assistance, as it is known at present, was unknown. Fortunately for the professors the enrollment in agriculture was low, their teaching duties were light, and they had time to make the desirable contacts. The personal conference and correspondence type of extension has been very effective throughout the years, and it is still an important part of the work of both the researcher and extension worker of the Morrill land-grant college system.

Farmers' Institutes

Farmers' Institutes were organized conferences or meetings of farmers and the professors of agriculture. In general, any given conference or session had a chairman to introduce the speakers and maintain parliamentary decorum, and a secretary to record the minutes of the meeting and assist the chairman in the performance of his duties. A unique feature of these institutes was the active participation of the farmers and the professors. In other words, the farmers and the professors entered into the discussions quite freely. Thus, the Farmers' Institutes encouraged the free interchange of opinions and ideas. This was extremely beneficial. The farmers discovered that the agricultural college was anxious to help them, and the professors became acquainted with the production and marketing problems of the farmers. This, in turn, greatly assisted the professors in establishing effective research, resident teaching, and extension programs.[1]

Growth and Development. In general, Farmers' Institutes started in the Midwest—in Kansas in 1868, in Illinois and Missouri in 1869, in Iowa in 1870, in Nebraska in 1872, in Michigan in 1875, and in Wisconsin in 1885. From these states the movement spread rapidly to other states. In fact, from the time the Institutes started, the growth of the movement was quite rapid, not only within a state but also for the nation as a whole. Further, in 1896 the directors of Farmers' Institutes of the several states banded themselves together in the formation of the American Association of Farm Institute Workers. These workers met annually until 1919 to exchange ideas and to compare experiences. "No two states had the same plan but the plan of each state had its good points about which the workers sought to be informed. They felt that the workers should meet together and acknowledge their mistakes so that others need not experience the same failures." Moreover, in 1899, Congress recognized the significance of the movement by appropriating funds to provide for a Farm Institute Specialist in the U.S. Department of Agriculture. In general, this officer worked with the directors of the Farmers' Institutes in the several colleges in developing outlines for various courses and in preparing slides and charts for use in the discussions.

Accomplishments and Decline. In general, the Farmers' Institute program was decidedly beneficial to the agriculture faculty and to the farmers. As previously stated, the professors became familiar with the problems of the farmers, and the farmers realized that the professors were anxious to help them in the solution of their problems. This again is an excellent example of two groups working together for the welfare of the whole. However, as indicated in table 6-1, the numbers of Farmers' Institutes rapidly declined from 1914 to 1920. This decline was largely due to the passage of the Smith-Lever Act of 1914, which established a cooperative program in agricultural and home economics extension between the United States Department of Agriculture and each of the several states. With this cooperative and coordinated program the work of the Farmers' Institutes was no longer necessary.

---

[1] In many states the women of the farmers' families attended the Farmers' Institutes. For example, the farm women of Illinois formed an auxiliary organization known as The Association of Domestic Science.

Table 6-1.

GROWTH AND DECLINE OF FARMERS' INSTITUTES
IN THE UNITED STATES FROM 1902 TO 1920*

Year	Total Number of Institutes	Total Persons Attending	Total Funds Allotted (Dollars)
1902	2,772	820,000	163,124
1907	3,927	1,569,877	284,450
1912	6,778	2,549,200	533,972
1914	8,861	3,050,150	449,882
1920	2,991	Not stated	158,000

*From Alfred C. True, 1928, *History of Agriculture Work in the United States.* U.S. Department of Agriculture Miscellaneous Publication 15, Washington, DC.

Agriculture Trains

Agriculture trains were especially equipped trains sent out to provide an opportunity for farmers to consider the use of recommended varieties and practices. In general, they were a cooperative enterprise between the railroad company and the land-grant college of the state through which the trains ran, with the railroad company furnishing at its own expense the locomotive, baggage cars, and coaches, and with the land-grant college furnishing the exhibits and lecturers or teachers. Naturally, the route of each train was well advertised in advance by the use of posters and announcements in local newspapers giving the time of arrival and departure from each depot, the nature of the exhibits to be shown, and the topics to be discussed. When the train arrived at any given depot the farmers were welcomed aboard to view the exhibits, to attend the lectures, and to take part in the discussions, and to receive pamphlets, circulars, or bulletins on recommended practices.

Growth and Decline. Agriculture trains were first operated in co-operation with the School of Agriculture of Iowa State College and two railway companies in 1904. From 1904 to 1911 this type of extension developed rapidly. In 1906 the land-grant colleges and the railroad companies operated agricultural trains in 21 states and in 1911 they operated 71 trains in 28 states with a total attendance of 995,220 people. However, with the passage of the Smith-Lever Act, which contained a section prohibiting the use of extension funds for the operation of trains, the number of trains declined to 34 in 1914, and soon after they passed out of existence. But, as Professor I. O. Schaub, the past director of agricultural extension of North Carolina, said, "It was a wonderful idea for the ten years it lasted."

Farmers' Week or Farm and Home Week

Farmers' Week or Farm and Home Week differs from the past Farmers' Institutes and agricultural trains in that the farmer and his family go to the college. There are definite reasons for this: (1) the period of one week provides an opportunity for the farmer and his family to become acquainted with their Morrill land-grant college and (2) the professors are able to present the results of applied research to the farmer and his family. In general, and for any given institution, the program usually consists of the giving of addresses on subjects of general interest to farm families by persons of national or international prominence, discussing the results of research by members of the experiment station and the extension service, preparing and setting up exhibits, usually by students of various vocational clubs in the several fields of agriculture, and home economics, and parading prize livestock, usually by the students and faculty of the animal husbandry department.

Actually, Farmers' Week or Farm and Home Week is an outgrowth of the Farmers' Institutes. They began during the first and second decades of the twentieth century, at Massachusetts Agricultural College and Pennsylvania State College in 1907, at Ohio State University in 1911, and at Michigan Agricultural College in 1914. Since that time and to the present (1975) many land-grant colleges and universities have continuously held an annual Farmers' Week. Examples are Cornell, Michigan State, Pennsylvania State, Kentucky, and Missouri. Attendance has varied somewhat in proportion to the rural population density and economic conditions within any given state.

Other related activities are Farmers' Day or Farmers' Fair. In general, these are held on a specific day during the summer and they provide an opportunity for the farmer and his family to inspect the crop-plant plots of the experiment station and the livestock under experimental tests, to witness demonstrations of new machinery and farm implements, and to enjoy the companionship of other farmers. On many campuses an added feature is the Farmers' Picnic, usually held on that part of the campus especially developed for picnics. In this way, the farmer and his family enjoy the fruits of the picnic basket and the visits with their friends under pleasant surroundings.

Direct from the Agricultural Experiment Station to the Grower

In this type of extension the professor of the experiment station applies the results of research directly to the farmer's farm. For example, in 1893 the grape vineyards of the Finger Lake district of New York were badly infected with a destructive fungus, which rapidly induced rotting and mumification of the individual fruits. Mr. S. F. Nixon, a prominent grower of the district and a member of the state legislature, asked the agricultural experiment station at Cornell University for help. "We have no funds to cover a request of this type," said the station. Nevertheless, Professor L. H. Bailey, the professor of horticulture, went to the Finger Lake district to inspect the plants. He immediately identified the disease as black rot, and, from the results of previous investigations at the Cornell and other state experiment stations, Professor Bailey knew just what the grower should do to destroy the fungus on the infected fruit and to prevent its infection of healthy fruit. Mr. Nixon was so delighted with the results that he introduced a bill in the state legislature that appropriated $8,000 for experimental work on the production of grapes. This initial appropriation led to further annual appropriations, with part of the money spent for actual research and part for the dissemination of the results. In fact, by 1896, the agricultural experiment station of Cornell University had published thirty-eight bulletins and conducted many meetings of grape growers. According to the historian of Cornell University, this was the first instance of agricultural extension work in the state of New York.[2]

Many instances of this type of extension performed by other state experiment stations during the early period could be cited. In fact, the attitude of the professors in the department of agriculture or the experiment station to the farmer was similar to that of the practicing physician to his patients. Whenever the farmer requested help from the agricultural college, the professors responded to the call regardless of whether funds were available to pay for the trips. In general, this attitude on the part of the professors explains, partially at least, the wide popularity and public acclaim the colleges of agriculture have enjoyed throughout the years.

THE INTERMEDIATE PERIOD (1910-1940)

The intermediate period is highlighted by the work of Dr. Seaman A. Knapp, the employment of the first county agricultural agents, and the passage of the Smith-Lever Act.

The Work of Seaman A. Knapp

The late Dr. Seaman A. Knapp is generally considered the originator or father of the demonstration method of agricultural extension. He was born in New York state in 1833, graduated from Union College in 1855, and taught in several academies in the states of New York and

---

[2]Morris Bishop. 1962. *A History of Cornell*. Cornell University Press, Ithaca, NY.

Vermont until about 1865, when he sustained an accident that seriously impaired his health. To regain health and vigor Dr. Knapp moved to a farm near Big Grove, Iowa, and became a successful breeder of Shorthorn cattle and Poland China pigs, and a contributor to farm newspapers and magazines. In 1879 Knapp was appointed professor of agriculture at Iowa Agricultural College, and in 1884 he was elected its president. But, because of an unstable condition within the Board of Trustees, Knapp resigned his position in 1886 and went to St. Charles, Louisiana, to take charge of the development of a large tract of land in western Louisiana. To demonstrate the value of using improved practices, based on the results of research, he got one farmer in each township to follow his directions and to allow farmers to observe the results. This plan was so successful that thousands of farmers settled in this area and even the descendents of the original settlers adopted Knapp's recommendations.

At the turn of the twentieth century the cotton boll weevil was inflicting severe damage to cotton plants in eastern Texas. To get the growers to adopt practices that would reduce the damage to a minimum, Dr. Knapp submitted a plan to a group of farmers and businessmen at Tyler, Texas, in 1903. In this plan specialists of the Department of Agriculture supplied the technical information underlying the improved practices, and the farmers and businessmen of the local community supplied the individual farmer with an insurance fund of $1,000 to cover any loss the farmer might sustain by following the recommendations of the specialists. Farmer W. C. Porter offered his farm of seventy acres for a demonstration. Despite the damage done by the boll weevil, Farmer Porter estimated that he obtained an additional $700 profit by discarding the old practices and adopting the new.

The First County Agricultural Agents

The good news of the Porter demonstration spread rapidly throughout Tyler and adjacent communities and resulted in a heavy demand for similar demonstrations throughout the state. In fact, in the fall of 1903 the U.S. secretary of agriculture and his chief of the Bureau of Plant Industry visited the demonstration. These officials were so impressed with the results that they persuaded Congress to make an emergency appropriation of $250,000 and assigned $40,000 of this fund to Dr. Knapp for the appointment of specialists or agents for additional demonstrations. With the assistance of this fund appointments for the 1904 growing season increased rapidly to twenty in Texas, to three in Louisiana, and to one in Arkansas. These demonstrations were so successful that Dr. Knapp, the officials of the U.S. Department of Agriculture, the presidents of the Morrill land-grant colleges, and the directors of the agricultural experiment stations realized the desirability of supporting this type of extension throughout the land. This in turn led to the beginning of demonstrations with the county as the administrative unit and to the appointment of county agricultural agents or advisors. According to the authorities, Texas first adopted this plan with the appointment of W. C. Stallings as the county agent of Smith County. Other states quickly followed the example of Texas: North Carolina in 1907, Michigan in 1908, Mississippi in 1909, and Ohio in 1910. Practically all of the remaining states had adopted this plan by 1912.

The Smith-Lever Act

The Smith-Lever Act established a nationwide system of extension work in agriculture and home economics. In other words, what the Hatch Act did for research in agriculture and home economics, and what the second Morrill Act did for formal instruction also in agriculture and home economics, the Smith-Lever Act did for extension work in these two fields. As with the Hatch Act and the Second Morrill Act, its principal sponsor was the American Association of Land-Grant Colleges and Experiment Stations. For some time this organization had realized the need to strengthen extension work throughout the nation. In fact, in 1905 a committee on extension work included in its report the following statements: "The extension work in the land-grant colleges differentiates itself sharply from research work on the one hand and from instruction of resident students on the other. There is little chance of argument upon the proposition that the organization of resident instruction in agriculture through the Morrill and Nelson Acts and the organization of research and experimentation through the Hatch and Adams Acts is chiefly responsible for the progress in agricultural education that has been made during the past few decades. . . . We can think of no argument that is ever applied or does now apply to the federal appropriations for agricultural colleges and experiment stations that does not equally apply to extension work which is organic and vital to the development of the functions of the institutions which we represent."

From 1909 to 1913 the American Association of Land-Grant Colleges and Experiment Stations continued to present to members of the Congress reasons for a federal endowment of extension work. Its efforts were crowned with success when, on September 6, 1913, Mr. Hoke Smith, the senior senator from Georgia, introduced a bill in the Senate for the federal endowment of extension work in agriculture and home economics, and Mr. A. L. Lever, a representative from South Carolina, introduced a similar bill in the House. After the differences between each of these two bills were reconciled, the joint Smith-Lever Bill was passed by both Houses and signed by President Wilson on May 8, 1914.

Thus, this date may be considered the birthday of this important phase of nationwide agricultural and home economics education.

Two significant paragraphs of the Act are presented herewith: "That in order to aid in the diffusing among the people of the United States useful and practical information on subjects relating to agriculture and home economics, and to encourage the application of the same, there may be inaugurated in connection with the college or colleges of each State now receiving or which may hereafter receive the benefits of the Land-Grant Act of 1862 and the Morrill College Endowment Act of 1890, agricultural extension work which shall be carried on in coopera- tion with the U.S. Department of Agriculture."

"That the cooperative agricultural extension work shall consist of the giving of instruction and practical demonstrations in agriculture and home economics to persons not attending or resident in said colleges in the several communities, and imparting to such persons information of said subjects through field demonstrations, publications, and other- wise; and this work shall be carried on in such manner as may be mutually agreed upon by the Secretary of Agriculture and the state agricultural college or colleges receiving the benefits of this Act." Note that the Act states that extension in agriculture and home economics shall be a coordinated and cooperative effort between the U.S. Depart- ment of Agriculture and each of the several land-grant colleges. This has led to the assigning of definite responsibilities to each of these groups, and these in turn are covered by a memorandum of understand- ing or agreement between each of the land-grant colleges on the one hand and the U.S. Department of Agriculture on the other. In general, each of the land-grant colleges agreed to establish and maintain a distinct administrative unit through which all extension work in agri- culture and home economics shall be handled and to cooperate with the U.S. Department of Agriculture in the planning of the work. The U.S. Department of Agriculture in turn agreed to channel all of its work in any given state through the Morrill land-grant college. Thus, the Morrill land-grant college of any given state is the headquarters for all extension work in agriculture and home economics.

THE MODERN PERIOD (1940-1970)

The modern period is characterized by (1) a refinement of the demonstration method, (2) the development of the pilot-plant system of research-demonstration, and (3) the development of the survey method. Examples of the first method are the growing of a newly developed variety side by side with a conventional variety, the growing of a strip of inoculated seed alongside a strip of noninoculated seed, and the effect of different rations on the growth and health of comparable lots of beef animals, pigs, and chickens or on the production of milk. Examples of the second method are the establishment of plots on the farmers' farm according to an approved experimental design by a research worker, recording of the data by the extension specialist or the county agent, and the analysis of the data by the research worker or the extension specialist or both. In this way, the effect of a new variety or a superior practice is more accurately measured and determined than by mere observation alone or by conducting a test in one location. Examples of the third method are ascertaining the status of destructive pests in any given community, e.g., the fungus that causes southern leaf blight of corn, the worm that destroys the bolls of cotton, or the cyst nematode, which reduces the yields of soybeans. Thus, during the modern period both the researcher and the extension worker work together in the solution of the farmers' problems. A similar situation exists between the researcher in home economics and the home demonstration specialists and agents.

Source of Funds

In general, extension work in agriculture and home economics is funded through four main sources: from the three levels of government, federal, state and county, and from farm organizations and other private groups: the federal government through the Smith-Lever Act of 1914; both the federal and each state government through the Capper-Ketcham Act of 1928 and the Bankhead-Jones Act of 1936; each state government by action of its legislators; and each county through its Board of Commissioners. Finally, private organizations and groups provide funds for the development of specific projects. In all cases the funds for any given state are administered by the agricultural and home economic extension unit of the local Morrill land-grant university. In general, these funds have increased throughout the years from $17.8 million in 1923 to $131.0 million in 1970. This increase in funds testifies in itself to the desire of the people to maintain a strong agriculture and to keep the farmer a first-class citizen.

Organization of Extension in Agriculture

Note the table of organization in figure 6.1.

The Farmer. Naturally, the farmer is placed at the head of this system, since all of the extension work in agriculture is done for his benefit. As with other citizens, the farmer is sovereign for two reasons: (1) he has the freedom to accept or reject the results of any experiment or demonstration or any recommendation, and (2) he has the freedom to communicate directly with any member of the extension staff, with any member of the experiment station staff, with the president of any one land-grant university, with any member of the U.S. Department of Agriculture, with any member of Congress, and with the president of the United States. In other words, extension in agriculture is a form of education in that it provides an opportunity for the farmer to increase his efficiency, to put more money in his pocketbook, and thereby improve his standard of living.

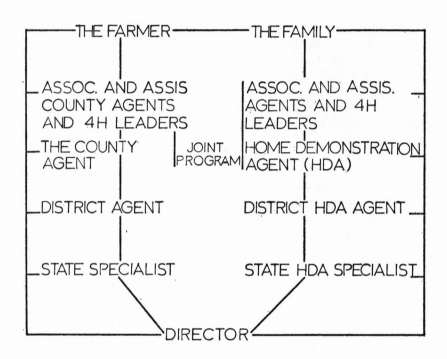

FIGURE 6.1. *Table of organization of extension work in agriculture and home economics. Note that the individual farmer and family are placed at the head of the table, since according to the Constitution of the United States they are "supreme in power."*

The County Agricultural Agent or Advisor. The county agricultural agent or advisor is the county representative of the local Morrill land-grant university. He is primarily an educator and his chief function is putting "knowledge to work." In general, the county agent does this by conducting demonstrations. Examples are the growing of a superior variety along side a conventional variety, comparing the yield of crops on limed and unlimed strips of a very acid soil, and determining the effect of different rations on milk production of cows. Quite often these demonstrations are carried out with the assistance of the extension specialists and/or the research specialists. The county agent also works with industrial firms and commercial companies that wish to demonstrate their particular products, arranges for tours of farms both within and outside the county, writes articles for local newspapers, conducts an enormous amount of correspondence with farmers and others, and keeps in touch with the work of his fellow county agents in adjacent counties. All of this work is greatly facilitated by the use of the telephone.

The District Agricultural Agent. The district agricultural agent is essentially an assistant director of extension. In common with the county agent he is primarily an educator and his chief function is to assist the county agent to put "knowledge to work" and to serve as the connecting link between the county agent and the director of extension or the extension specialist. In general, the district agricultural agent does this by coordinating the work of the county agents in a group of contiguous counties, consults with the extension specialists on the giving of demonstrations, and confers with the extension director on extension policies.

The Extension Specialist. The extension specialist is an expert within a given area of the great field of agriculture. Thus, there are extension specialists in agronomy, agricultural economics, animal science, dairy science, entomology, forestry, horticulture, poultry, rural sociology, soils, and veterinary medicine. In general, he has a working knowledge of the results of research in his field and of the problems of the growers, and his chief function is to interpret the results of research in relation to the solution of pertinent problems. In this way, the specialist serves as a connecting link between the experiment station and the agricultural extension service. Accordingly, he resides at the home of the land-grant college and maintains a continuous liaison with his corresponding colleagues in the experiment station. In fact, in some Morrill land-grant institutions, the extension specialist and the corresponding research specialist occupy the same office; in other institutions they occupy adjacent offices on the same floor or in the same building; while in other institutions they have offices in separate but usually adjacent buildings.

The Director of Extension. In sharp contrast to the county agricultural agents and the district agents, the director of extension is primarily an administrator. His chief function is to direct the work according to the Smith-Lever Act and subsequent acts and to have general supervision of all of the work. He also determines the general policies of the extension service of his particular state, ascertains in consultation with the district agents the projects that shall be conducted, maintains liaison between the federal extension office of the U.S. Department of Agriculture, and channels pertinent information between the U.S. Department of Agriculture and other agencies on the one hand and his own extension staff on the other. As would be expected, he resides at the home of the Morrill land-grant college and he and his staff usually have offices in the Cooperative Agricultural Extension Service Building.

Organization of Extension in Home Economics. In Great Britain and Europe the farmers' homes are cloistered together in the form of villages or hamlets, and the farmers' land is situated some distance from these villages. This is in sharp contrast to the situation in the United States. Most of the farmland in this country is occupied by family farms, and the farmer's home is an integral part of the farmer's farm. In other words, the farmer's home and the farmer's farm in the United States are inseparable, and all the members of the family work together as a unit. For these reasons Congress, through the Smith-Lever Act, provided for extension in home economics under the same conditions as for extension in agriculture.

The Farmer's Family. As with the farmer, all of the extension work in home economics is done for the benefit of the farmer's family, and each member of the family has the freedom to accept or reject the results of any demonstration or recommendation, and to communicate directly with any member of the extension service, the experiment station, or the U.S. Department of Agriculture. Further, as with extension work in agriculture, extension in home economics is primarily a form of education—an opportunity for the farmer's family to apply the results of research to the development of their individual selves in particular and to the welfare of the home and family life in general.

The Home Demonstration Agent. The home demonstration agent is the female counterpart of the county agricultural agent. Thus, she is primarily an educator and her duties and responsibilities to the farmer's family are practically the same as those of the county agricultural agent to the farmer.

The District Home Demonstration Agent. The district home demonstration agent is the female counterpart of the district agricultural agent. Thus, she is primarily a teacher. In general, the district agent supervises the work of the home demonstration agents of a group of contiguous counties, confers with the home economics extension specialists with reference to problems within her district, and confers with the extension director on extension policies.

The Extension Specialist in Home Economics. The extension specialist in home economics is the female counterpart of the extension specialist in the various fields of agriculture. Thus, each specialist is an authority on a rather narrow area in the wide field of home economics. For example, there are extension specialists in development of the family, in economics of the home, in food and human nutrition and meal management, in home furnishings and decoration, and in textiles and clothing. As with the extension specialist in agriculture, her functions are that of an educator, with special emphasis on the interpretation of the results of research in home economics to the welfare of the farmer's family. Further, the specialist serves as the connecting link between the home economics division of the experiment station on the one hand and the extension service on the other.

The State Home Demonstration Agent. The state home demonstration agent is primarily an administrator. For any given state she resides at the home of the land-grant college of that state and has offices for herself and staff in the Cooperative Agricultural Extension Service Building. Usually these offices are adjacent to those of the director of extension to whom the state agent is directly responsible.

GROWTH AND DEVELOPMENT OF 4-H CLUBS

I pledge my head to clearer thinking, my heart to greater loyalty, my hands to greater service and my health to better living for my club, my community, and my country.

—THE 4-H PLEDGE

The First Clubs for Young Men

In October, 1854, at the Watertown Fair of the state of New York young Franklin B. Spaulding received $50 as first prize for growing one acre of Dutton's Yellow Dent field corn, and for exhibiting a representative sample of ears of that corn. As required by the contest, Spaulding kept a record of his expenses in growing the corn, a panel of impartial judges measured the yield, and from this Spaulding determined his profits. His expenses, including cost of the seed, cost of hauling and spreading manure, cultivating and harvesting and renting the land, came to $28.50. The judges found that the yield was 152 bushels of ears per acre (170 kilograms per hectare), and from this Spaulding realized $20 from the yield of the stalks and $76 from the yield of the ears. Thus, with a gross income of $96 and an outgo of $28.50, Spaulding realized a net return of $67.50. Incidentally, the donor of this first prize was Mr. Horace Greeley, famed editor of the *New York Tribune* and promoter of agricultural science and education.

In 1855, sixteen-year-old Wilbert La Tourrette of Muscatine County, Iowa, won a premium for growing 95.5 bushels of field corn on a measured acre. Both the land that grew the corn and the yield were measured and sworn to by a surveyor.

In the spring of 1882 Dr. J. A. Reinhart, professor of agriculture, Delaware Agricultural College, announced a statewide corn contest for boys between the ages of eight and eighteen. According to instructions from the college, each competing plot was one-quarter acre in area, each boy might have the land plowed and harrowed for him, but all other work, fertilizing, planting, cultivating and harvesting had to be done by himself, and the harvesting had to be done within three days of October 18 under the supervision of three practical farmers of the vicinity. The prizes consisted of cash awards, subscriptions to the *American Agriculturist*, and books. Other instances of boys' contests before 1900 could be cited. However, they were conducted in the same way as those of the three previously described contests, and, since they were scattered and isolated from each other, there was no continuity of effort.

The Land-Grant Colleges Assist in the Program

As stated in chapter 4 the professors of agriculture started to conduct experiments soon after the colleges were established (1855-1890). Thus, by the turn of the twentieth century a considerable amount of experimental data was available and, as explained in chapter 5, the professors of agriculture used every conceivable means to carry this new knowledge to the farmer. In general, they found that an effective means was the conducting of demonstrations by boys' and girls' clubs. Two examples are presented herewith. In 1902, Mr. A. B. Graham, superintendent of schools of Spaulding Township, Clark County, Ohio, conceived the idea that boys and girls of family farms could advantageously demonstrate the results of research on their parents' farm. In this way, since "seeing is believing," the period between the time the experimental results are obtained and their application by the farmer is reduced to a minimum. Accordingly, Mr. Graham discussed the idea with a selected group of farm boys and girls, in conjunction with the dean of the School of Agriculture, the director of the Agricultural Experiment Station of the Ohio State University and the secretary of the Agriculture Students' Union, a group of former students who were applying the recommendations of the agricultural experiment station to their own farms. The boys and girls selected many projects: for example, the growing of corn, the testing of soil for the degree of acidity, the growing of vegetables in the home garden, and the growing of flowers. The dean and the director were delighted and greatly impressed with Graham's work. In fact, they brought him to the Ohio State campus as the first superintendent of agricultural extension. Under his direction, the number of boys' and girls' clubs increased rapidly. In fact, by 1906 he had developed a total of sixty clubs with an enrollment of about three thousand young men and young women.

On February 22, 1902, Mr. O. J. Kern, superintendent of schools of Winebago County, Illinois, assembled thirty-seven boys in his office at the county courthouse in Rockford for talks by two professors from the College of Agriculture of the University of Illinois: Dr. C. A. Shammel, professor of agriculture, and Professor Fred Rankin, superintendent of agricultural extension and farmers' institutes. These professors outlined plans whereby each boy could conduct demonstrations on superior varieties or improved techniques on his father's farm. The college would supply the seeds and directions for planting the seeds, and the culture of the crop, and the teachers of the local schools would supervise the work. According to Reck, 1951,[3] the boys tested seeds for viability, grew corn and sugar beets under recommended practices, ascertained the feasibility of growing sugar beets in northern Illinois, and determined the percentage of smut-infected oat plants in commercial plantings. Further, at the annual meeting of the Winebago County Farmers' Institute the boys gave reports on the behavior of their crops, and the fathers and teachers discussed ways and means whereby they could be helpful in the future. Thus, Kern's work was highly commendable in that he linked the experiment station and the extension service of the college with the family farm and the rural school. His book *Among Rural Schools*, which gave his experiences with farm boys, undoubtedly inspired other county superintendents of education to undertake similar projects. At any rate, boys' clubs spread rapidly to other states: to Texas in 1903, to Iowa and Indiana in 1904, to Nebraska, North Dakota, and Wisconsin in 1905, and to Kansas and Georgia in 1906.

In February, 1907, Mr. W. H. Smith, superintendent of education of Holmes County, Mississippi, invited one hundred and twenty farm boys together with their fathers and teachers for a meeting at the county courthouse in Lexington. Mr. Smith called this meeting for three reasons: (1) A one-crop system of agriculture prevailed in the county, (2) credit could be extended only to this one crop—cotton, and (3) when the time came to settle accounts at the supply store after any one growing season most farmers had very little, if any, money left. Thus, since farmers could obtain credit for the growing of cotton only, an unfavorable cycle existed, with the individual farmer getting very little, if any, return for his labors and investments. Smith explained the situation as follows: "It has been demonstrated that our soil and climate are capable of producing 100 bushels of corn per acre (112 kilograms per hectare) yet our average is less than 20 bushels. We have good pastures and cornland yet we are bringing in wheat and corn from the West. This need not be, with the raising of corn we could feed our mules, a group of hogs, a flock of chickens and one or more cows." Mr. Smith suggested that each boy grow one-half acre of corn (0.2 hectare), Professor W. R. Perkins of Mississippi A and M College supplied seed of a recommended variety, the fathers provided the free use of mules, plows, and cultiva-

[3]F. H. Reck. 1951. *The 4-H Story: A History of 4-H Club Work.* Iowa State University Press, Ames, IA.

tors, and Mr. Smith, Professor Perkins and the teachers of the college gave advice and supplied bulletins on the care and culture of the crop. Mr. Smith, in turn, kept in touch with the progress of these half-acre corn plots during the growing season, and in October he reported that some of these plots produced yields as high as 120 bushels per acre (134 kilograms per hectare). Later in October, 82 of the original 120 boys exhibited their best ears of corn at the county fair at Lexington while local merchants provided prize money and ribbons.

The Federal Government Joins the Program

By 1907 Dr. Knapp's program, as discussed in preceding paragraphs, to reduce the havoc of the boll weevil in weevil-infested areas, and to promote crop diversification in nonweevil areas, had been going on for four years. As a result, many of Knapp's agents were conducting demonstrations in Mississippi. One of these agents, Mr. A. F. Meharg, attended the meeting at Lexington, observed the plants on the half-acre plots at intervals during the growing season, and informed his chief, Dr. Knapp, of the success of the project at the end of the season. Dr. Knapp was greatly impressed. He concluded that the time had come to enlist the aid of young men to demonstrate the results of research on their fathers' farms, and to enlist the aid of Mr. Smith in a further promotion of the work. Accordingly, on December 11, 1907, Dr. Knapp appointed Mr. Smith as a collaborator of the U.S. Department of Agriculture at a salary of a dollar a year. The important feature of this appointment was that Mr. Smith became an official of the U.S. Department of Agriculture and thereby obtained the franking privilege to mail, postage free, correspondence on official business and circulars and bulletins on agricultural matters. Thus, Mr. Smith became the first man to be named by the federal government to do club work with rural young men and young women.

Another important feature of the appointment was the bringing together of local, state, and federal officials in a cooperative and co-ordinated effort in the boys' club program. In other words, the county superintendents of education, the professors of agriculture of the land-grant colleges, and Dr. Knapp's agents worked together with considerable goodwill. As a result, the movement spread rapidly throughout the South, from Holmes County in 1907 to Yalobusha and other counties in Mississippi in 1908, to several counties in Alabama, North Carolina, and Georgia in 1909, and to South Carolina in 1910. This rapid development necessitated the creation of two new officials: a federal official to coordinate the work of a group of adjacent states, and a state official to coordinate the work of the clubs within a state. The former became known as the 4-H Club leader of the U.S. Department of Agriculture, and the latter the 4-H Club state leader.

The First Clubs for Young Women

With the success of the farm boys' clubs, it was only natural that farm home projects be made available to farm girls. Although the results of research in home economics were meager, there was plenty of constructive work that could be done. According to Reck,[4] in the spring of 1904 Cap E. Miller, superintendent of schools of Keokuk County, Iowa, suggested that the teachers organize girls' home culture clubs, that the girls in turn develop projects directly related to the farm home, and that they exhibit samples of their handiwork at the school fair in the fall. The number and quality of the exhibits exceeded expectations and received favorable comments, particularly from the professors of agriculture and home economics of Iowa State College and editors of farm magazines and papers within the state. Here is another example of the effectiveness of an enthusiastic and inspirational teacher on the development of young people.

Soon superintendents in adjacent counties and neighboring states began to organize girls' clubs. In fact, by 1910 home culture girls' clubs or home life girls' clubs were in operation in Illinois, Indiana, Mississippi, Nebraska, New York, North Dakota, Ohio, Pennsylvania, and Virginia. In general, most of the projects were on needlework and sewing, on canning, and on bread and cake making.

As soon as the young men's clubs had convinced Dr. Knapp that they could effectively demonstrate the results of research and recommended practices, he was ready to enlist the aid of the young women. He suggested the growing and canning of tomatoes. Each girl of any given club would grow plants on one-tenth-acre plots according to recommendations of the horticulturalist of the local experiment station and can the fruit of these plants according to recommendations of the home economist also of the local experiment station. The reason Dr. Knapp recommended the tomato is that the plant is well adapted to most soils and climates of the United States, the canning procedure of the fruit has been well worked out, and each girl after supplying the needs of the family would have some fruit for sale, that is, some pocket money to spend on her own. This is a matter of considerable importance and frequently overlooked by many writers.

According to Shaub,[5] Mr. O. B. Martin, a righthand man of Dr. Knapp, outlined plans for the proposed tomato garden and canning project at the annual meeting of the South Carolina Teachers Association in 1909. Schaub states, "The teachers listened with interest but

---

[4]F. H. Reck. 1951. *The 4-H Story: A History of 4-H Club Work*, Iowa State University Press, Ames IA.

[5]O. B. Shaub. 1953. *Agricultural Extension Work: A Brief History*. North Carolina Agriculture Extension Service Circular 377.

only one responded with definite action. Miss Marie S. Cromer from Aiken County (South Carolina) went home and spent her Saturdays writing letters to girls trying to enlist them in the project." By spring she had forty-six volunteers. Miss Cromer's project was highly successful and received wide publicity. For example, one fourteen-year-old girl produced on her one-tenth acre plot sufficient fruit to fill 512 No. 3 cans and realized a profit estimated at $40. As a result, girls' canning clubs quickly developed in adjacent counties in South Carolina and in counties in adjacent states, particularly in Virginia, North Carolina, Mississippi, and Tennessee. This in turn led to the appointment of home economists to head the work in each state. These were given the title of State Agents in Charge of Canning and somewhat later they became officially known as Home Demonstration Agents.

THE MODERN 4-H CLUB

Use and Adoption of the Term "4-H"

Prior to 1920 farm youth clubs were called boys' clubs, agriculture clubs, girls' clubs, home life clubs, or home economics clubs. In general, these names are not specific and are without distinction. However, in the early 1920s, the 4-H emblem began to appear on the label of canned tomatoes and on pens as a mark of membership in any given club. As a result, people in general began to refer to these farm youth clubs as 4-H clubs. Finally, in 1923 the term "4-H" was adopted as the official name of the youth clubs in America.

The Emblem, Motto, Colors, and Pledge

The emblem is used as a badge of membership and as a label denoting various kinds of 4-H work. It was adopted in 1911 and first described in U.S. Department of Agriculture Circular 66, in 1920. In general, the emblem consists of an open book, a four-leaflet leaf of clover with an *H* superimposed on each leaflet, and a kernel of corn or a boll of cotton (for young men) or a tomato (for young women), superimposed on the center of the leaf. The meaning of each of the four *H*s is as follows: the head to think, plan, and reason; the heart to be kind, true and sympathetic; the hands to be useful, helpful, and skillful; and health to enable one to enjoy life, resist disease, and increase efficiency. The colors are green and white. Green, the predominating color of the outdoors, signifies the close relationship of photosynthesis and 4-H work to nature and to crop-plants and crop-animals. White signifies purity and freedom from destructive thoughts. The pledge further elicits the meaning of each of the four *H*s: "I *pledge my head to clearer thinking, my heart to greater loyalty, my hands to greater service, and my health to better living for my club, my community, and my country."*

Organization

The Individual Club and the Local Leaders. An individual 4-H club consists of young men and young women between the ages of ten and fourteen and at least two voluntary leaders. In general, the boys and girls within each club belong to the same community, quite often they attend the same school, and are well acquainted with each other. Each boy and girl has the right to select his own projects and to communicate directly with any member of the teaching, research, and extension staff of the college of agriculture or any other member of society. In other words, as with the farmer and the farmer's family, the object of 4-H club work is to provide opportunities for young men and women to develop their potentialities. The local leaders serve as advisors or counselors. In general, they are past 4-H club members, have had training in counseling and guidance, and are familiar with the youth needs of the local community.

The County and State 4-H Leaders. The county 4-H leader is the counterpart of the county agricultural agent and the county home demonstration agent. In other words, what the county agricultural agent and the county home demonstration agent are to the farmer and the farmer's family, respectively, the county 4-H leader is to the boys and girls of the individual clubs. In general, he has had training in the counseling and guidance of young people; he has a working knowledge of the needs of young people; and he coordinates the activities of the several 4-H clubs in his county.

The state 4-H leaders are analogous to the state agricultural agents and the state home demonstration agents in that they coordinate the work of all of the clubs within any given state. In many states the 4-H club leader has two assistants, an associate leader in charge of boys' work and an associate leader in charge of girls' work, and several assistant leaders. In general, the assistant leaders work with the county agricultural agents, county home demonstration agents, and volunteer leaders in order to develop effective and well-rounded programs. Since 4-H club work is a type of extension education in agriculture and home economics, the administrative direction of the work for any given state is the responsibility of the state director of the cooperative agricultural extension work.

The Number and Nature of Projects. In general, the projects are of two types: individual and collective or club. Examples of individual projects involve photography, dressmaking, gardening, canning, tractor driving and maintenance, and room improvement. Examples of club projects are painting and printing names on rural mailboxes, picking up trash and distributing litter bags to help keep the roadside neat and attractive, placing first-aid kits in schools, putting signs on the major roads to caution motorists to drive carefully, raising funds for landscaping the grounds of new schools, participating in drives for funds to support health organizations, contributing books to libraries of elementary schools, preparing baskets for patients in nursing homes, soliciting donors of blood, buying wheelchairs for use in a community, and providing some items of equipment for hospitals. In other words, the projects are many and varied and include all phases in the lives of young men and young women. This is a far cry from the original boys' corn club of 1907 and the original girls' tomato club of 1909. However, the motto "to make the best better" remains the same and, as the young men and young women have discovered, there are many different ways "to make the best better."

The District, State, and National Conventions. The district, state, and national conventions provide opportunities for the recognition of outstanding work in 4-H, for these outstanding members to become acquainted with each other, and for each member to receive training in leadership. The outstanding work is recognized by various prizes and awards. In general, these prizes and awards are made by both private corporations and industrial firms that are interested in promoting the growth and development of the 4-H club movement. An important and necessary feature of the prizes and awards is that they are made primarily to promote the development of the winners rather than to advertise the products of the donor.

In general, the district winners attend the state convention, and the state winners in turn attend the national convention or national camp. For the most part each state convention has the following characteristics: (1) It is held on the campus of the local land-grant college or at a city with facilities for the lectures, addresses, demonstrations, and exhibits; (2) it receives statewide publicity, since the editors of local newspapers and farm magazines join in saluting the achievements of 4-H; (3) it is well attended; and (4) its program includes practically all phases in the life of the 4-H'er. For example, the state convention of Mississippi in 1967 was attended by about five hundred boys and girls. They held talent shows, fashion revues, listened to an address by a former Miss America, participated in special-interest panel discussions, and enjoyed a program of entertainment and study. Five private and public service agencies sponsored special luncheons and banquets for the group.

From 1927 to 1949 the national convention or camp was held at Washington, D.C., under the auspices of the U.S. Department of

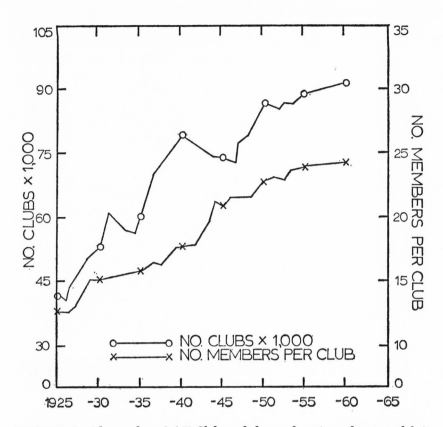

FIGURE 6.2. *The number of 4-H Clubs and the number of members per club in the United States from 1925 to 1960. Adapted from A. S. Gordy, 1962. Statistical Summary of 4-H Club Work. U.S. Department of Agriculture Extension Service Circular 540.*

Agriculture. Since that time it has been held in other cities. In general, the national convention receives nationwide publicity, and the program includes receptions, tours, addresses by national leaders, symposia on the training of the voluntary leaders, and, most important, panel and informal discussions of ideas that may promote the work of the 4-H movement as a whole. The individual delegates usually go back to their individual clubs with new ideas "to make the best better."

Growth of 4-H Clubs

Various aspects of the growth of 4-H clubs in the United States are depicted in figures 6.2 and 6.3. Figure 6.2 shows the trends in number of clubs and in number of members per club. Note the sharp

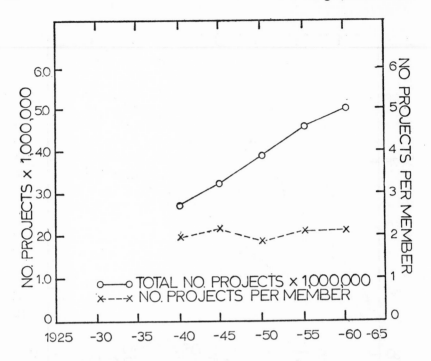

FIGURE 6.3. *Total number of projects and average number of projects per member in the United States from 1940 to 1960. Adapted with permission from H. S. Gordy, 1962. Statistical summary of 4-H Club work. U.S. Department of Agriculture Extension Service Circular 540.*

increases from 1926 to 1931, from 1934 to 1940, and from 1946 to 1950; and the slight decrease from 1931 to 1934; and from 1940 to 1946. Despite the setback during these two periods, the general trend is remarkably upward. Also note that the number of members per club increased from an average of 12 in 1925 to about 24 in 1960. This increase was quite rapid from about 1929 to 1950, when an average membership of 23 was attained. This indicates that from the standpoint of efficiency the maximum number of members per club lies between 20 and 25.

Figure 6.3 shows the total number of projects for the United States as a whole and the average number of projects carried by each club member. The number of projects carried by each club member is remarkably constant for the period studied. This means that the marked upward trend in number of projects is primarily due to the increase in number of clubs and the increase in number of members per club. As explained previously, a distinct feature of 4-H club work is the participation of voluntary leaders. In other words, as the clubs gained in experience they realized the necessity to lower the number of students for each counselor in order for the leader to give a relatively large amount of time to any given member. This in itself attests to the remarkable growth and success of the 4-H club movement in the United States.

4-H Club Work Overseas

Since the means of communication remain open between people of friendly countries, it was inevitable that the 4-H movement would soon go overseas. About 1920 Lord Northcliff, the energetic editor of the London *Daily Mail*, visited the United States and Canada. He was much impressed by the excellent work of the 4-H clubs in each country. He felt that a similar organization for young farmers in Great Britain would promote their development and well-being. He accordingly started organizing clubs in 1921, and his newspaper, the *Daily Mail*, supported them financially until 1924, when the government agencies of Parliament rendered support. The number of clubs rapidly increased throughout the United Kingdom, and by 1960 there were more than 1,500, with over 50,000 members. They associated themselves together as the National Federation of Young Farmers Clubs.

In 1921 the Extension Service of the U.S. Department of Agriculture loaned one of its workers, Danish-born F. D. Lund, to Denmark for the establishment of 4-H club work. He held meetings with agricultural societies in the fall and winter of 1923-1924 and started club work in the spring of 1924. During this first year more than 700 boys and girls enrolled in the 4-H club program, and by 1927 about 6,600 were engaged in the work. They adopted the four-leaflet clover as the emblem and the four *Hs*, *Hoved, Hjerte, Haande,* and *Halbred,* the Danish words for head, heart, hand, and health as the motto.

In 1920 Mr. Bertel Rockstrom, a native of Finland, was serving his country as the agricultural commissioner to the United States and Canada. He visited the Northwoods section of Minnesota, where colonies of Finns had settled. While there he learned from 4-H State Leader Mr. T. A. Erickson that a Finnish girl had won the state potato club championship with a yield of 664 bushels per acre (744 kilograms per hectare). On his return to Finland, Rockstrom recommended that 4-H clubs be started in Finland, and, with the financial assistance of the International Education Board, the work was officially established under Baron Mannerheim in 1926. The Finnish boys and girls also adopted the four-leaflet clover as the official emblem and the four *Hs* as the official motto. During this early period 4-H clubs were established in Sweden in 1925, in Belgium in 1927, in Austria in 1928, in North Ireland and France in 1929, in the Netherlands in 1930, in Australia and New Zealand in 1933, in Central and South America between 1939 and 1962, and in many countries across the Pacific between 1946 and 1959. Thus, the boys and girls of many countries now have the opportunity to be engaged in 4-H club work. In fact, by 1960 there were seventy-six countries with a 4-H or 4-H-type organization.

Some of the countries have a comparatively large number of clubs as, for example, Poland with 24,386, South Korea with 18,874, Japan with 13,000, and the Philippines with 4,770. These figures compare with the 94,664 clubs for the United States as a whole. An interesting feature of some of these clubs is the use of symbols other than 4-H. For example, there are 4-S clubs in Bolivia, Brazil, Colombia, Costa Rica, Honduras, Nicaragua, and Guatemala, with the Ss meaning *Saber*—to know, *Serbir* —to serve, *Sentir*—to feel, and *Ser*—to be or *Asaude*—for health; 4-C clubs exist in Chile, El Salvador, and Paraguay, with the Cs meaning *Cabeza*—head, *Corizon*—heart, *Capercidad*—ability, and *Cooperacion*— cooperation; 4-K clubs exist in Turkey, with the Ks meaning *Kafa*—head, *Kol*—hand or arm, *Kubdete*—health or strength.

AGRICULTURAL EXTENSION SERVICE PUBLICATIONS

As the name suggests, agricultural extension service publications are written for wide dissemination and for use by all of the people. In general, they contain no primary experimental data, very few if any technical terms, and they are usually well illustrated either by actual photographs or by line drawings or both, and their authors use simple, understandable words. Further, an important feature of these publications is that their statements and recommendations are based on the results of experimental work. In other words, they are one of the end products of scientific research. Thus, these extension publications are sound, reliable, and extremely useful.

Quite often, scientists of the experiment stations collaborate or work with members of the extension service in the writing of extension service publications. This again reflects the close working relationship between the agricultural scientists on the one hand, and the extension workers on the other, both groups working together to promote the welfare of all the people.

Relation of the County Agricultural Extension Service to Other County Organizations

In addition to working directly with farmers, the county agricultural agent and his assistants work with other groups to promote the welfare of all the people. Some of these organizations are the Farm Home Administration, an agency for the issuance of short-term loans to farmers; the Production and Marketing Administration, an agency for giving financial assistance to farmers to adopt experiment station and extension service recommended practices; the Soil Conservation Service, an agency given over entirely to the conservation of soil; the State Sanitation Livestock Board, an agency primarily for the testing of livestock for serious diseases; and the State Plant Board, a regulatory agency for the inspection and movement of plants or plant products. Naturally, the county agricultural agent must be familiar with the function and operation of each of these agencies.

REFERENCES

Baker, Gladys. 1939. *The County Agent*, chapter 9. University of Chicago Press, Chicago, IL.
    The author, after a study of the work of the county agricultural agent from 1862 to 1931, makes suggestions for improving the effectiveness of county agent work.

Gouin, Francis R. 1975. "4-H Horticulture in Maryland," *HortScience*, 10, No. 5, 466.
    A brief discussion on the success of 4-H club work in horticulture throughout the state of Maryland from 1968 to 1975.

Hamilton, J. 1906. *History of Farmers' Institutes in the United States.* U.S. Department of Agriculture Office Experiment Stations Bulletin 174.
    The author, a former Farm Institute Specialist of the U.S. Department of Agriculture, presents information on the origin and progress of Farmers' Institutes in the several states and territories from 1868 to 1904.

Reck, F. H. 1951. *The 4-H Story: A History of 4-H Club Work.* Iowa State University Press, Ames, IA.
    This three-hundred-page book is dedicated to all volunteer 4-H club leaders, and presents a comprehensive account on the origin, growth, and development of 4-H in the United States and countries overseas.

Shaub, O. B. 1953. *Agricultural Extension Work: A Brief History.* North Carolina Agricultural Extension Service Circular 377.
    A former director of the North Carolina Agricultural Extension Service discusses the origin of the Morrill land-grant colleges and the development of the extension dimension in agriculture and home economics. Principal topics includes the Morrill Act, the work of Dr. S. A. Knapp, acknowledged father of the extension dimension in agriculture, girls' club and home demonstration work, and the Smith-Lever Act.

Stemmons, Walter. 1931. *Connecticut Agricultural College—A History,* chapter 13, "The College Goes to the People." Connecticut Agricultural College, Storrs, CT.
    An account of the development of extension work in the agriculture of Connecticut from 1893 to 1931.

7

THE THREE DIMENSIONS
IN OPERATION
AND COORDINATION

Man's mind stretched to a new idea never goes back to its original dimension.

The three dimensions are research, resident teaching, and extension. As explained in chapters 4, 5, and 6, respectively, research consists of securing data that have a bearing on a specific problem or a group of related problems. Resident teaching in the classroom or laboratory consists of using these data or knowledge in the preparation of young men and young women for their life's work. Finally, extension consists of disseminating this knowledge in the education of all adults and their families. In other words, research, resident teaching, and extension are always utilitarian in nature. The research worker obtains the data, and the teacher and the extension worker and even the ordinary citizen apply the data to the solution of his particular problem. As Reuther has said, "We do not learn for the sake of learning; only by its use does basic knowledge bear fruit of benefit to man."[1]

Research—the Foundation

Of the three dimensions, research is the foundation. There are definite reasons for this. As stated previously, the results of research within any given field constitute the scientific literature of that particular field, and this literature in turn is the basis for all resident teaching and extension work in that same field, whether that field is agriculture, home economics, engineering, business and industry, chemistry, or some other field of constructive endeavor. In other words, there cannot be excellence in resident teaching or excellence in extension without excellence in research.

---

[1]Walter Reuther. 1963. *Proceedings of the American Society for Horticultural Science,* 83:855-61.

THE THREE DIMENSIONS IN AGRICULTURE
AND HOME ECONOMICS

Agriculture is not just the most essential industry, it is the only essential industry.
—BOYSIE E. DAY

As previously stated, the great field of agriculture consists of a large number of more or less distinct industries. Examples are the small grain, the corn, the soybean, the beef cattle, the dairy, the tree-fruit, the vegetable crop, the floriculture, and plant nursery industries. How are the problems solved within any given industry? In general, the investigator obtains answers to a given problem in a series of important and sequential steps: (1) the conducting of a survey usually in consultation with knowledgeable growers to ascertain the pertinent problems, (2) the setting up of experiments at one or more places within the industry with an appropriate experimental design in order to obtain reliable data or experimental information, (3) the arranging with the county agent or farm advisor for field days so that the growers may inspect the plants or animals of the experimental plots (Since seeing is believing, field days of this type are very effective in getting the growers to adopt the best treatments or varieties in a short time.), (4) presenting the results to growers during the next nongrowing season to acquaint them with the progress of the work and to modify if necessary the experiments for the next season, and (5) preparing a report, usually as an experiment station or extension service bulletin or circular, which embodies the data on which recommendations are made. Naturally, a similar procedure is used in the wide field of home economics, particularly in the field of human nutrition.

In general, this method of operation is very effective, efficient, worthwhile, and enjoyable. Effective because the farmers quickly adopt the superior practice(s) or superior variety(ies). Efficient because the taxpayer's dollar yields comparatively high returns from the money invested. Enjoyable because everyone concerned is provided with happy experiences. The research worker finds satisfaction in helping the farmer, the farmer makes more money, the teacher is provided with new knowledge for the training of the students, the consumer is assured a superior product at reasonable cost, and the taxpayers receive high returns for the money they have invested.

The So-Called Hybrids

The term "hybrid" refers to a member of the faculty of the colleges of agriculture or the colleges of home economics who spends part of his time as an investigator and part of his time as a teacher. In general, this research and teaching are done within the same area of crop-plant or crop-animal production or home economics. For example, a member of the department of agronomy may do research on the production of alfalfa or clover and teach "forage crops"; a member of the department of poultry science may do research on the housing, feeding, or control of diseases of broilers and teach broiler production, or a member of the department of home economics may do research on the relative value of spinach and turnip greens in the human diet and teach courses in the selection and preparation of foods for home canning and drying.

This type of arrangement is very effective. From the standpoint of the teacher it promotes confidence, because the teacher as an investigator is familiar with the methods and results of his own research and that of workers in related fields. From the standpoint of research it promotes the development of a broad outlook, because the research worker as a teacher has a working knowledge of disciplines related to his own fields of interest. The effectiveness of this arrangement explains why most members of the faculty of the colleges of agriculture and home economics are employed as combination research workers and teachers. Note from the data in table 7.1 that at each of the nine Morrill land-grant universities most of the faculty of the colleges of agriculture are hybrids. That is, they do research and teach within their special fields of interest. A similar situation exists with the colleges of home economics, and with both the colleges of agriculture and home economics at most of the other fifty-nine Morrill land-grant institutions.

Another effective arrangement is the research-extension combination; that is, an individual may spend part of his time doing research on a particular problem and part of his time showing growers how to solve that problem. For example, a member of the plant pathology extension department may conduct experiments on the behavior of the root lesion nematode on soybeans and teach growers of soybeans how to control this destructive pest. Naturally, with this arrangement there is little, if any, lag between the time the new knowledge is secured and the time it is applied.

From the Three Dimensions Combined in One Individual
to the Three Dimensions Operating as Teams

During the early period of research in agriculture and home economics, in general from 1862 to 1930, most of the problems for any given crop or situation were solved by one individual. In other words, each of the three parts of the great triad, research, resident teaching and extension, was vested in one individual. He or she had the re-

Table 7-1.

TYPE OF PROFESSIONAL WORKERS IN THE COLLEGE
OF AGRICULTURE OF NINE MORRILL LAND-GRANT UNIVERSITIES[*]

University	Teach[a]	Res[b]	Ext[c]	Teach-Res[d]	Teach-Ext[e]	Res-Ext[f]	Teach-Res-Ext[g]
Illinois	4	44	14	83	0	12	12
Kansas State	2	28	36	74	0	5	4
Louisiana State	6	44	18	41	0	0	0
Michigan State	10	14	8	47	5	22	10
Mississippi State	7	7	25	53	0	0	5
Nebraska	4	20	13	35	1	9	10
New Jersey	9	12	20	41	0	9	2
New Mexico State	3	3	8	35	1	0	0
Oregon State	5	12	14	41	1	4	6
TOTAL	50	184	156	490	8	61	49

[*]From U.S. Department of Agriculture Handbook 305, 1975.
[a]Full-time teaching.
[b]Full-time research.
[c]Full-time extension.
[d]Part-time teaching and part-time research.
[e]Part-time teaching and part-time extension.
[f]Part-time research and part-time extension.
[g]Part-time teaching, part-time research, and part-time extension.

sponsibility to do the research and to use the data for the education of students in class and/or laboratory and/or for the benefit of farmers or the farmer's family. The effectiveness of the single investigator-teacher-extension combination is manifested by the fact that numerous problems were solved during this early period. In other words, many sick industries were brought back to health, stability, and profitability. Examples are the cabbage industries in Wisconsin and New York, the cantaloupe industries in California, Colorado, and Michigan, the garden pea industry in Wisconsin, the pickle industries in Michigan and Mississippi, the onion industries of California, Michigan, New York, and Mississippi, and the sweet corn industries of Illinois and Maryland. Many other examples could be cited.

During the modern period, in general from 1930 to 1975, agricultural biometricians developed experimental plot techniques by which a large number of variables can be compared in a single overall experiment. For this reason the team approach to the solution of many agriculture and home economic problems developed, with each member of the team serving as a specialist or authority in a related science or discipline. For example, in a crop-plan production research program the team may include a plant geneticist and plant breeder, a plant physiologist, a plant biochemist, a plant pathologist, a nematologist, an entomologist, a marketing specialist, and an agricultural engineer. In a milk production program the team may include an animal cytologist, an animal geneticist, an animal physiologist and biochemist, a doctor of veterinary medicine, a dairy manufacturing specialist, and an agricultural engineer. In a human nutrition program the team may include a horticulturist, a plant physiologist, a statistician, and a human nutritionist.

In general, any given team may consist of two or more individuals working together within a given area or state, or two or more individuals working together within a region or group of states. An example of the former is the cotton production research program of Mississippi in which the crop-plant scientists of five substations work together, and an example of the latter is the U.S. National Potato Improvement Program, in which potato specialists of the twenty-five to thirty commercially important states are involved. Other examples of team research are the National Boll Weevil Eradication Program, the National Sweet Potato Research Program, the Southern Tomato Experimental Program, and the National Pickle Production and Processing Program. This team approach to the solution of problems does not mean that there is no place for the lone individual type of research, since experience has shown that certain individuals have ability to "think through a problem" and are quite productive in the solution of problems when they are working independently.

The Solution of Problems with Experiments
Conducted in Farmers' Fields

A striking example is the research-teaching-extension work with growers of tung from 1938 to 1964. Three groups were involved: (1) research workers of the U.S. Department of Agriculture, (2) research workers and teachers of four state stations, and (3) private growers of tung. The disciplines represented were plant physiology, plant pathology, plant genetics, plant breeding, and agricultural engineering, and the growers' orchards were scattered more or less at random throughout the industry from northeast Florida to southern Louisiana. Practically all phases of tung nut production were investigated. Because the growers could not help but observe the results of the experimental plots, they quickly adopted superior practices. As a result, marketable yields within the tung belt rapidly increased from 0.5 ton per acre (56 kg per hectare) in 1938 to 1.5 tons per acre (168 kg per hectare) in 1964. Thus, a unique feature of this type of research is the constant stimulus the research workers receive because of continuous contact with farmers and their operations. There is no danger of failure to recognize and investigate the problems of an industry on the part of the scientists, and no danger on the part of the growers of adopting an unprofitable practice.

The Relation of Efficiency in Agriculture to Prosperity of the Nation

The increasing efficiency of agriculture in the United States throughout the years is shown by the data in table 7-2. Note that as the number of farm workers required to produce the nation's food, feed, and fiber gradually decreased, the number of workers available for industries other than that of food, feed, and fiber production correspondingly increased. This is a notable and highly beneficial achievement, since a relatively large number of workers have become available for the development of a wide variety of goods and services characteristic of the prosperous society. Unquestionably, a strong and highly efficient agriculture is the basis of prosperity of any nation.

The Factors. Although many factors are concerned in promoting the efficiency of agriculture in the United States, the primary factor is the work of the agricultural experiment stations and the agricultural extension services of the Morrill land-grant colleges and universities. The plant scientists of these sixty-eight institutions have developed new and superior varieties of crop plants and new and improved cultural practices, and the animal scientists have developed new and superior types of farm animals combined with new and superior cultural and feeding practices. The extension workers have disseminated and in many cases demonstrated the results of research to the growers and farmers. The farmers in turn have accepted the results with alacrity. As a result, yields and quality per unit area of crop-plant or per crop-animal have progressively increased.

Other factors associated with the increased efficiency of American agriculture are the physiographic and geographic position of the United States, the large areas of fertile land, the relatively large number of family farms, and the enlightened capitalistic system, which rewards individual initiative and effort. The geographic and physiographic position of the United States refers to its temperature level, its light supply, and its water supply. Since the contiguous forty-eight states are located between 25° and 50° latitude north, their temperature level and light supply are sufficiently high to promote the production of a larger number of cool-temperate, warm-temperate, and subtropical crops. Further, the annual rainfall, despite its uneven distribution, is sufficient for comparatively high yields per crop-plant and per crop-animal from one year to the next. The large areas of fertile soil, combined with the wide differences in temperature and rainfall within these areas, have

Table 7-2.

THE INCREASING EFFICIENCY OF THE AMERICAN FARMER
AS MEASURED BY THE RATIO OF FARM WORKERS
TO THE TOTAL POPULATION*

	Total Number Persons (Millions) (A)	Total Persons Employed All Industries (Millions)	Employed All Farms (Millions) (B)	Farm Workers Compared to Total Workers (Percent)	The Ratio† Number Farm Workers to Total Population (A/B)
1870	39.8	12.5	5.9	47	6.7
1880	50.2	17.4	7.7	43	6.5
1890	62.9	22.7	9.0	40	7.0
1900	76.0	29.3	10.4	36	7.3
1910	92.0	38.2	12.7	33	7.2
1920	105.7	41.6	11.0	24	9.6
1930	122.8	48.8	10.5	21	11.7
1940	131.7	45.2	8.5	19	15.5
1950	151.3	59.6	7.4	12	20.5
1960	179.3	66.7	5.4	8	33.2
1970	203.2	78.4	3.2	4	63.5

*From *Reports of the U.S. Census* and *Statistical Abstracts of the United States*.
†These ratios or indices are rough measures at best. In former times the farmer had to spend considerable time to raise food for his horses and/or mules, which were needed to pull the plows, harrows, drills, cultivators, mowers, and other types of farm tools and machinery. However, in modern times the farmers use tractors to power their machinery and they buy the fuel for their operation. In other words, the time that farmers spent in caring for horses and/or mules is no longer necessary. Thus, the farmer can spend more of his time in raising products for human consumption and enjoyment. This in turn has increased the farmer's efficiency.

favored the development of distinct crop-plant and crop-animal producing regions. Six regions are set forth in table 7-3. Note the differences in location and kinds of crops grown between any two of these regions, and for the forty-eight contiguous states as a whole the production of a wide variety of high-quality food, feed, and fiber crops is possible.

The Large Number of Family Farms

The establishment of a large number of family farms was made possible by the passage of the Homestead Act (1862) and by grants of land to railroad companies. As stated in chapter 2, to qualify for a homestead the prospective farmer was required to be the head of a family or over twenty-one years of age and either a citizen of the

Table 7-3.

PRINCIPAL CROPS OF SIX CLIMATIC REGIONS
OF THE CONTINENTAL UNITED STATES*

Region	States	Principal Crops
Northeast	New England NY, PA, NJ	Pastures, hay, dairy and beef livestock, cool and moderately warm season fruits, vegetables, and ornamentals
Southeast	MD, DE, VA, NC, SC, GA, FL, AL, MS, LA, AR, TN, KY	Tobacco, peanuts, soybean, cotton, cool and warm season fruits, vegetables and ornamentals, citrus, dairy, beef, and poultry production
Midwest	OH, IN, MI, WI, IL, MN, IA, MO	Corn, soybeans, alfalfa, cool and warm season fruits, vegetables and ornamentals, dairy, beef, and pigs
Prairie	ND, SD, NB, KS, OK, TX	Wheat, soybeans, corn, cotton, beef
Intermountain Valleys of	MT, ID, WY, NV, UT, CO, AZ, NM	Winter wheat Sheep
Pacific Coast	Intermountain Valleys of WA, OR, CA	Cool and warm season fruits, vegetables and ornamentals, citrus in CA, livestock

*Adapted from U.S. Department of Agriculture Yearbook for 1957.

United States or a noncitizen who had declared his intention of becoming a citizen. Further, he was required to cultivate the land for a period of five years before he could obtain title to it. At first the prospective owner was entitled to 160 acres; later, in 1909, Congress increased the individual allotment to 320 acres, and, as settlement extended into the semiarid and arid areas, Congress in 1916 increased the individual allotment to 640 acres. Other acts of Congress that helped the citizen or prospective citizen to own a farm were the Pre-Emption Act of 1841, the Timber Culture Act of 1873, and the Desert Land Act of 1877.

Grants of land to railway companies, usually consisting of alternate sections on the right of way, also promoted immigration and settlement. For example, the Northern Pacific established numerous offices in the British Isles to acquaint prospective immigrants with the opportunities to own a farm, sold land to the immigrants as they arrived in the United States, and actually assisted the prospective owners to get started in the business. To the poor immigrants the prospect of owning and operating a farm exceeded all of their expectations. It fired their ambitions to develop their potentialities and to become independent and free. As a result, thousands and thousands of so-called poor people came to this country. Other examples of railway companies that received land grants and promoted settlement were Gulf, Mobile and Ohio; Illinois Central; the Pere Marquette; and the transcontinental line consisting of Chicago and Northwestern, Union Pacific, and Central Pacific.

The Relation of Agricultural Abundance to the Standard of Living and the Development of the Individual

What is the meaning of standard of living and development of the individual? In the author's opinion, these terms refer to the goods and services by which any individual may develop his potentialities into actualities. This is an essential part of the American dream or tradition that each individual shall have opportunity to develop himself to his fullest capacity without injury to others. In this way, each individual can make the greatest contribution not only to himself but also to his fellow man.

There are many fields of human endeavor and there is a wide diversity of human talent or ability among respective fields. Some individuals have ability to do excellent work in one of the professions, for example, medicine, law, or education; others do their best work in the manufacturing field, for example, the making of autos, radios, and TV sets, while others excel in fields pertaining to the feeding, clothing, and sheltering of the human race, for example, the farmer, the food processor, the food marketer, the maker of clothes, and the grower of wood. However, the fact remains that any one individual cannot enter his chosen field or develop his potentialities on an empty stomach, or an unwholesome diet, or without adequate clothing and shelter. In other words, there cannot be a strong education program or a strong liberal arts program, or a strong program in any other field of human endeavor without a strong agriculture. To look at the situation in another way, if most of the workers of any given country had to occupy themselves in the production of food, feed, and fiber, there would be very few workers left for the making of automobiles, TV sets, radios, or other materials characteristic of a highly developed and prosperous society.

Should there be a moratorium on agricultural research, resident teaching, and extension? In the past, particularly during the Great Depression, certain so-called authorities suggested that research in agriculture be terminated or at least drastically curtailed. Even in recent times (1975), since the number of farmers in the United States is becoming smaller and smaller, certain so-called authorities state that, since farmers are becoming few in number, they are not entitled to representation in a cabinet department of the federal government and that the functions of the department be strongly reduced and attached to another department, for example, the Department of Interior.[2] Since an efficient agriculture is the foundation for the development of prosperity, the great triad in agriculture should be strengthened rather than weakened. There is a major reason for this: All of the members of mankind, all of the many kinds of animals, all of the many species of fungi, and most kinds of bacteria are dependent on the products of photosynthesis for their growth and development. The farmer is the warden of crop-plant photosynthesis. He is continuously fighting the members of these other groups for the products of this basic reaction. For example, the farmer is continually fighting insects that reduce crop-plant yields and certain fungi and bacteria that cause disease. These organisms are continuously mutating in the direction of greater virulence or destructiveness, which if allowed to grow and develop would finally gain the upper hand of the crop-plant, and our abundant supply of food and fiber would gradually disappear.

A case in point is the T-strain of a fungus that causes Southern Leaf Blight in corn. This virulent strain first appeared in fields of hybrid corn in Florida in the spring of 1970. Since its spores are carried by the wind, this virulent fungus had infected fields of hybrid corn in Georgia, Alabama, and Mississippi by late spring, and fields of hybrid corn in Illinois and Iowa by early summer. In all of these states the leaves became badly infected. As a result, the chlorophyll content of the leaves was low, the rate of net photosynthesis was low, and the yields were accordingly low. In fact, corn plant scientists of the various states and of the U.S. Department of Agriculture estimated that the disease had caused a loss of five billion bushels in 1970. Fortunately, for the welfare of the people and the nation, corn-plant agronomists, geneticists, and pathologists found that certain varieties of corn were resistant to this virulent T-strain of the leaf blight fungus and they immediately began a program to incorporate this resistance in recommended hybrid varieties. Many other examples of the appearance of "sudden death" to our valuable crop-plants could be cited. For these reasons alone, funds for research in agriculture should not be turned on or off as many misguided persons have suggested. Further, the American farmer should be complimented rather than penalized for his efficiency.

THE THREE DIMENSIONS IN ENGINEERING

The three dimensions in engineering are practically the same as those for agriculture and home economics. As with all other fields, research is the foundation for the education of young men and women

---

[2]Before the U.S. Department of Agriculture was established in 1862, the agricultural affairs of the nation were part of the Department of Interior.

in engineering and for the continuing education of engineers after graduation. In other words, the same system that has been so successful for the family farm is also successful for the industrial enterprise. This is particularly true for the so-called small industries in any given community. In general, the owner(s) of any small industry has neither the time nor the money to employ expensive research scientists and buy expensive equipment for the solution of his problems.

The So-Called Hybrids

In common with agriculture and other fields, certain members of the engineering faculty are full-time researchers or teachers or extension workers, and others are hybrids; that is, they are part-time researchers and part-time teachers, or part-time extension workers. Any one of these two combinations is always within a specific field of constructive endeavor. For example, a civil engineer may study the structural properties of soils and teach courses in highway construction, or a chemical engineer may study the relative efficiency of various types of internal combustion engines and teach courses in thermodynamics. As with agriculture, this arrangement is effective and efficient. The researcher as a teacher is familiar with the results of his research and that of others in the same or related fields, and acquires a broad outlook on the problems of his own field. In general, this explains why most of the engineering faculty are hybrids. For example, according to the Engineering Experiment Station Record for 1921 by far the majority of the Engineering faculty in the Morrill land-grant colleges were part-time researchers and part-time teachers.

Research Teams in Engineering

As pointed out in chapter 4 research in agriculture has universal appeal. In other words, its results are likely to benefit, either directly or indirectly, all members of society. However, in sharp contrast to agriculture, research in engineering may or may not have universal appeal. In other words, its results may benefit a large segment of the population or only a relatively small group. For this reason, research teams within and between the various branches of engineering have not developed to the same extent as those within and between the various phases of agriculture. Nevertheless, a significant feature is that communication lines between any two individuals working on the same or related problems are open and free. To this extent a certain amount of cooperation and/or coordination exists in research in engineering.

REFERENCES

Gibson, W. L., Jr. 1959. *Research and Education in Agriculture.* Virginia Agricultural Extension Service Bulletin 260.

An elucidation of the fact that the industrial power of a nation is based on an effective and efficient agriculture.

Kilby, W. W. 1969. *History and Literature of the Domestic Tung Oil Industry.* Mississippi Agricultural Experiment Station Technical Bulletin 56.

The author, an authority of tung production, discusses methods used in solving tung production problems during the fifth and sixth decades of the twentieth century.

Grayson, Lawrence P. 1977. *A Brief History of Engineering Education in the United States.* American Society for Engineering Education:68, No. 3, 246-64.

A comprehensive account on the growth and development of the many fields of engineering and the impact of engineering technology on American society.

8

THE MORRILL
LAND-GRANT COLLEGES
EXTEND THEIR SERVICES

The Entire State Becomes The Campus.

Reasons for Service Extension

As pointed out previously, the Morrill land-grant colleges and universities are for the most part tax-money-supported institutions. Although this tax money goes to each college from both the federal and state treasuries, its ultimate source is the people. Thus, it is only fair and equitable that the services of these institutions should extend to all of the people.

During colonial times and the first four or five decades in the life of the nation, agriculture and the mechanic arts were the principal occupations of the people. However, with an increase in efficiency in agriculture and with the consequent development of nonagricultural industries, society as a whole began to consist of a relatively large number of highly specialized groups. Since the Morrill land-grant colleges had demonstrated their worth and usefulness to agriculture, engineering, and home economics, it seemed logical and inevitable that this usefulness should be extended to the people engaged in other fields.

Obligations and Responsibilities of the Morrill Act

Section 4 of the Morrill Act as approved by Congress on July 2, 1862, states in part: *"Where the leading object shall be without excluding other scientific and classical studies to teach agriculture and the mechanic arts in order to promote the liberal and classical education of the industrial (working) classes in the several pursuits and professions in life."* Note that the Act provides not only for instruction and training in agriculture and engineering, but also for instruction and training in other fields. In this way, the founding fathers in their wisdom provided opportunities for the education of all of the people and for greater service on the part of the Morrill land-grant colleges and universities.

The response of these tax-supported colleges and universities to this obligation and responsibility, and the opportunity to be of greater service to the people as a whole, is briefly discussed as follows.

Growth and Development of the Schools of Agriculture, Engineering, and Home Economics

Agriculture. As previously stated in chapter 1, the Agricultural College of the State of Michigan was the first of the first four people's colleges. It was established on February 12, 1855, under the laws of the State of Michigan, which included the following statement: *"This institution shall combine physical with intellectual education, and shall be a high seminary of learning in which the graduate of the common schools shall commence, pursue, and finish a course of study terminating in thorough theoretical and practical instructions in those sciences and arts which bear directly upon agriculture and kindred industrial pursuits."* Since no high schools existed at the time, and since the students varied in scholastic attainment at the end of grade school, the faculty required all prospective students to take an examination in arithmetic, geography, grammar, reading, spelling, and penmanship. Students who failed the examination were required to take a preparatory course, which included advanced arithmetic, algebra, physics, geography, natural philosophy, English grammar, and rhetoric, before they became eligible for the four-year college course. The college courses for each of the undergraduate years in 1861 are presented in table 8-1. Note that these courses were designed to educate the student on a broad basis; that is, they were designed to educate the whole man rather than his agricultural side only. The college opened its doors for the teaching of students in April, 1857, when sixty-three young men matriculated, and its first commencement took place in 1861, when seven young men were awarded the bachelor of science degree in agriculture. In general, the other agricultural and agricultural and mechanical colleges followed the example of the Michigan College in the development of the curricula along a broad field.

Engineering. The growth and development of the school of engineering may be divided into three stages: the initial, the intermediate, and the modern. The initial stage began in 1862 and is characterized by providing opportunities for the student to acquire skills in the various mechanical and industrial trades, skills in carpentry with the repair of farm buildings, and skills in blacksmithing with the repair of farm equipment and the shoeing of horses and mules. Naturally, the colleges provided shops for woodworking and for blacksmithing, and the teachers were men who had acquired skills and practical experience in the various trades.

Table 8-1.

COURSES OF STUDY FOR EACH YEAR OF THE FOUR YEARS
AT MICHIGAN AGRICULTURAL COLLEGE IN 1861*

Year	*First Term*	*Second Term*
FRESHMAN	Geology Meteorology History	Trigonometry Surveying Chemistry English Literature Bookkeeping
SOPHOMORE	Physics Plant Physiology Horticulture Rhetoric	Civil Engineering Botany Horticulture Mineralogy Inductive Logic
JUNIOR	Drawing Rural Engineering Geology Philosophy	Astronomy Zoology Moral Philosophy
SENIOR	Analytical Chemistry Political Economy Animal Physiology	Agricultural Chemistry Entomology Veterinary Medicine Botany Household and Rural Economy

*From W. J. Beal, 1915, *History of the Michigan Agricultural College.* Michigan
State University Press, East Lansing, MI.

The intermediate stage began about 1900 and is characterized by a
gradual change in classroom and laboratory work. With increasing
specialization in industry a need for the development of creative ideas
became evident, and this in turn required instruction in theory as well
as in practice. Thus, the shops became laboratories, the term "mechanic
arts" was changed to engineering, and the five original or traditional
departments of engineering made their appearance: mechanical, civil,
electrical, chemical, and agricultural.

The modern period is characterized by a continuous need for the
development of creative ideas, with a correspondingly greater emphasis
on the "why" rather than on the "how." Thus, the shops continued as
laboratories to provide opportunities for the students to develop new
ideas, the teachers became highly specialized in the wide field of
engineering, and opportunities in new fields became available—in nuclear

and aerospace engineering and, in certain Morrill land-grant institutions, in marine and petroleum engineering.

Home Economics. An outstanding feature of the Magnificent Charter is that it provides equal opportunity to both men and women to acquire a college education. Since the charter provides for teaching and research for the benefit of the men of the farm, a similar provision for the benefit of the women of the farm was an inevitable development. In this respect, Iowa Agricultural College and Farm was the pioneer. Mrs. Mary Welch, the wife of the first president, gave the first course in home economics in 1871. She called it domestic chemistry. Other members of the women's faculty gave additional courses: cooking in 1877, and sewing and dressmaking in 1879. In 1909 the college established a four-year curriculum leading to the degree of bachelor of domestic science. Other Morrill land-grant colleges soon followed the example of the Iowa College in establishing courses and curricula in home economics: Kansas Agricultural College in 1873, Michigan Agricultural College in 1895, the Ohio State University in 1896, the University of Illinois in 1900, and the University of Wisconsin in 1903. In fact, by 1940 most of the Morrill land-grant colleges had developed four-year curricula for the education of young women (and men) in the wide field of home economics.

"THE SEVERAL PURSUITS AND PROFESSIONS IN LIFE"

Growth and Development in Additional Fields

The Morrill land-grant law states that men and women shall be educated in the several pursuits and professions in life. This means that the founding fathers provided for the education and training of men and women in all constructive fields. Further, with the development of both the agricultural and nonagricultural industries by the turn of the twentieth century, American society began to consist of a large number of highly specialized groups, with each group having special educational needs and requirements. Moreover, in order to promote the welfare of society as a whole the educational needs of any one particular special group shall not be neglected. How did the Morrill land-grant colleges meet the provision stated by the founding fathers and how did they provide opportunities for the education and training of young men and young women in fields other than agriculture, engineering, and home economics?

In general, the growth and development of curricula in any one field began with the giving of one or two courses, usually but not always by a teacher in a related field. As a first example, take the development of curricula in the field of veterinary medicine or veterinary science. The initial course involved the care and health of farm animals, and this course was usually given by a professor in the department of animal husbandry in the school of agriculture. As a second example, take the development of curricula in the field of forestry. The initial course was concerned with the care and management of the farm woodlot and was usually given by a professor in the department of horticulture. As a third example, take the development of courses in the field of journalism. The initial course was usually given by a teacher in the department of English and consisted of acquiring practical experience in the production of the campus newspaper: gathering and reporting the news, taking of subscriptions, and handling the circulation. As a fourth example, take the development of the curricula in business and industry at Mississippi Agricultural and Mechanical College. Professor J. B. Bowen, a member of the foreign languages department, gave the first course, the principles of commerce, in 1911. By 1916 he had developed an entire curriculum in the field of business and commerce, the first of its kind in the United States. Table 8-2 presents examples of originating departments, the original course developed by any given department, and the department that developed from any one individual course. Note that for the most part the curricula in any given field originated from a course given in a related field.

THE CHANGE IN NAME OF THE SEPARATE MORRILL LAND-GRANT COLLEGES

As shown in table 2-1, the legislatures of each of twenty-one states located their respective Morrill land-grant college at a place other than that of the first state university. With the exception of Alabama Polytechnic Institute, Virginia Polytechnic Institute, and Purdue University, these colleges were officially named "Agricultural" or "Agricultural and Mechanical" (A and M) colleges, and, in accordance with the Morrill Act of 1862, they developed research, teaching, and extension programs, first in the field of agriculture and subsequently in the fields of engineering and home economics. With a further interpretation of the Magnificent Charter and in accordance with the needs and demands of the people, the agricultural and agricultural and mechanical colleges, in common with the colleges that were attached to the first state universities, or that developed into the first state universities, developed research, teaching, and extension programs in other fields, particularly the fields of applied science, business and industry, education, and postgraduate. Since the term "agricultural" implied that only agriculture was given at the agricultural colleges and only agriculture and engineering were given at the agricultural and mechanical colleges,

Table 8-2.

COMMON EXAMPLES OF ORIGINATNG DEPARTMENTS,
ORIGINAL COURSES, AND NEW DEPARTMENTS

Originating Departments	*Original Courses*	*New Departments*
Agriculture	Bookkeeping	Business and Commerce
Agronomy	Surveying and Draining	Agriculture Engineering
Animal Husbandry	Anatomy and Physiology of Farm Animals	Veterinary Medicine
Bacteriology	Basic Bacteriology	Sanitary Engineering
Business	Management of Cafeterias	Institutional Management
Civil Engineering	Principles of Flight	Aeronautical Engineering
Dairy Husbandry	Milk Products	Dairy Manufactures
Education	Teaching of Agriculture in High Schools	Agricultural Education
English	Writing for Newspapers	Journalism
Home Economics	The Preparation and Serving of Food	Home Management
Home Economics	Food Preparation	Dietetics and Human Nutrition
Horticulture	Principles of Flower Production	Floriculture
Horticulture	Processing of Fruits and Vegetables	Food Science
Horticulture	Landscaping the Home Grounds	Landscape Architecture
Horticulture	Care of Farm Woodlots	Forestry
Horticulture	Production of Grapes for Wine	Enology
Liberal Arts	Music Appreciation	Music Education
Mechanical Engineering	Farm Engines and Machines	Agricultural Engineering

students and alumni began to agitate for the adoption of more representative names. For example, C. B. Collinwood, an engineering graduate of Michigan Agricultural College, stated in an address before the alumni association: "I wish we could change the name of our college. . . . It receives funds from the federal and state governments for a broader pursuit than for a mere school of agriculture. I would like to have it called the Michigan School of Applied Science."[1] One morning in 1911 the students of Michigan Agricultural College found posters under the doors of their rooms reading "MAC or MSC." At this time agitation for

[1]From W. J. Beal, 1915, *History of Michigan Agricultural College.* Michigan State University Press, East Lansing, MI.

more representative names was going on at Oregon Agricultural College, Kansas Agricultural College, and at other agricultural and agricultural and mechanical colleges. In fact, by the end of the third decade all of the seventeen institutions established as agricultural or as agricultural and mechanical (A and M) colleges and listed in Table 2-1, except Texas A and M College and Clemson Agricultural College, eliminated either the term "agricultural" or "agricultural and mechanical" and substituted the term "State," usually with the additional notation, "State College of Agriculture and Applied Science." In this way, a more representative and satisfactory name was provided.

Table 8-3.

THE CHANGE IN NAME TO A MORE INCLUSIVE AND
REPRESENTATIVE NAME OF SEVENTEEN MORRILL
LAND-GRANT COLLEGES

First Official Name	*New Name and Year*
Colorado Agricultural College, 1876	Colorado Agriculture and Mechanical College, 1888
Iowa Agricultural College and State Farm, 1859	Iowa State College, 1898
Kansas Agricultural College, 1863	Kansas State College, 1931
Maryland Agricultural College, 1857	Maryland State College, 1916
Massachusetts Agricultural College, 1863	Massachusetts State College, 1933
The Agricultural College of the State of Michigan, 1855	Michigan State College, 1924
Mississippi A and M College, 1878	Mississippi State College, 1932
New Mexico A and M College, 1888	New Mexico State College
North Carolina College of Agriculture and Mechanic Arts, 1887	North Carolina State College, 1917
North Dakota Agricultural College, 1890	North Dakota State University, 1960
Oklahoma Agricultural and Mechanical College, 1890	Oklahoma State University, 1957
Oregon Agricultural College, 1868	Oregon State College, 1907
Farmers' High School of Pennsylvania, 1855	Pennsylvania State College, 1874
Rhode Island Agricultural College, 1892	Rhode Island State College, 1909
South Dakota Agricultural College, 1881	South Dakota State College, 1907
Utah Agricultural College, 1888	Utah State University, 1957
Washington Agricultural and Mechanical College, 1890	Washington State College, 1905

Significance and Summary

During the second and third decades of the twentieth century and in accordance with the provisions of the Magnificent Charter the Morrill land-grant colleges extended their services to practically all fields and professions. They greatly strengthened their research, teaching, and extension programs in agriculture, engineering, and home economics, and they started research, teaching, and extension programs in many other fields. Further, with the extension of their services to all fields, these institutions extended the right to every individual—the right to develop himself to his fullest capacity without harm or injury to others. Moreover, the people as a whole began to realize that these institutions could be most helpful in the solution of their problems and in the creation and application of useful knowledge. As a result, the Morrill land-grant colleges grew rapidly, both in enrollment and in service and influence. In fact, the idea began to take root throughout the United States that these institutions are indispensable to the growth, development, and progress of the people and the nation.

REFERENCES

Bettersworth, John K. 1953. *People's College: A History of Mississippi State*, chapter 16, "A New Name and a New Peril." University of Alabama Press, Tuscaloosa, AL.

Cary, Harold W. 1962. *The University of Massachusetts: A History of One Hundred Years*, chapter 9, "From MAC to MSC." University of Massachusetts, Amherst, MA.

Kuhn, Madison. 1955. *Michigan State: The First Hundred Years*, "MAC Becomes MSC." Michigan State University Press, East Lansing, MI.

The chapters of the above references are typical of the foresight of the Morrill land-grant colleges in extending their services to all of the people.

9

THE MORRILL
LAND-GRANT COLLEGES
AND WORLD WAR I

Enthusiasm is at the bottom of all progress. With it there is accomplishment, without it there are only alibis.

—HENRY FORD

PRINCIPAL REASONS FOR THE ENTRY
OF THE UNITED STATES INTO THE WAR

World War I began in 1914. Prior to 1917 the major antagonists were Germany, Austria-Hungary, and Turkey on one side; and Great Britain, France, Italy, and Russia, the so-called Allies, on the other. The United States entered the war on the side of the Allies on April 7, 1917. There were at least three reasons for this decision on the part of the people: (1) Germany's resumption of unrestricted and irresponsible submarine warfare on the open seas; (2) Germany's promise to award the states of Texas, Arizona, New Mexico, and California to Mexico and Japan, provided these countries entered the war against the United States; and (3) Germany was winning the war. By the latter part of 1917 the Russian armies had collapsed, and the British and French armies had failed to stop the German forces on the Western Front. Further, the people of Great Britain, Ireland, and France had lost thousands upon thousands of brave and courageous men.

WORLD WAR I AND THE MORRILL ACT OF 1862

As stated in chapter 2, the Morrill Act of 1862 requires instruction and training in military science and tactics. Note the phrase "where the leading object shall be, without excluding other scientific and classical studies, *and including military tactics* to teach such branches of learning as are related to agriculture and the mechanic arts." However, the Act does not state how the instruction and training shall be implemented. Should instruction and training in military science and tactics be compulsory or voluntary? In view of the emergency brought on by World War I, the presidents and faculties interpreted the act to mean that the military requirement shall be compulsory. Consequently,

116

as described in chapter 14, programs were set up that organized the men of the student body into cadet companies with their cadet officers, and, as a result, the life of the students from 1917 to 1918 was regulated by the "military bugle."

THE NATIONAL DEFENSE ACT OF 1916

Among other things, the National Defense Act of 1916 provided for the establishment of units of the Reserve Officers Training Corps, ROTC, on the campuses of the Morrill land-grant colleges. The prime reason for the formation of these units is that the nation would have a splendid corps of educated men for leadership positions in the armed forces during any emergency. To develop this type of leadership, instruction in military science and tactics was changed from one or two years to four years, with the granting of reserve commissions at the end of the fourth year. However, this program had just nicely gotten started when the people, through their representatives in Congress, declared war on Germany in April, 1917.

EFFECTS OF THE DECLARATION OF WAR

As would be expected, the declaration of war disrupted the peace-time activities of the colleges. In fact, the presidents and faculty placed all of their resources at the disposal of the federal and state governments in order to help the people to defend and safeguard their way of life. As a result, each respective campus began to look like a military post. Pertinent factors are briefly discussed as follows.

Reaction of Students and Faculty

Many students enlisted in the armed forces; others left the campus to work on farms or in war-related factories. The same situation existed with the faculty. Those with commissions left to join their respective units; others enlisted, while others remained on campus to teach the military units or to join the agricultural research or extension services in the production and conservation of food. Thus, with both students and faculty, the preservation of the nation's way of life took precedence over that of the individual.

Suspension of ROTC and Establishment of the Student Army Training Corps, SATC

As previously stated, the curriculum of ROTC required a period of four years. Under the critical conditions of the spring of 1917 a program was needed to discover and develop officers in a relatively short time. Thus, the ROTC program was temporarily suspended, and the Student Army Training Corps, SATC, program was initiated in its stead. Actually, the organization consisted of soldiers of the National Army,[1] and, as such, each individual received rations, clothes, and the pay of a private —$30 a month. There were two distinct groups: the collegiate and the mechanic. In general, the collegiate group was trained to qualify as officers or noncommissioned officers, and the mechanic group was trained to become proficient as auto mechanics, blacksmiths, machinists, or surveyors. A unique feature was the induction ceremony. It was held simultaneously at all of the colleges on October 1, 1918, at 12:00 hours, Eastern Standard Time, and consisted in the raising of the colors, the administration of the oath, the reading of a message from President Wilson and from General Marsh, the Army Chief of Staff, and an address by a prominent citizen. Since the Armistice occurred on November 11, 1918, only forty-two days had elapsed after the program had officially started, an insufficient time for a full and comprehensive appraisal or evaluation of the program.

Special Units

A unique and distinct organization was the Ames Ambulance Unit. This unit consisted of thirty-six students recruited on the Iowa State College campus. It left the campus on May 31, 1917, for a year's training at Camp Crane, Allentown, Pennsylvania, and finally it was assigned to active duty on the Italian-Austrian front. Its effective service won a U.S. Army Corps Citation and the Italian Cross of War. Other special units include the radio school of the University of Maryland, where about six hundred men received training in communication techniques, and the aviation-ground school of the Ohio State University, where 1,510 men received training as aviation pilots or balloonists.

The Farmer and His Research and Extension Workers

A slogan of World War I was "Food Will Win the War." In fact, there was an urgent need to increase the production and conservation of food, since the submarine blockade had seriously reduced the food supplies of the British, and the Allied blockade had seriously reduced the food supplies of the Germans and Austrians. Consequently, crop-plant and crop-animal specialists of the experiment stations and

---

[1]During World War I and from the standpoint of source and origin of the soldiers, there were three groups: soldiers of the Regular Army, the National Guard, and the National Army.

the extension services put on intensive campaigns to increase the production of food, and the food specialists in home economics and the home demonstration agents put on intensive campaigns to promote the conservation of food. This was particularly the case for crops raised in the home vegetable garden. Extensive demonstrations were held on the home canning and home drying of fruits and vegetables. In a further attempt to conserve food the federal government requested civilians to refrain from eating meat and using sugar at least one day each week. In this way, the so-called meatless and sugarless days each week were started and continued until the end of the war.

THE EPIDEMIC OF INFLUENZA

An epidemic of influenza, the so-called Spanish flu, broke out on practically all college campuses in the fall of 1918. Since at that time the cause of the disease was unknown, no vaccine had been developed. The disease proved to be highly contagious and it spread like wildfire. Within a matter of hours college hospitals on each campus became overcrowded and other buildings were rapidly pressed into service as temporary hospitals or wards—the YMCA, the gymnasium, the fieldhouse, fraternity houses, and churches of the local community. Women on the faculty and wives and daughters of the faculty assisted the regular nurses and dietitians in feeding and caring for the sick. Under these conditions, all classes were suspended and all assemblies within buildings were postponed. However, with the maintenance of strict sanitary conditions and the isolation of the sick from the healthy, the number of new cases gradually declined and classes and drill periods were resumed by the last week of October or the first week of November.

THE EFFECT OF THE ARMISTICE

The Armistice was signed on November 11, 1918. As a result, the military activities of each campus gradually decreased and the civilian or peacetime activities gradually assumed their prewar status. Old students returned to complete their education, new students matriculated to begin theirs, and members of the faculty on leave with the armed forces or on special assignment returned to take up their respective positions. Thus, each Morrill land-grant college assumed its peacetime position as a center of higher education in its respective state.

Of particular interest was the reestablishment of ROTC in 1920, as originally conceived in 1916, with its four-year curriculum and commissioning of its graduates as reserve officers. As stated in chapter 14, a splendid corps of reserve officers has developed throughout the years—young men and young women who have always stood guard for America in times of peace, and who have always fought for America in times of war.

THE REHABILITATION PROGRAM FOR DISABLED VETERANS

The federal government in cooperation with certain selected Morrill land-grant colleges conducted educational and training programs for veterans who were unable to pursue the respective vocations in which they were engaged when they entered the service. Essentially, the program was similar to that embodied in the GI Bill of World War II, except that the benefits were limited to the in-line-of-duty disabled. In general, the Veterans Bureau supplied funds to pay the subsistence, tuition, books, and laboratory materials of the students, and the colleges provided the teachers, classroom, laboratory, and library facilities. There were two distinct groups: the collegiate and the vocational. The collegiate group took the regular four-year course within any given field leading toward the B.S. degree, whereas the vocational group took special semi-technical courses leading toward the granting of a certificate. Of the two groups, the vocational was in greater demand. For example, at Kansas State College a total of 946 took the vocational course, and 498 took the four-year regular course. Of the two groups the collegiate received the greater benefits, since the members received a well-rounded college education at little expense to themselves. In this way, they qualified for positions of leadership and responsibility in their respective communities.

THE MEMORIALS

During the first part of the third decade of this century several of the Morrill land-grant colleges erected memorials on each of their respective campuses. The object of these memorials was to honor the soldiers and sailors who gave their lives during the war and to serve as a constant reminder to the present and future generations of the sacrifices each of these men and women had made. Although these memorials are of various types, all of them were made possible by gifts of money from students, faculty, alumni, and friends, and all of them combine beauty and love of country with usefulness and utility. Examples are the Memorial Student Unions of Iowa State and Michigan State; the Memorial Stadiums or Gymnasiums of Ohio State, Kansas State, University of California-Berkeley, and Purdue; the Carillon Towers at the University of Missouri-Columbia, and at North Carolina State;

the Monuments at Mississippi State and Virginia Polytechnic Institute and State University; and the Bronze Cabinet in the library of the University of Arkansas.

CONTRIBUTIONS DURING THE WAR

The trying days of World War I proved the first real test of the Magnificent Charter of the Morrill land-grant colleges to the life and well-being of the nation during a period of extreme emergency. In particular, the research workers and teachers in schools of agriculture joined with the agricultural extension workers in assisting the farmer to go all out in the production of food. In like manner, the research workers and teachers in the schools of home economics joined hands with the home demonstration agents and 4-H leaders in assisting all families in the preservation of foods. Indeed, the need for the production and preservation of food was quite urgent, since the people of many countries overseas were on the verge of starvation. These countries included both those that had fought with and those that had fought against the Allies. To promote the production and preservation of food Congress appropriated emergency funds for the employment of county and home demonstration agents in counties without the services of either one or both of these specialists. In fact, by the end of 1919 more than seventy-five percent of the counties in the United States had a county agent, and at least thirty-five percent had a home demonstration agent.

In addition the teachers of the schools of engineering established courses for the training of soldiers in the National Army as auto mechanics, machinists, blacksmiths, and carpenters. (The artillery caissons and supply wagons of the United States Army were pulled by mules.)

Moreover, many administrative officers and members of the faculty accepted assignments more directly connected with the war effort. For example, Dr. R. A. Pearson, president of Iowa State, served as special assistant to the secretary of agriculture in the production and preservation of food; Dr. W. O. Thompson, president of the Ohio State University, served as a member of the National Industrial Board; Dr. Max Levine, professor of bacteriology at Iowa State, was in charge of a bacteriological laboratory at Dyon, France; Vice Director H. V. Bemis, also of Iowa State, and four colleagues helped direct the veterinary science program of the American Expeditionary Forces; Professor H. D. Eustace, head of the Department of Horticulture, Michigan Agricultural College, served as associate head of the Perishable Food Division under Food Administrator Herbert Hoover; Professor A. A. Pollard, dean of engineering at Kansas State, from September 1 through September 11, 1918, supervised instruction in mechanics at several engineering schools in the Midwest; and Professor D. J. Baker, director of agricultural extension, Connecticut Agricultural College, served as director of the Farm School at Allery, France.

Last and not least the Morrill land-grant colleges established preparatory courses for returned soldiers and sailors who had not completed their high school education and who intended to go on to college.

REFERENCES

Ross, Earl D. 1942. *A History of Iowa State College*, chapter 13, "Over Here and Over There." Iowa State University Press, Ames, IA.
Willard, Julius T. 1940. *History of Kansas State College of Agriculture and Applied Science*, chapter 10, "The College and the World War." Kansas State University Press, Manhatten, KS.
Stemmons, Walter. 1931. *Connecticut Agricultural College—A History*, chapter 8, "The College During the War." Connecticut Agricultural College, Storrs, CT.

In the chapters cited the authors present comprehensive discussions of the contributions of each of the Morrill land-grant colleges during World War I.

10

THE MORRILL LAND-GRANT COLLEGES AND THE GREAT DEPRESSION

Nothing would be done at all if man waited until he could do it so well that no one could find fault with it.
—Cardinal Newman

THE GREAT DEPRESSION: ITS CAUSE AND EXTENT

The Great Depression was the period of severe economic stagnation that occurred throughout the United States and the remainder of the world during the third decade of the twentieth century. Some authorities state that it started in the United States with the stock market crash of October 23, 1929. Actually, it started several years before that time. During World War I the Allies needed large quantities of food. To meet this need the farmers of the United States mortgaged their farms at wartime prices to buy more land to produce this food. As a result, the farm debt due to mortgages markedly increased. For example, the average mortgage debt per acre in 1920 was 2.5 times that of 1910. With the cessation of hostilities, farmers overseas rebuilt their agriculture and set up tariffs to stem the flow of food and fiber from the United States. With the overseas market virtually cut off and with the American farmer producing food and fiber on the same acreage as he did during World War I, supplies greatly exceeded demand and prices fell.

As prices declined the farmer increased his production in an attempt to maintain his income to pay off the mortgages. This only added to the surplus, and prices further declined. In fact, farm income in the United States declined more than one-half between 1919 and 1930. In 1932 wheat and corn were selling at 38 and 32 cents per bushel, respectively, and cotton and hogs were selling at 6 and 4 cents per pound, respectively. In fact, foreclosures increased from 3.1 per 1,000 farms in 1919 to 38.8 per 1,000 farms in 1933, and nearly 15,000 banks closed their doors between 1920 and 1933. Further, farmers of the Corn Belt and the Prairie States had to contend with severe crop-yield-reducing droughts—droughts accompanied by hot-dry dust-storm-producing winds,

123

the like of which has not been seen since. Under these conditions, crop-plants wilted beyond recovery, crop-animals sought shade, the ditches drifted full, the skies filled with silt and darkened. This in turn caused people to drive with their lights on. In fact, almost everything that people ate, touched, or wore felt gritty, even the sheets on the bed.[1] Moreover, with the farmer's income greatly decreased, money for the purchase of industrial goods correspondingly decreased. This resulted in the laying off of large numbers of industrial workers. Unemployment increased and thousands of industrial workers went on relief.

EFFECT ON STATE TAX REVENUES AND APPROPRIATIONS

As pointed out, the income of both the farmers and factory workers taken as a whole was low. In fact, thousands of farmers lost their farms, and thousands of factory workers lost their jobs. As a result, these people could not pay their taxes, and tax delinquency was prevalent throughout the country. This prevailing delinquency markedly reduced the amount of money flowing into the state treasuries. For example, the legislature of Mississippi at its meeting in 1930 made appropriations of about $15.5 million for the next biennium 1931-33, but from an esti-mate of the amount of money flowing into the treasury in early 1931 the state could receive only $8 million. This situation was similar, though not as severe in degree, in all of the other states. Thus, the legislatures were obliged to retrench—to reduce appropriations and expenses.

How Did the Colleges Absorb the Cuts?

Since the Morrill land-grant colleges are tax-supported institutions, reductions in appropriations to each college were inevitable. How did the colleges absorb the reductions in operating funds? In general, the reductions were absorbed not by eliminating any of the employees, but by reducing the salaries of all the employees, from the president to the deans, the various grades of professors, the graduate students and laboratory assistants, the secretaries, janitors, and maintenance men. The cuts varied with the year for any given college and with the college for any given year. For example, the University of Arkansas reduced all salaries 8 percent for 1932-33, and 14 percent for 1933-34, and, for 1932-33, Kansas State College reduced all salaries by 10 percent, whereas Mississippi State College reduced all salaries by 25 percent. Despite these adverse circumstances, the research workers, the teachers, and the

---

[1]Carl Hamilton, 1974, *In No Time at All*. Iowa State University Press, Ames, IA.

extension staffs carried on with full programs. The research workers continued with their projects, the resident teachers met all of their classes and laboratories, and the extension workers continued to disseminate and demonstrate the results of research to the farmers and homemakers.

THE NEW STATE REVENUE-RAISING PROGRAM

As stated previously, tax delinquency was quite prevalent during the first part of the third decade of the twentieth century. Since the taxes were largely based on the value of the property, and since property values had declined and many property owners could not pay their taxes, tax authorities recognized the futility of relying wholly on real estate taxes to replenish the state treasuries. Consequently, they began to look for other means either to supplement or entirely replace the property taxes. On the assumption that everyone should contribute to the support of public schools, colleges, and universities, tax authorities suggested the establishment of a general sales tax. Mississippi established this type of tax in 1932. Within a matter of months the treasury of the state was replenished, and the credit of the state government was entirely restored. More importantly, and contrary to expectations, businessmen found that the tax was not detrimental to the transaction of business. As a result, the outlook of the people changed from one of futility and despair to one of optimism and hope. The success of the Mississippi sales tax encouraged other states to establish this type of tax in rapid succession: Pennsylvania in 1932; Arizona, Illinois, Indiana, New York, Utah, Michigan, North Carolina, South Dakota, Oklahoma, and Washington in 1933; Missouri, Iowa, West Virginia, and Kentucky in 1934; Ohio, Colorado, Idaho, Maryland, Wyoming, Arkansas, North Dakota, and New Mexico in 1935; Louisiana in 1936; and Alabama and Kansas in 1937.[2]

THE FEDERAL GOVERNMENT-LAND-GRANT
COLLEGE COOPERATIVE PROGRAMS

The National Youth Administration Program (NYA)

The object of the NYA program was to provide an opportunity for high school graduates of poor Depression-stricken families to work their way through college. The federal government supplied the funds, and

---

[2]From Neil S. Jacoby, 1938, *Retail Sales Taxation*. Commerce Clearing House, Inc., New York, NY.

the land-grant colleges supplied the faculty and facilities for doing constructive work. (No leaf-raking or similar boondoggling projects were allowed.) For any given college a member of the faculty had overall charge of the program. In general, he carefully selected each student on the basis of his high school scholastic record, his potentialities for success in college, and his financial need, and assigned each student to one or more members of the faculty. The members of the faculty in turn trained the students to be useful in a wide variety of constructive activities. Examples are caring for experimental crop-plant plots in the greenhouse or field, or for experimental crop-animals, recording and analyzing data of the crop-plant or crop-animal research projects, and serving as assistants in chemical research or regulatory laboratories, in the library, or as typists. As the historian of the University of Minnesota points out, "In field and in laboratory, in engine room and library, they, the students, performed routine tasks which would otherwise have absorbed the energy of the investigator."[3] Thus, the NYA program was extremely beneficial. The impoverished student was given an opportunity to acquire a college education at little or no expense to himself or his family, and the teacher and investigator of the college obtained valuable assistance in the development of his respective projects. One wonders why this program was not continued even in the more prosperous times. The data presented in table 10-1 show the years, the number of students, and the expenditures per student in the NYA program at Kansas State College. Note that both men and women students were benefited.

The Work Progress Administration Program (WPA)

WPA programs provided for the development of projects that could be initiated at the onset of the Depression and finished in a relatively short time. Examples are the building of concrete sidewalks and gravel or hard-surface roads on the various campuses, the installation of drain tile on the campus and/or on the experimental farm, the repair and painting of farm buildings of the college, the development of tennis courts and running tracks of the athletic departments, the finishing of incomplete parts of campus buildings, the landscaping and planting of trees and shrubs on the campuses, and the binding of valuable library materials. In this way, constructive work was made available to a large number of unemployed, and the appearance and utility of each campus were considerably enhanced.

---

[3]James Gray. 1951. *The University of Minnesota, 1851-1951.* University of Minnesota Press, Minneapolis, MN.

Table 10-1.

THE YEARS, NUMBER OF STUDENTS, AND EXPENDITURES
PER STUDENT AT KANSAS STATE COLLEGE, 1933-1939*

Years	Number of Students Men	Women	Total	Average Amount per Student
1933-34	154	76	230	56.09
1934-35	211	111	322	104.89
1935-36	286	122	408	104.08
1936-37	407	160	567	106.78
1937-38	252	118	370	111.95
1938-39	257	135	392	105.86
TOTAL	1,567	722	2,289	101.62

*From J. T. Willard, 1940, *History of Kansas State College of Agriculture and Applied Science*, p. 332. Kansas State College Press, Manhatten, KS.

The Public Works Administration Program (PWA)

The PWA programs provided funds for the erection and furnishing of needed buildings on each campus. In this way, a comparatively large number of both local and nonlocal people was employed. Here again, the federal government supplied most of the funds, and the college supplied the remainder of the funds and the site for each building. Examples are the Center for Continuation Study at the University of Minnesota, two men's dormitories, and a combination gymnasium-fieldhouse at Michigan State College, the home economics building and the natural science hall at the Virginia Polytechnic Institute, and an agricultural hall at Clemson College. Many other examples could be cited. A unique case is the building of Seitz Hall for the agricultural engineering department at Virginia Polytechnic Institute. The historian states: "Instead of letting the erection of the building out to contractors, the agricultural engineering staff designed the building and then trained transient labor in the skills of stone cutting, masonry, plumbing, carpentry, and electricity. Then having trained its own working force, the staff supervised much of the actual erection of the building. This on-the-job training made everybody happy. The college got a much needed building, the workmen got paychecks during the Depression, and the state got a boost in the number of skilled workers."[4] In common with other states, the state of Virginia also got a boost in that its land-grant

[4]Duncan L. Kinnear. 1972. *The First 100 Years, A History of Virginia Polytechnic Insttiute and State University*, p. 308. VPI Educational Foundation, Blacksburg, VA.

college could proceed unabated with its work toward promoting the
welfare of the people.

The Agricultural Adjustment Act (AAA)

As pointed out previously, the farmer during the post-World War I
period continued to produce large quantities of basic commodities such
as corn, wheat, and cotton. At the same time, the demand for these
and other products markedly declined. In fact, by 1932 the prices available to the farmer were often lower than his costs of production. This
was certainly out of line with the profit motive on which American
industry is based. As a result, the farmer could not pay his taxes, or
the mortgages, or buy apparel for the members of his family, or send
his children to college.

To help the farmer reduce his production more in line with market
demand, Congress passed the Agricultural Adjustment Act (AAA) in
1933. Only five crops—wheat, corn, cotton, peanuts, and tobacco—and
two animal products—hogs and milk—were involved. To reduce production of these crops and products, Congress authorized the secretary
of agriculture to make compensatory payments to farmers in return
for their agreement to curtail their acreage or production for market.
The secretary of agriculture in turn authorized the director of the
agricultural extension service in each of the respective states to implement the program, and he in turn authorized the county agents to
support and conduct the program. Thus, the county agents or farm
advisors during the Depression were busy persons. In general, an
individual agent acquainted the farmers with the nature and purpose
of the AAA program, the method by which the production of any given
crop would be reduced, and how compensatory payments would be
made. With the outbreak of World War II in 1939 the demand for
the seven commodities increased and the need for curtailing their
production accordingly decreased. A distinct and noteworthy feature
of the Depression days is that, with the exception of growers of potatoes, all growers of horticulture crops—fruits, vegetables, and orna-
mentals—weathered the production-market demand storms without assistance from the federal government.

FURTHER ENDOWMENT OF THE
MORRILL LAND-GRANT COLLEGES

The Purnell Act

In 1925 Congress passed the Purnell Act. The purpose of this act
as stated in the title is as follows: "An Act to authorize the more complete endowment of agricultural experiment stations and for other

purposes." In general, this endowment consisted of an annual allotment of $60,000 to the agricultural experiment station of each state or territory. Before this allotment was made the federal grants to each station were $30,000 a year: $15,000 from each of the Hatch and Adams Acts. With an additional $60,000 a total of $90,000 was available. This permitted each experiment station director to greatly broaden the scope of research at each station, and to start projects on certain phases of rural life that had not heretofore been encompassed. For the most part, these phases pertained to the marketing of agricultural products and to the economic and social aspects of rural life.

The Bankhead-Jones Act

In 1935 the Congress of the United States passed the Bankhead-Jones Act. The purpose of this act as stated in the title is "to provide for research into basic laws and principles relating to agriculture and to provide for the further development of cooperative agricultural extension work and the more complete endowment and support of the [Morrill] land-grant colleges." Thus, the Act is rather comprehensive in nature, in that it provides funds for the support and further endowment of each of the three great dimensions in agriculture: research, resident teaching, and extension. In general, the research dimension was strengthened by including projects on the heredity and genetics of principal crop-plants and crop-animals; the resident teaching dimension by establishing new courses and building new facilities for the giving of these courses; and the extension dimension by developing new methods in extension teaching. In general, the amount allotted varied with each of the three dimensions. For example, according to the historian of Kansas State College, the school of agriculture received an annual allotment of $61,250 for research, $43,000 for resident teaching, and $274,000 for extension. Similar allotments were made to the schools of agriculture and home economics of other Morrill land-grant colleges.

GROWTH AND DEVELOPMENT DURING THE GREAT DEPRESSION

In general, the Morrill land-grant colleges expanded their facilities for service to all the people quite rapidly during the Great Depression. This marked growth and development were made possible by various agencies of the federal government. The Purnell and Bankhead-Jones Acts provided funds for expanding and strengthening each of the great dimensions in agriculture and home economics. Of special significance was the NYA program, since it provided funds that enabled thousands of selected young men and young women to acquire a college education. The WPA and PWA programs provided funds for the improvement of many campuses, and the erection and refurbishing of many needed buildings and laboratories. In fact, most of the Morrill land-grant colleges enjoyed a great building boom during the Depression. For example, in the fall of 1936 seven new buildings were in various stages of completion on the campus of the University of Missouri (Columbia); by 1939 six dormitories, a chemistry building, a textile building, a fieldhouse, a new dairy plant, and several buildings for agronomy and plant pathology had been completed on the North Carolina State campus, and also by 1939 an administration, agricultural engineering, home economics, and natural science building, plus two dormitories and a student activities building, had been erected on the Virginia Polytechnic Institute campus. A striking and singular method for the funding and erection of buildings was developed at Michigan State College. The president and faculty discovered that dormitories could be successfully financed by people willing to invest their money in the immediate future of the college. The Board of Trustees sold revenue bonds to the general public for the funding and erection of any given dormitory, and they gradually retired these bonds by the income from the use of the building. Several new men's and women's dormitories were successfully erected and operated under this plan.

REFERENCES

Hamilton, Carl. 1974. *In No Time At All.* Iowa State University Press, Ames, IA.
       A spicy, well-illustrated, firsthand account of the indomitable courage of four farm families of northwest Iowa during the Great Depression. A reader states: "I like the integrity with which you [the author] have treated the events described in the book."
Kuhn, Madison. 1955. *Michigan State University, The First 100 Years, 1855-1955,* "Depression Decade." Michigan State University Press, East Lansing, MI.
       How a land-grant college balanced its budget, strengthened its finances, and actually expanded its services to the people during the dark days of the Great Depression.
Statdman, Verne A. 1970. *The University of California, 1868-1968,* chapter 18, "The Students Between Two Wars."
       A discussion of the forces that shaped student life at the University of California-Berkeley and the University of California-Los Angeles. The interaction among the presidents, faculty, and student body and the development of the so-called California spirit.
Terkel, Studs. 1970. *Hard Times: An Oral History of the Great Depression.* Pantheon, New York, NY.
       The author, using a tape recorder, interviewed more than a hundred and fifty people: farmers, miners, stockbrokers, whites, blacks, businessmen, lawyers, and teachers. From these interviews he developed an outstanding anthology of the memory of the American people. A reviewer stated, "To read this book will reassure your faith in all of us."

11

THE MORRILL
LAND-GRANT COLLEGES
AND WORLD WAR II

*A people that mean to be their own masters should arm them-
selves with the power that knowledge brings.*
                                        —JAMES MADISON

THE EFFECT OF THE BLITZKRIEG AND
THE BOMBING OF PEARL HARBOR

World War II started in the fall of 1939. The Nazis invaded Poland,
and the people of Great Britain and France declared war on the Nazis.
Prior to this time the Nazis had developed a type of land warfare
called *Blitzkrieg* ("lightning war"). Essentially, this consisted of using
a large number of bomb-dropping planes within a small area to demor-
alize the populace and/or defending troops, and a large number of
armored gun carriers (tanks) to occupy and defend the invaded land.
Since the Polish, British, and French troops had not developed an
adequate defense against this type of land warfare (they clung to the
type of defense used in World War I), the Nazi forces took over and
occupied large areas of land in rapid succession: all of Poland, all of
France except the strip along the Mediterranean, all of Czechoslovakia,
Austria, Hungary, Rumania, Bulgaria, and Greece, and most of the
Ukraine, and, with the help of Italy, they also took over a strip of land
on the south shore of the Mediterranean extending from Tunis in Tunisia
to El Alamein in Egypt.

On December 7, 1941, the Japanese bombed ships and shore installations of the U.S. Navy at Pearl Harbor, Hawaii. The United States
immediately declared war on Japan, and, because of a previous treaty
with Japan, the Nazis declared war on the United States. At this time
the United States and its territories were inadequately prepared to
defend themselves. Thus, as with the Nazis, the Japanese took and
occupied large areas of land within a relatively short time: all of the
Philippines, Taiwan, Malaysia, and numerous islands of the South
Pacific. In fact, during the dark days of 1942 the Mediterranean was
virtually a German-Italian lake and Nazi troops had stormed beyond
Kharkov and were driving toward the River Don, and the outskirts of

131

Stalingrad, Moscow, and Leningrad. The Japanese, in turn, had severely reduced the fighting effectiveness of the United States forces in the Pacific.

THE BOLD AND COURAGEOUS COUNTERATTACKS

Nevertheless, in spite of this gloomy situation, Franklin D. Roosevelt, president of the United States, and Winston S. Churchill, prime minister of Great Britain, together with their respective staffs planned bold and courageous counterattacks. On the Atlantic side, American and British naval forces overcame the menace of German submarines by devising a means by which these ships could be detected and destroyed. This provided for the shipping of large quantities of war matériel to the Russian port of Murmansk via the North Atlantic and the Bering Sea, and the development of huge training and staging areas in Great Britain. The valiant American, British, and French troops eliminated the German and Italian forces on the strip of land on the south shore of the Mediterranean, successfully invaded the southern half of Italy, and successfully attacked the German forces on the beaches of Normandy and in the Rhone River valley. At the same time, the Russian troops stopped the German offensives in Stalingrad and on the outskirts of Moscow, and with counterattacks caused the Nazis to retreat. With continued attacks by the American, British, and French forces in the West, and by the Russian forces in the East, the German forces continued to retreat until they surrendered on May 7, 1945.

On the Pacific side, American naval forces overcame the menace of the Japanese submarine by breaking the Japanese naval code and by developing huge training and staging areas in Queensland, Australia, and on the islands of New Caledonia and Espíritu Santo. The valiant American, Australian, and New Zealand troops stopped the march of the Japanese toward Australia and New Zealand, started a march of their own toward the Philippines and the Marianas, and continued with this march until the Japanese surrendered on the U.S. battleship *Missouri* on August 14, 1945.

THE EFFECTS OF THE WAR ON THE RESEARCH,
TEACHING, AND EXTENSION DIMENSIONS

Immediately after the infamy of the Japanese at Pearl Harbor the issue of survival of the American people was at stake. Accordingly, the presidents, faculty, and students of each land-grant institution immediately set about to assist the people to eliminate the peril across the Atlantic and the peril across the Pacific. In general, the presidents of each institution placed the campus on a wartime basis. The faculty who were members of the reserves joined their respective units; others qualified for commissions in the armed forces or for special assignments in the war effort as civilians, while others remained on campus to teach subjects of the special military training program, to assist the agricultural extension service in the production of food and fiber, to assist the engineering experiment station in the making of synthetic rubber and other compounds, and to teach students enrolled in the regular courses.

For the most part, the students belonged to one of three groups: the members of ROTC, the members of the Selective Service Corps, and the regular students. Those of the first group immediately joined the armed forces, those of the second waited until they were called to the colors, and those of the third continued with their education.

The Research Dimension

Agriculture. Because of the severe nature of the World War II crises most peacetime research projects were placed on a standby basis; that is, experimental plants and animals were maintained, but experiments with them were reduced to a minimum. This provided time for investigations of problems directly related to the war effort. Examples are (1) the dehydration of eggs, potatoes, beets, carrots, onions, and sweet potatoes in cooperation with the U.S. Army Quartermaster Subsistence Laboratory (these investigations were necessary to conserve valuable shipping space and to eliminate the need for and expense of cold storage); (2) the growing of vegetable crops without soil (certain islands of the Atlantic and the Pacific had very little, if any, soil, and the soil of Japan was infested with the dysentery organism); (3) the development of high-yield varieties of rice (when the Japanese took Burma, French Indochina, Thailand, and the Philippines, supplies of rice were cut off from other rice-eating countries); (4) a search for satisfactory compounds to take the place of mercuric chloride as a disinfectant (mercuric chloride was unavailable to farmers during World War II); (5) investigations with guayule as a source of natural rubber in cooperation with the U.S. Department of Agriculture (as stated previously, almost all supplies of natural rubber were cut off); and (6) the development of farm laborsaving machines—planters, cultivators, and harvesters. During World War II many workers left the farm to join the armed forces or to work in war-related factories. As a result, farm labor became scarce. This acute shortage of labor, combined with the need for high production on the part of the farmer, emphasized the need for laborsaving machines.

Home Economics. Examples of projects are (1) studies of the sealing performance of canning jar rings under conditions of home canning (because supplies of natural rubber to the United States had been cut off, and since American housewives canned billions of jars of food during the war, investigations were needed on the sealing ability of reclaimed rubber); (2) investigations on the rate of heat penetration within glass jars and tin cans packed with several kinds of vegetables; (3) studies of the quality of foods dried at home (in general, home gardeners were encouraged to grow their food so that commercial gardeners would be free to grow food for the armed forces); and (4) research on a satisfactory design of work clothes for the women (during World War II thousands upon thousands of women worked on farms and in factories, and clothes for specific types of work were unavailable). Many other examples could be cited.

Engineering. Examples of projects are (1) investigations with different types of soil combined with different types of stabilizing materials for use as runways of airports (these studies were part of a nationwide project for the development of airports throughout the nation); (2) studies on the recovery of fats and oils from garbage (during World War II critical shortages existed in the supply of fats, and there was some concern over the possibility of the shortage of food); (3) studies of the use of lead as a substitute for zinc and tin in the protective coating of iron and steel (a vigorous experimental program with lead was necessary when the Japanese seized the tin mines of Malaya and Indonesia); (4) research for the U.S. Army Ordnance Department (this research included the behavior of gun barrels under various conditions of firing); and (5) the development of microwave radar sets. Many other examples could be cited.

Chemistry. Examples of projects are: (1) investigations on the making of synthetic rubber (prior to World War II all automobile tires were made from natural rubber, a secretion of the rubber tree *Heva braziliensis* (L.) most plantations were in the South Pacific; when the Japanese invaded these regions, supplies to the United States ceased); (2) a search for satisfactory antimalarial compounds (quinine and atabrine, the commonly used antimalarials, had side effects); and (3) the preparation and study of organic compounds containing fluorine. Many other examples could be cited.

The Teaching Dimension

The teaching dimension is divided into two rather significant types of work: (1) instruction in regular courses and (2) instruction in special wartime courses.

Instruction in Regular Courses. As previously stated, right after the bombing of Pearl Harbor many male students joined the armed forces. As a result enrollment of male students declined and the need for the usual number of professors correspondingly declined. In this way professors became available for the teaching of wartime courses. Further, with the decline in male students and lack of decline in women students the ratio of men to women students decreased. For example, on the Illinois campus the ratio was three to one in 1941 and one to three in 1942. Moreover, the giving of regular courses was accelerated. In general, institutions on a two-semester or three-quarter basis changed over to a three-semester, sixteen-week basis or a four-quarter, twelve-week basis.

Instruction in the Wartime Courses. These courses were developed to meet the needs of two groups: the military and the civilian. The military courses included those for the Army Specialized Training Program (ASTP), the Officer Candidate School (OCS), and the Navy College Training Program designated as V5, V7, and V13. The ASTP program was given at most of the Morrill land-grant colleges, and for any given campus the students came in groups or units for training in specific fields. Some units were trained in physics and mathematics, others in psychology and languages, and others in basic courses in engineering, mathematics, chemistry, and geology. For example, this program was established on the Purdue campus in March, 1943, and discontinued in March, 1944. Between these dates a total of 3,566 men received training.

The OCS program was designed to provide an opportunity for promising enlisted men in the United States Army to qualify as officers. For example, a school opened at the North Dakota State College campus in September, 1942, and closed in June, 1943. Between these dates a unit consisting of 335 men was admitted every four weeks, with an individual course lasting eight weeks. A total of 2,139 young men graduated and were commissioned as second lieutenants in the United States Army. A similar course was given at Mississippi State for the training of officer candidates in the U.S. Army Transportation Corps.

The Navy College Training Program was usually referred to as the V5, V7, and V13 programs. These programs were designed to develop a reservoir of trained personnel to staff the rapidly expanding Atlantic and Pacific fleets. For example, at Purdue University and between July, 1943, and July, 1944, a total of 2,730 men took training under this program, and about 400 of these graduated with the B.S. degree. Other special courses were the Signal Corps Training Program at the University of California-Davis, the Training Program for Meteorologists at the University of California-Los Angeles, and the Cadet Nurses Training Program at the University of Minnesota.

Civilian courses included programs for factory workers and programs for civilian protection. The program for industrial workers for any given state consisted of establishing training centers in cities where manufacturing plants existed and of giving the workers training to qualify for positions in the making of planes, munitions, and other war matériel.

For example, Purdue University, in cooperation with the War Department, now part of the Department of Defense, established 14 centers for instruction the first year, 68 centers for instruction the second year, and more than a hundred centers of instruction the third year. A total of 44,200 workers received training. A similar program was conducted by other Morrill land-grant colleges in other industrial states.

The program for civilian protection was sponsored and conducted by the Office of Civilian Defense (OCD). In general, this program consisted of organizing the members of any given community into teams, with each team trained for a specific purpose. Examples are teams to survey public buildings for use as bomb shelters, teams to spot planes, teams to defuse unexploded bombs, teams to demolish damaged buildings, and teams to give first aid.

The Extension Dimension

On the Atlantic side of the struggle, the Nazis forces invaded, overran, and occupied many countries—Poland, Czechoslovakia, Austria, Rumania, Bulgaria, Albania, Greece, and the Ukrainian USSR. Within each of these countries there were areas given over to the production of food, and both the attackers and the defenders impaired the food-producing capacity of these areas. Much the same situation existed on the Pacific side. The Japanese invaded, overran, and occupied many countries—Taiwan, the Philippines, Indochina, Cambodia, Thailand, Malaya, and Indonesia. Here again, there were areas given over to the production of food, and both the attackers and the defenders impaired the food-producing capacity of these areas. Fortunately for the United States and the rest of the world its land was not invaded and its food-producing areas remained intact. In other words, the farmers of the United States were free to produce food not only for their own people and the armed forces but for the people of the Allies and their armed forces, and, with the end of the war, for the people of the conquered countries. Thus, as in World War I, the farmers of the United States were urged to go all out in the production of major food crops—corn, wheat, rice, sugarcane, sugar beets, potatoes, and sweet potatoes. Principal factors concerned were (1) production goals of each major crop, (2) the farm labor supply, and (3) the Victory Gardens.

Production Goals. Production goals were established by the War Production Board of the U.S. Department of Agriculture. A panel of specialists on any given crop determined the number of acres required for that crop, since these specialists were familiar with the seed supply, the commercial fertilizer supply, and more particularly with the past performance of the crop based on the average yield. These estimates were made on a county basis and under the leadership of the county agricultural agent and his staff, since he had a working knowledge of the performance of any given crop in his county. Specialists of the extension service were always available to assist him in this important endeavor.

The Labor Supply. During World War II many farm laborers joined the armed forces or worked in plane, munition, or other war-related factories. As a result, labor for work on farms became scarce. The agricultural extension service of the U.S. Department of Agriculture and that of each of the Morrill land-grant colleges combined their efforts to solve this problem. They arranged for the following groups to work on farms: prisoners of war (POWs) from across the Atlantic, laborers from the West Indies, and laborers from Mexico. In this connection the work of the agricultural extension service was quite impressive. For example, for 1943-44-45 the extension service of Purdue University arranged placements for about 200 year-round positions, and work for about 10,000 POWs and about 55,000 seasonal laborers.

The Victory Gardens. Of special significance in the production of food were the so-called Victory Gardens. Where possible, all families in the United States were urged to grow vegetables in their home gardens, not only for immediate use but also for canning and drying. In fact, the resources of the U.S. Department of Agriculture and those of every Morrill land-grant college were used in this important endeavor. The U.S. Department of Agriculture published and widely disseminated bulletins on the production and preservation of vegetable crops for home use from the standpoint of the country as a whole, and the land-grant college(s) within each state through its extension service(s) published directions for the growing of these crops within each of the states. In general, both rural and urban families throughout the country accepted this project with enthusiasm. For any given year throughout the war, thousands upon thousands of Victory Gardens were evident in all of the communities throughout the country. Even vacant city lots and similar nonculitvated areas were used in the growing of vegetables. In this way, civilian communities throughout the country grew sufficient vegetables to supply most of their needs, and this in turn enabled the commercial growers of vegetables more adequately to supply vegetable crop products to the armed forces and to starving civilians of the war-ravaged countries.

SOME OUTSTANDING ACHIEVEMENTS

1. *The Production of Food.* With the removal of government restrictions on food production American farmers were urged to go all out in the production of basic foods—e.g., wheat, corn, meat, and milk. They produced enormous quantities of these basic products. Thus, the

armed forces and civilians were constantly supplied with nutritious food, and, with other factors favorable, their morale and fighting stamina were sustained.

2. *The Production of Rice in the Western Hemisphere.* Before the War, Burma, Indochina, and Thailand exported large quantities of rice. When the Japanese invaded these countries, exports of rice to the United States and other Allied countries were cut off. To resolve this critical situation, production of rice in the Western Hemisphere was greatly expanded, from a pre-World War II average of 153 million bushels to more than 225 million bushels in 1945. This increase was largely due to increases in Brazil and the United States.

3. *The Dehydration of Eggs and Certain Vegetables.* Dehydration of vegetables consists of removing sufficient water from the product to prevent it from spoiling in storage. Entire armies, together with their hospital and clerical staffs, were engaged in both the Atlantic and Pacific areas, and supplies for the troops had to be shipped across the Atlantic and across the Pacific. In fact, the need for the hardware type of war matériel was so great that shipping space for fresh eggs and fresh vegetables was unavailable. Consequently, large quantities of eggs and certain vegetables—potatoes, onions, carrots, beets, and sweet potatoes—were dehydrated before they were shipped and rehydrated when they were prepared for the mess.

4. *The Use of DDT.* The discovery that dichloro-diphenyl-trichloro-ethane, abbreviated DDT, a chlorinated hydrocarbon, controlled typhus and malaria was of major significance. Typhus and malaria have serious debilitating or weakening effects on the human race. Typhus is caused by a virus, and it is carried and spread by body lice. Malaria is caused by a protozoa, and the organism is carried and spread by the Anopheles mosquito. The discovery that DDT kills these harmful insects was a very important contribution to the war effort. Its use was particularly valuable in the South Pacific in that it removed the scourge of malaria from hospital and staging areas. In this way the physical stamina of the troops was sustained.

5. *The Growing of Vegetable Crops without Soil.* The growing of crops without soil consists of growing crop-plants with their root systems in water or in fine-textured sand. In either case, the essential raw materials for crop-plant production, for example, the nitrate ion, the phosphate ion, or the potassium ion, are applied in the form of highly water-soluble commercial fertilizers. This method was necessary to supply the troops with fresh vegetables in places where no soil was available, for example, Ascension Island in the mid-Atlantic, Atkinson Field in British Guinea, and Iwo Jima in the Pacific, or where the soil was infested with the dysentery organism, for example in Japan. In fact, during the American occupation of Japan large installations of growing vegetable

crops without soil were developed in order to supply the troops with fresh vegetables free from the dysentery organism.

6. *The Discovery of Streptomycin.* Streptomycin is an antibiotic. It was discovered by Dr. S. A. Waksman and his co-workers at the New Jersey Agricultural Experiment Station in 1943. Streptomycin is particularly useful in treating forms of tuberculosis and in the manufacture of B_{12}. Other antibiotics discovered about the same time are auromycin, terramycin, and bacitiacin.

REFERENCES

Anon. 1943. *Commercial Dehydration of Fruits and Vegetables in War Time.* U.S. Department of Agriculture Miscellaneous Publication 524, U.S. Department of Agriculture, Washington, DC.

    A summary of the results of investigations throughout the United States on the dehydration of fruits and vegetables during World War II.

Anon. 1947. "Science in Farming," *The Yearbook of Agriculture, 1943-1947.* U.S. Department of Agriculture, Washington, DC.

    A comprehensive report on the application of science up to 1947, covering all phases of agriculture. A notable feature is the excellent photographs of new varieties of crop-plants and crop-animals, and the development of new practices, new products, work clothes, and laborsaving machinery.

Knoll, E. B. 1947. 1944-1945. "A Record of a University in the War Years," *The Archives of Purdue,* No. 4. Purdue University Press, Lafayette, IN.

    A comprehensive report on the contributions of Purdue University, the land-grant university of Indiana, during World War II. Principal topics are Wartime Training and Education; Research in Science and Engineering; Research, Teaching, and Extension in the School of Agriculture; Contributions by Other Departments; Staff and Alumni Activities.

Hunter, William C. 1961. *Beacon Across the Prairie: North Dakota's Land-Grant College,* chapter 11. North Dakota Institute for Regional Studies, Fargo, ND.

    A concise statement on how North Dakota's land-grant college assisted the nation during World War II.

12

THE MORRILL
LAND-GRANT COLLEGES BECOME
STATEWIDE UNIVERSITIES

The proper sphere for all human beings is the largest and highest they can attain.

As pointed out in chapters 4, 5, and 6, the three principal functions of the Morrill land-grant colleges are research, resident teaching, and extension. At first these functions were applied to agriculture and home economics. As shown in tables 7-2 and 12-1, these three activities in combination have been markedly successful in promoting the efficiency of the American farmer and in developing a strong agriculture. In 1860 the American farmer produced enough food for himself and four others, and in 1960, a century later, he produced sufficient food for himself and fifty-four others. This in itself is a notable achievement, since it released a large number of individuals for work in other fields. As discussed in chapter 8, the president and faculty of each institution applied these functions to fields other than agriculture and home economics, in particular to engineering, business and industry, teacher training, and science. Here again the results of research in these fields and their application to the solution of problems have been extremely beneficial. Finally, the presidents and faculties extended the three primary functions to all fields where the scientific method of inquiry is applicable. In this way and as with agriculture a large amount of experimental information within any given field has become available and the scientific knowledge of any given field has accumulated. Further, since the Morrill land-grant colleges obtained most of their financial support from all of the people in the form of taxes, they extended their knowledge and facilities to all of the people. In fact, a very close and affectionate relationship has developed throughout the years between each land-grant college and the people it is destined to serve. In other words, the Morrill land-grant colleges together with the first state universities have become the joy and pride of the people.

EXPANSION OF THE RESEARCH DIMENSION

Prior to World War II most funds for research were limited to three closely related fields: agriculture, veterinary science, and home economics,

Table 12-1.

MEAN YIELDS OF CERTAIN MAJOR CROPS PRODUCED IN
THE UNITED STATES AT AN EARLY AND A RECENT DATE*

		Mean Yield	
		Early	Recent
Crop	*Unit*	*Date*	*Date*
Corn	Bu/A	23	87
		(1887)	(1975)
Wheat	Bu/A	13	31
		(1887)	(1975)
Dry edible beans	lbs/A	714	1,209
		(1919)	(1973)
Peanuts	lbs/A	719	2,323
		(1919)	(1973)
Potatoes	cwt/A	56	228
		(1891)	(1973)
Sweet potatoes	cwt/A	52	109
		(1930)	(1973)
Tomatoes for processing	Tons/A	4	20
		(1919)	(1973)
Onions	cwt/A	134	280
		(1939)	(1973)
Milk	lbs/day/cow	4.2	10.3
		(1924)	(1974)
Eggs	No/yr/bird	103	227
		(1939)	(1973)
Soybeans	Bu/A	18	28
		(1915)	(1973)
Cotton	lbs/A	220	519
		(1890)	(1973)

*From *Agricultural Statistics,* U.S. Department of Agriculture, Washington, DC.

and to the field of engineering. During World War II research was necessary not only in these fields but also in the fields of physics, chemistry, and human health. Striking examples of this type of research are those that led to the development of sonar for the discovery of enemy submarines, the walkie-talkie for the maintenance of liaison between groups, and the atomic bomb. Consequently, the people and their representatives in Congress became aware of the fact that research, if properly conducted, pays enormous dividends. As a result, Congress appropriated relatively large sums of money for research in many fields. For example, in 1953, the University of Maryland received about $2 million for research, principally for agriculture and home economics, but in 1965 the University received more than $14 million, principally for research in the additional fields of physics, chemistry, and the health sciences.

Source of Funds

At present (1976), the sources of funds for research and subsequent teaching and extension are many and varied. In general, these funds come from the citizens in the form of taxes, the so-called public funds, or as gifts, the so-called private funds. Examples of organizations that dispense public funds and that allocate private funds are presented in table 12-2. Note that funds are available for research and its application to the solution of problems in practically all fields of human endeavor.

Table 12-2.

EXAMPLES OF PUBLIC AND PRIVATE AGENCIES THAT
DISPENSE PUBLIC OR PRIVATE FUNDS FOR RESEARCH

Federal Agencies

National Science Foundation, National Institutes of Public Health, Atomic Energy Commission, U.S. Space Administration, National Fish and Wildlife Administration, Office of Naval Research, Environmental Protection Agency.

Federal and State Agencies

U.S. Department of Agriculture and the government of each state. Pollution research centers. Pesticide research centers.

State Agencies

Business research centers. Computer science research centers. Social science research centers. Chemical Biodynamics Laboratory (California). Institute of Human Development (Maryland, Minnesota, and California).

Funds Provided by Gifts

THE FOUNDATIONS

The Carnegie and Rockefeller Foundations. Ford Foundation. Alumni foundation of each college.

PRIVATE COMPANIES OR INDIVIDUALS

Du Pont Chemical. Dow Chemical.

EXPANSION OF THE TEACHING DIMENSION

The GI Bill of World War II

On June 23, 1944, the Congress of the United States passed the Serviceman's Readjustment Act, commonly known as the GI Bill of Rights. Among other things, the Act provided for the training and education of veterans on the college and university level. In general, the federal government (the taxpayers) paid for the tuition and texts for each veteran and $65 per month to the single veterans and $90 per month to the married. Of the 11.5 million who received some form of training, about 5.1 million attended college. Since most of them enrolled in 1945, 1946, and 1947, they accounted for the marked increase in enrollment during these years.

More importantly, from the standpoint of the development of the individual, the veteran changed the attitude of the nonveteran toward study and learning. As compared to the prewar student, the veterans had seen war and its destructive effects; they were more mature, more serious in their work, and more determined to get the most out of their education. As Nathan M. Pusey, president of Harvard University, said, "The veterans taking the regular college courses were an able, mature, and energetic student body."

The Housing and Classroom Shortage

With the rapid influx of students from 1945 to 1948, adequate housing and teaching facilities became a serious problem of practically all college campuses. Fortunately, at this time a comparatively large amount of war surplus material became available in the form of wheelless trailers, Quonset huts, and abandoned barracks. These structures were used for both the housing and teaching of the students. Moreover, because of the large increase in enrollment, the legislatures of the various states were quite liberal in appropriating funds for the erection of dormitories, classroom and laboratory buildings, and libraries. In addition, practically all institutions extended the usual working day. For example, at Mississippi State classes began at 7:00 A.M., and at Michigan State classes began at 8:00 A.M. and continued in some instances to 10:00 P.M. Despite the crowded conditions, the administration, faculty, and students of each institution performed each of their respective tasks with zest, cooperation, and harmony.

"Putting Hubby Through" (Ph.T.). An interesting sidelight of the late 1940s and early 1950s was a unique project known as "Putting Hubby Through" (Ph.T.). This project referred to a graduate student working toward his master's or doctorate—and his wife. At that time, stipends from research fellowships were not very large, and the wife worked usually as a secretary or in a similar capacity until her husband acquired his degree. At many land-grant colleges and universities the Ph.T. wives banded themselves in the formation of a Ph.T. club, with officers and committees characteristic of clubs of this nature. An interesting feature was the annual commencement with its speaker and the award of certificates of wives who had successfully "put her hubby through." These were very delightful and happy occasions.

Growth and Development in Teaching

The land-grant institutions now as universities include the major fields of human activity. In other words, expansion has occurred in the traditional fields of agriculture, home economics, and engineering, but courses have been added for instruction in new fields. For example, agriculture has expanded to include the closely related fields of forestry, conservation of natural resources, the development of fisheries, and the development and maintenance of wildlife and recreational areas. In most institutions curricula have been established on weed science, turf and turf grass management, food science and technology, with interdisciplinary programs involving animal science, dairy science, and poultry science. In 102 instances the school of veterinary medicine has split off to become a college of its own. Engineering has proliferated to include the engineering phases of aerospace, nuclear reactions, biology, and petroleum production. Home economics has expanded to include curricula in consumer economy and in teaching research and extension in home economics. Business and industry have expanded to include curricula in the processing of data and in the preparation for law. Education has expanded to include curricula in the administration and development of the community college, in industrial arts and technology, and in counseling education. Science has expanded to include curricula for premedicine, predentistry, and prepharmacy courses and in physical therapy, while science and the arts have expanded to include curricula in anthropology and preparation of students for the ministry, and the colleges of business and engineering have expanded to include programs leading toward the B.S.-M.B.A. degree.

Problems Pertaining to Tuition

Prior to the establishment of tax-supported colleges and universities, tuition, matriculation fees, and other student expenses were very high—in fact, much higher than the farmer and industrial worker could afford. Thus, the founding fathers realized that, in order to reach a large number of the working class, the expenses of the student should be kept at a minimum. This explains why the Morrill land-grant colleges when they were established specified either free tuition or tuition at a low rate. This situation prevailed until about 1940. By that time the cost of supporting the colleges and universities had markedly increased. Consequently, the idea developed that the student's family should make a contribution to the student's education. As a result, the Boards of Trustees abandoned the principle of "free tuition" and adopted the principle that the student or his family should make a contribution to his education in the form of tuition. Nevertheless, charges for tuition at the Morrill land-grant colleges are significantly lower than those at private colleges and universities.

Within recent years two organizations, the Carnegie Commission on Higher Education, and the Committee for Economic Development, an organization of businessmen, have suggested that "there should be a substantial increase in charges for tuition at public-supported universities." They state that an increase in fees and tuition would put the private universities in a more competitive position for the recruitment of students with that of the public universities. Comments on this suggestion follow:

"It [is] time to build a better understanding of what the abandonment of the low tuition principle—which keeps the financial threshold for entry into the public universities low—would mean: that it would spell the end of public higher education as we know it."[1]

"Tuition charges are unsound because they are based on an erroneous principle: that higher education is a luxury and a privilege, not a service and a necessity.

"If higher education were indeed a luxury in which the state indulged a few privileged young men and women, then it would be quite logical to require them to pay for the privilege. But if it is preparation for services essential to the well-being of the community we are no more justified in charging for it than we would be in charging for elementary and high school education."[2]

Essentially, if the charge for tuition at the public-supported universities were the same as that for the private universities the American system of higher education as it is known today would gradually disappear. In other words, it would revert to the system of education that existed before the passage of the Morrill Land-Grant Act of 1862. More importantly, the opportunity for every individual to develop himself to his fullest capacity would decline, and the productive capacity of the people would accordingly decline.

EXPANSION OF THE EXTENSION DIMENSION— CONTINUING OR CONTINUATION EDUCATION

I would found an institution where any person can study any subject.

—EZRA CORNELL
Founder of Cornell University

Essentially continuation education in all fields is an outgrowth of extension work in agriculture and home economics. As discussed in

---

[1]"Education for Whom and at What Price?" *News of Iowa State,* January-February, 1974.

[2]*Ibid.*

chapter 6, extension work in agriculture started with the development of Farmers' Institutes. These were held both on and off the campus. The farmers varied in educational attainment. Some had gone to college, others had completed the eight grades, others had partially completed these grades, while others had not attended grade school. However, they all had one thing in common. They wanted to learn how to improve their proficiency as farmers. In other words, every farmer wanted to know how to put more money in his pocketbook. Since extension work in agriculture has promoted the welfare of the farmer and the farming industry in general, the trustees and faculties of the Morrill land-grant colleges believed that extension work in other fields would be correspondingly beneficial. This has turned out to be the case. Thus, continuing or continuation education in the modern land-grant university includes instruction in all fields of constructive endeavor and to all individuals within each field, regardless of race, color, creed, sex, or educational attainment. Here again, for any given land-grant university the entire state is the campus, and for the sixty-eight Morrill land-grant universities as a whole the entire country is the campus.

Reasons for Continuing Education

The reasons for continuing education in all fields are quite similar to those for continuing education in agriculture. All types of human endeavor are dynamic; that is, changes are continually taking place. Many of these changes are due to the results of research, and these results may or may not be beneficial. Consequently, it behooves individuals within a given field to keep up with the results of research in that field. This is particularly the case for members within fields where vigorous and progressive research programs are being conducted.

Why the Land-Grant University?

As stated in chapter 4, research is the foundation of all types of teaching. Thus, it is the foundation of continuation education. The research within any given field, in turn, is conducted by members of the faculty, with each member a regional, or national and quite often an international, authority within that field. Therefore the land-grant university is the logical place for the development and maintenance of continuation education programs. Further, the land-grant university is supported largely by taxes in the form of federal and state funds. To this extent the university is in the service of the people.

Organization

In general, the continuation education program for any given state is conducted by a headquarters station and by one or more branches or substations. The headquarters station is situated on the main campus and houses the dean of continuation education and his administrative staff. Each branch has an assistant dean or director with his administrative staff. For the most part each branch is located some distance away from the main campus and at a large center of population. Usually the number of branches within any given state varies with the density of population in that state. For example, Michigan State has about ten branches and Mississippi State has two.

Types of Work

To meet the needs of all of the people two types of work are available: (1) academic and (2) nonacademic. In general, academic courses are taken for credit leading toward the bachelor's or master's degree, and in some institutions leading toward the high school diploma. Naturally, the amount and quality of the work required for any one course and for any one degree are the same as those on the headquarters campus and may comprise (1) attending lectures or recitations; (2) a combination of 1 and laboratory; (3) correspondence courses, and (4) a combination of 1, 2, and 3. In general, nonacademic courses are taken to become familiar with the results of recent research and/or practices. They comprise institutes, short courses, conferences, workshops, and tours. Institutes and short courses are given for the benefit of specific groups who want to become familiar with the results of the latest research. Examples are corn or soybean growers, commercial fertilizer manufacturers, farm implement makers or dealers, pesticide makers or dealers, supermarket operators, nursery and landscape designers, poultry producers, egg producers, and even farriers. Conferences are held so that leaders of any given enterprise can develop projects within or closely related to the enterprise, and tours are organized to enable members of any given industry to inspect any segment of the industry. Of special significance are correspondence courses. A wide range of subjects is offered, and the student may start any given course at any time and at any place.

Facilities

Facilities for doing the work are practically the same as those for students enrolled in any regular course. In other words, the classrooms, laboratories, and equipment are the same as those for the regular students. However, several institutions have built hotel-type structures with eating and sleeping facilities and rooms for lectures, laboratories, conferences, short courses, and workshops. Examples are Kellogg Center at Michigan State; Pleasant Hall at Louisiana State; and the Extension Service Center at the University of Georgia.

ALUMNI ORGANIZATIONS, DEVELOPMENT FOUNDATIONS, AND UNIVERSITY PRESSES

The alumni consist of students who have attended any given institution. They are organized by classes. At some institutions induction occurs when the student has finished his first semester or term, at others when he has graduated, with the induction ceremony as part of the graduation exercises. The purpose of alumni organizations is to promote an everlasting interest on the part of the individual in Alma Mater. In general, this interest is manifested by gifts of money, and this money in turn is used to promote excellence in research, in resident teaching, and in extension.

Development Foundations for any given university consist of individuals or organizations that donate money or property to the university either in a restrictive or a nonrestrictive form. Restricted gifts are used for a specific purpose only, whereas nonrestricted gifts are used to promote excellence in research, in resident teaching, and in extension.

University presses have developed to encourage faculty publication of books that have rather limited interest or appeal. For example, the library of Mississippi State contains a history of most of the Morrill land-grant colleges and universities. The history of any given university has been published by its university press or by its state historical society.

THE FIRST STATE UNIVERSITIES AND THE MORRILL LAND-GRANT UNIVERSITIES[3]

As stated in chapter 1, when any given territory within the Northwest territory was organized, Congress granted an entire township to the territorial government for the establishment of a seminary of learning. Later, when any given state was organized from any given territory, Congress granted a township for the establishment of a state university. Quite often these two grants were combined, as in the case of Louisiana, Michigan, and Wisconsin. Thus, the first state universities got started from a land-grant, and for this reason they may be considered as land-grant institutions. In general, the first state universities and the Morrill land-

---

[3]As stated in chapter 2, certain states established their respective first state university and its Morrill land-grant university at separate locations; other states attached their respective Morrill land-grant college to their first state university, and in other states the Morrill land-grant college developed into their first state university.

grant universities have many things in common: (1) they are supported largely by federal and state funds (taxes); (2) they are dedicated to the service of all of the people through their research, resident teaching, and extension; and (3) they have banded themselves together in the formation of an organization known as the Association of Land-Grant Colleges and Universities with a headquarters staff in Washington, D.C. This organization meets each year to discuss mutual and pertinent problems, and issues reports of its deliberations.

REFERENCES

Barrons, Keith C. 1971. "Environmental Benefits of Intensive Crop Production," *Down to Earth,* 27: No. 3, Dow Chemical Corp., Midland, MI.

A distinguished crop-plant scientist presents convincing evidence that continuous crop-plant research and its application are necessary to produce adequate supplies of food, feed, and fiber to all the people.

Curti, M. 1949. *The University of Wisconsin: A History,* chapter 17, "The Wider Campus—Extension," pp. 549-624. University of Wisconsin Press, Madison, WI.

A discussion on the growth and development of extension in Wisconsin, from the formation of Farmers' Institutes in 1885 to the dissemination of knowledge to all groups in all constructive fields from 1891 to 1976.

Pell, Claiborne. 1975. "A New Approach to Higher Education," *Saturday Evening Post,* 247, No. 9, December.

A proposal that the people as a whole extend tuition-free education from the twelfth year of high school to the fourth year of college or university.

13

THE MORRILL
LAND-GRANT COLLEGES
AND THEIR
INTERNATIONAL DIMENSION

Give a man a bowel of rice, and he will eat for a day. Teach a man how to grow rice (or any other valuable crop), and he will eat for a lifetime.

THE STATUS OF AGRICULTURE AND EDUCATION IN THE UNITED STATES, 1855-1975

The Status of Agriculture

As previously stated, the farmer of the United States has become highly efficient. In 1860 he produced enough food for himself and four others, but in 1970 he produced enough food for himself and sixty others. As discussed in chapters 4, 5, 6, and 7, this marked increase in efficiency has been largely due to (1) the work of the agricultural experiment stations, the creation of knowledge, (2) the work of the agricultural extension services, the dissemination of this knowledge, (3) the preparation and application of chemical compounds needed for the production and marketing of crop-plant and crop-animal products,[1] (4) the development of laborsaving machines for planting, cultivating, spraying and harvesting, and (5) the incentives centered around the profit motive. As is generally accepted in the United States, the farmer is entitled to a reasonable profit from his work and his investments. Thus, as Harrar stated, "A nation cannot have cheap food, if cheap food means that the money that the farmer gets for any given product is lower than his costs of producing that product."[2]

In addition to his high efficiency, the American farmer enjoys the same social status as that of workers in other fields—engineering, business and industry, science, education, medicine, the ministry, and law. Dr. Don Paarberg, a graduate of Purdue University and an economist with

---

[1]Examples are commercial fertilizers, herbicides, pesticides, and growth regulators.

[2]J. G. Harrar. 1966. "Principles for Progress in World Agriculture," *National Agricultural Chemical News and Pesticide Review*, 25, No. 1, October.

150

the U.S. Department of Agriculture, states, "It has been my privilege to travel in many countries, and to meet the farm people in these countries. What readily meets the eye is the better agricultural science and technology one generally finds when he returns to the United States, largely as a result of the Morrill land-grant college system. More subtle, but perhaps more important, is the fact that American farmers enjoy social status on a par with that of workers in other vocations, whereas in many other countries this is not the case. The difference between an American farmer and the farmers in most other countries is not just a difference in farming methods; it is the greater self-respect one finds among our own farm people. The land-grant colleges not only helped the farmer to escape peasant or serf farm methods, but they also helped him to escape the peasant or serf mentality." Thus, two striking features of agriculture in the United States are (1) the high efficiency of the individual farmer and (2) his status as a first-class citizen, combined with the right to make his own decisions.

Relation of Farm Efficiency to the Development of Nonfarm Industries. As shown in table 7-2, the efficiency of the American farmer has gradually increased over the years. With this increase in efficiency there has been a corresponding increase in the number of workers available for employment in other fields. For example, in 1870, forty-seven percent of the population was necessary to produce the food and fiber supply, whereas in 1970 only about four percent was needed. Thus, in the development of the affluent and prosperous society, a highly efficient and strong agriculture is necessary.

The Status of Education

The people of the United States believe that every individual has the right to develop himself to his fullest potential, provided he does not induce injury to others. This requires a certain amount of formal or basic education and explains why education through the eight grades and high school is generally tuition-free, and why education at technological institutions, in colleges or universities is available at relatively low tuition cost. As a result, the rate of literacy of the people is high and the productive capacity of the people is correspondingly high.

THE STATUS OF AGRICULTURE AND EDUCATION IN THE UNDERDEVELOPED COUNTRIES

The Status of Agriculture

In sharp contrast to the American farmer, the farmer in the underdeveloped countries is highly inefficient. Frequently, he has difficulty in producing enough food for himself and his family, let alone food for others. In particular, he does not have at his beck and call: (1) a corps of scientists to solve his problems, (2) a corps of extension workers to assist him to establish more efficient practices, (3) the money or credit to buy the chemical compounds necessary for high crop-plant and high crop-animal production, and (4) the profit motive. In other words, the farmer in underdeveloped countries is forced to stand helplessly alone without any assistance in the solution of his problems.

In addition, in many underdeveloped countries the prestige of agriculture is relatively low. This is undoubtedly due to the failure of the government to educate its people on the central role of agriculture in human affairs, that agriculture is the basic and only essential industry, and that a strong agriculture is prerequisite to a strong program in business, in engineering, in law, in medicine, in nonagricultural industries, in science and art, and in any other nonagricultural phase of human endeavor. How can a person study for proficiency in each of these fields, or enjoy and appreciate a concert, a painting, an inspiring book, or even watching the current events on TV, on an empty stomach?

The Status of Education

In sharp contrast to the children of the United States, the children of the underdeveloped countries rarely have an opportunity to go to grade school, let alone to high school, technological school, or college. As a result, the rate of illiteracy is high and the productive capacity of the people is correspondingly low. For example, the population of ten underdeveloped countries is close to 700 million. Of these 700 million, 500 million cannot read or write. This is a tremendous waste of human resources, and represents a total disregard of the principle that every individual has the right to develop himself to his fullest capacity without injury to others.

STEPS IN THE DEVELOPMENT OF
THE UNDERDEVELOPED COUNTRIES

The Development of a Strong, Highly Efficient Agriculture

The first step in the development of the people of the underdeveloped countries is to remove the scourge of hunger, combined with the development of a strong, highly efficient agriculture. Some authorities believe that hunger is the planet's number-one problem, and that it is difficult for the people of the well-developed countries to realize that malnutrition and dietary deficiencies are rampant throughout the underdeveloped countries.[3] Further, as pointed out previously, a hungry person or a person suffering from malnutrition cannot learn, even though he has the potential to do so. The removal of this scourge of hunger and the development of a strong agriculture depend largely on the development and production of crop-plants that produce high yields both in terms of quality and quantity where the crop is to be grown. In other words, the basis for an efficient agriculture is the behavior of the crop-plant. In general, this principle has been followed in the United States ever since the land-grant colleges started. As pointed out in chapter 4, when a given college first started, the professor of agriculture determined the pertinent problems of the farmers in the local community and began to conduct experiments to find the solution to these problems. This type of investigation has been in operation continuously since that time. As a result, the varieties and cultural practices in use today (1975) are far superior to the varieties and cultural practices that were used at the time the experiments were started (1862-1890). For any given crop, these methods consist of (1) making a survey of an industry to discover the pertinent problems, (2) establishing procedures for the development of superior varieties by breeding, and/or (3) establishing procedures for the development of superior cultural practices.

The Work of the Rockefeller Foundation. The adaptation of the methods developed by the land-grant colleges toward the development of a highly efficient agriculture in underdeveloped countries has been sponsored and financed by both private foundations and public (tax-supported) agencies. As an example, consider the development of high-yielding varieties of wheat in Mexico. This program was financed by the Rockefeller Foundation and conducted under the field leadership of Dr. J. George Harrar and Dr. Norman E. Borlaug.

Dr. J. George Harrar was born in Ohio in 1906. He received the B.A. at Oberlin College in 1928 and the M.S. in agronomy at Iowa State College in 1930. From 1930 to 1933 he taught botany and plant pathology in the School of Agriculture of the University of Puerto Rico, where he acquired a working knowledge of Spanish and the behavior of crop plants under tropical conditions. To complete his graduate work, Mr. Harrar accepted an assistantship in the Department of Plant Pathology of the University of Minnesota, where he was awarded the Ph.D. in 1935. From Minnesota Harrar moved to a research and teaching position in the Department of Biology of the Virginia Polytechnic Institute, where he rose to the rank of full professor of plant pathology within a period of six years. From 1941 to 1972 Dr. Harrar's advancement and responsibilities in his chosen field have been rapid and rewarding.

---

[3]Herbert J. Walters, Assistant Administrator, Agency for International Development (AID), U.S. Department of State, Washington, DC.

In 1941 he became head of the Department of Plant Pathology of Washington State University; in 1942 he was selected as leader of the Agricultural Development Program of the Rockefeller Foundation in Mexico; in 1952 he was appointed Deputy Director for Agriculture with headquarters at New York, and finally in 1961 Dr. Harrar was made President of the Rockefeller Foundation.

Dr. Norman E. Borlaug is a native of northeast Iowa. He earned the B.S., M.S., and Ph.D. degrees at the College of Agriculture of the University of Minnesota: the B.S. from the Department of Forestry in 1937, the M.S. and the Ph.D. from the Department of Plant Pathology in 1940 and 1942, respectively. He became a plant pathologist for Du Pont in 1942 and entered the service of the Rockefeller Foundation in 1944. He was placed in charge of the wheat improvement program in Mexico in 1944 and was appointed director of the International Improvement Wheat Program in 1959. He was awarded the Nobel Peace Prize for 1971.

At the beginning of the wheat improvement program, Drs. Harrar and Borlaug assembled a team of agricultural scientists of Mexico and the United States, with each member of the team a specialist in a distinct discipline, plant pathology, plant physiology, entomology, and soil technology. They found that the main problems in wheat production were the presence of virulent strains of the wheat rust, and the absence of improved cultural practices. The research program required a continuous effort for fifteen years for Mexico to become self-sufficient in the production of wheat. In fact, at the end of the fifteenth year Mexico began to export wheat, and in 1966 seed of the superior varieties developed in Mexico were used as foundation stocks for commercial production or for breeding programs in Colombia, Ecuador, Chile, Venezuela, India, Pakistan, the Philippines, and East and West Africa.

The Work of the International Rice Research Institute (IRRI). As a second example consider the development of superior varieties of rice at the International Rice Research Institute, Las Banos in the Philippines. This program was made possible through the cooperative efforts of three agencies: the Rockefeller Foundation, the Ford Foundation, and the Agricultural Experiment Station of the University of the Philippines.[4] The Rockefeller Foundation paid the salaries of key scientists, the Ford Foundation provided funds for construction of the laboratories and laboratory equipment, and the Agricultural Experiment Station furnished the land for the experimental work. The scientists discovered that yields were high in the rice-growing regions of Japan, Taiwan, and Korea, and that the plants growing in these countries had short, stout, and

---

[4]The University of the Philippines has developed on the same lines or under the same philosophy as the land-grant colleges of the United States.

erect stems that were resistant to lodging and responded well to the application of commercial fertilizers. Further, they produced a type of starch that is slightly sticky when cooked, a characteristic desired by the people of Japan, Taiwan, and Korea. In contrast, the scientists found that yields were low in the monsoon areas, Thailand, Indonesia, Cambodia, Viet Nam, and the Philippines, and that the plants in these countries had long, slender, weak stems that were susceptible to lodging and unresponsive to commercial fertilizers. In addition, they produced a type of grain that is nonsticky when cooked, a characteristic desired by the people of the monsoon areas. To combine the desirable characters of each of these types, the scientists crossed the plants of each type and selected outstanding plants of each generation for a period of six generations. The resulting hybrid combines the desirable characteristics of each type and constitutes the development of a new variety or type. It was released by the International Rice Research Institute as IR-8.

The Peace Corps Disseminates the New Variety. The Peace Corps, established by the late President John F. Kennedy, consists of a federally sponsored organization of men and women who want to partake of the rich experience of helping the nonwealthy to develop themselves or of helping the poor farmer to increase his efficiency. In 1967 several volunteers were helping the poor rice farmers in the Philippines when they learned about the new variety IR-8 developed at the International Rice Institute at Los Banos. Some of these volunteers went to the Institute to interview the scientists who had developed this new variety, and the scientists in turn outlined a program for use by the volunteers, which, if followed, would result in the successful dissemination and cultivation of the new variety. This program provided an opportunity for the volunteers to become familiar with the characteristics and cultural requirements of the new variety, to establish comparative demonstration plots containing the new variety and the conventional varieties in strategic places in any given community, and to invite the farmers to inspect the plots and compare the performance of the new with the old.

This is essentially the same type of program that has been followed by the crop-plant scientists of the Morrill land-grant colleges since their establishment between 1862 and 1902. The research scientists develop a new strain or variety, or an improved cultural practice, the extension specialists establish demonstration plots to compare the new variety or improved practice with the old, and, if necessary, the research scientists and the extension specialists work together to conduct short courses for the training of additional specialists.

In other words, seeing is believing and convincing. The farmer sees the performance of a new variety or a new practice as demonstrated under his particular set of conditions one year and exercises his right of decision to grow the new variety or adopt the new practice the next.

However, when the profit motive is involved and when more profits are indicated, there is no reluctance on the part of the farmer to grow the new variety or to adopt a new or improved practice. Thus, the introduction of IR-8 has been equally successful in the other monsoon rice-growing areas: in Hawaii, Thailand, Malaysia, Indonesia, Sri Lanka, and India.

Successful breeding and improvement programs have also been conducted with corn, the bread crop of the Mexicans, various kinds of beans, the protein crop of the Mexicans, potatoes, home garden vegetables, sorghum, and soybeans.

The Meaning of the Term "Green Revolution." The term "green" refers to the pigment chlorophyll,[5] the dominant and prevailing pigment of crop-plants, and the term "revolution" refers to the changes that take place when a country goes from the underdeveloped to the developed state. In other words, a chain reaction sets in that begins with the development of superior crop-plants and/or superior crop-plant production practices which eventually and inevitably leads to the development of the prosperous society. The superior crop-plants absorb more light per unit time from the life-giving sun.[6] As a result, they have high rates of net or apparent photosynthesis, and if these plants are grown in a favorable environment and under recommended cultural practices, they produce high yields of high-quality food. In this way, the scourge of hunger vanishes and food becomes available for making tools, machines, and chemical compounds that the farmer needs for the production of his crop-plants. Finally, with the further increase in efficiency of the farmer, food becomes available for export and/or for the establishment of industries characteristic of the prosperous and constructive society.

The Education and Development of All of the People

The second step in the development of underdeveloped countries is to lay the foundations for the education of all of the people. President Harry S Truman in his inaugural address on January 20, 1949, while speaking on the relationship of the United States to other countries, stated, "Our aim should be to help the free people of the world through their own efforts to produce more food, more clothing, more materials for housing, and more power to lighten their burdens." Shortly after

---

[5]Actually there are two pigments, chlorophyll *a* and chlorophyll *b*. Both operate together in the absorption of light.

[6]Statements have often been made that the United States is a wealthy nation. A prime reason for this is that its agriculture is comparatively efficient. In other words, its crop-plants capture comparatively large quantities of light per unit time and per unit area. This light energy is free, and is essentially the basis of the prosperous society.

the address Dr. John A. Hannah, president of Michigan State, in his capacity as president of the prestigious Association of Land-Grant Colleges and Universities, offered President Truman the active support of the Association[7] and all of the land-grant colleges. Dr. Hannah undoubtedly felt that the land-grant colleges and universities were in a unique position to assist President Truman in his program of helpfulness, since the philosophy of the land-grant colleges and universities has always been based on helpfulness and service to others. At the same time, the members of Congress were fully in sympathy with President Truman's proposal and they accordingly passed legislation that provided funds for joint programs between the federal government and the land-grant colleges and universities.

For this purpose Congress established a new agency called the U.S. Agency for International Development, abbreviated AID, and each land-grant college established a new division called the Division of International Programs. In this way, the excellent relationship that had existed between the federal government and each of the land-grant colleges and universities for the development of the people within the nation was now extended to the development of the people of other nations. In other words, as Dr. Hannah stated, *the entire world became the campus.*

Methods of Operation

The methods of operation are similar to those that have been developed for the solution of practical problems in the wide field of agriculture and home economics in the United States. As outlined in chapter 4, the research scientists make a survey of any given industry to determine the pertinent problems and develop in outline form procedures or plans for the solution of any given problem. This outline in turn is submitted for approval to the director of the local agricultural experiment station and to the appropriate administrative officer of the Office of Experimental Stations, U.S. Department of Agriculture, Washington, D.C. Thus in the solution of problems within the fields of agriculture and home economics, both state and federal officials are involved. With the international programs funded by AID the federal administrative officer is the director of the U.S. AID program, and he and his staff are located with other government agencies in Washington. The local administrative officer is the dean or director of international programs, and he and his staff are located on the campuses of the local land-grant university.

---

[7]This Association includes the Morrill land-grant colleges and universities and the first state universities.

Type of Projects or Programs. The assistance program was designed primarily to help the people to develop themselves. In other words, the program or project is conducted so that the people of any given under-developed country can take an active part in any given project. In this way, the people become acquainted with the problem at hand and acquire confidence in their ability to learn, to think for themselves, and finally to acquire the ability to teach others. In general, the type of project varies with the state of agricultural education in each country and falls into one of the following five groups:

1. Assisting in the establishment of a new land-grant-type of college or university with its agricultural experiment station and agricultural extension service. Examples are the University of Nigeria, the University of Ife (West Nigeria), Haile Selassie I University of Ethiopia, Uttar Pradesh Agriculture University of India, and the University of the Ryukyus on Okinawa.

2. Helping to strengthen the research, teaching, and extension programs at established colleges or universities. Examples are the Balcarce Agricultural College in Argentina, the University of São Paulo in Brazil, Bager Agricultural Institute in Indonesia, West Pakistan University at Lyallpur, and the College of Forestry of the University of the Philippines.

3. Training of extension workers in agriculture and home economics. Examples are Arapai Agricultural College in New Ghanda and the University of Malawa at Blantyre.

4. Assisting in establishing a new agricultural industry. An example is the development of a certified seed crop industry for the state of Brazil.

5. Developing student exchange programs. An example is the student exchange program between Michigan State and the University of Nigeria.

EVALUATION OF THE AID-LAND-GRANT COLLEGE PROGRAMS

In 1957 a committee consisting of members of the Association of Land-Grant Colleges and Universities evaluated the work of the AID-Land-Grant college program. They studied the results of 68 AID-land-grant college contracts and found that 16 had been in operation for 10 years or more, 11 had been in operation between 5 and 10 years, and the remainder, 41, had been in operation for less than 5 years.

Of the projects that had run ten years or more the committee found that (1) the underdeveloped countries had significantly increased their production of crops, (2) the teams of scientific workers were competent technically and anxious to help in the development of agriculture, (3) the cost of the AID program to the U.S. taxpayer in comparison to the benefits attained was relatively low, and (4) less than one percent of the scientists of the agricultural colleges has been engaged in the AID-Land-Grant College Program at any one time. The committee pointed out that, since a period of about fifty years was required for the Morrill land-grant colleges to extend and coordinate their research, teaching, and extension phases of agriculture and home economics, the building of a strong agriculture is a relatively long-time process.

On the other hand, the committee found that (1) in practically every underdeveloped country the teaching of agriculture was under the ministry of education, and the research work in agriculture was under the ministry of agriculture, (2) the basic sciences that underlie agriculture needed upgrading, (3) additional colleges of the land-grant type should be developed, and (4) since AID-Land-Grant programs are supported by the taxpayers of the United States, the people as a whole should be more fully informed about this beneficial, good-neighborly, and "helping others to develop themselves" program. The committee pointed out that (1) the development of a strong, highly efficient agriculture requires cooperation and coordination among each of the three dimensions, research, resident teaching, and extension, and that this coordination is attained under one administration, preferably located on the campus of the land-grant-type university, and (2) that as compared with the United States the population of the underdeveloped countries as a whole is ten times greater, the area of these countries is five times greater, and the number of colleges and universities of the land-grant-type is much lower.

REFERENCES

Anon. 1976. "America's Third Century Special Bicentennial Supplement," *U.S. News and World Report*, 81, No. 1, July.
  Several eminent authorities give insights on the near future of the United States.
Brown, L. R. 1970. *The Green Revolution: The Role of the Volunteer as a Manpower Link.* Office of Program Development, Peace Corps, Washington, DC.
  An excellent discussion of the work of the young men and women of the Peace Corps in extending the results of research to the poor farmers of underdeveloped countries.
Committee on Institutional Cooperation. 1968. *Building Institutions to Serve Agriculture.* Office of International Programs, Purdue University, LaFayette, IN.
  A summary report of the Committee on Institutional Cooperation (CIC) and the Agency for International Development (AID) on the progress made by underdeveloped countries.

Paarlberg, Don. 1976. "The Future of the Family Farm," *Saturday Evening Post,* 248, No. 2.
    The author, an eminent economist, discusses the changes in agriculture of the United States from the time the country was established, and the family farmer's right to make his own decisions.
Stakman, E. C., *et al.* 1967. *Campaigns Against Hunger.* Harvard University Press, Cambridge, MA.
    An informative and highly instructive book on how scientists educated in certain land-grant colleges adapted the land-grant philosophy to the solution of agricultural problems in certain underdeveloped countries.
Uribe, Irene. 1975. "George Harrar Sets Off the Green Revolution," pp. 312-313. U.S. Department of Agriculture Yearbook for 1975. Washington, DC.
    The author presents a precise account of how a professor of the Morrill land-grant college system applied his knowledge, training, and experience to the solution of crop-plant production problems in countries outside the United States, and how he assisted in the development of international programs in research, teaching, and extension of major crop-plants and crop-animals. In other words, the so-called "Green Revolution," which actually began in 1862 with the establishment of the Morrill land-grant college system, has been extended to many countries overseas.

14

THE DEVELOPMENT
OF STUDENT LIFE, CUSTOMS,
AND TRADITIONS

Never stop learning, never stop growing.
—MARIE M. MELONEY

The Morrill land-grant colleges and universities are primarily service institutions. This service involves conducting research on pertinent problems of local, regional, national, and worldwide importance, and providing opportunities for young men and young women and adults to develop their potentialities into actualities. This chapter deals with the major changes that have taken place in the lives of four-year undergraduates from 1855, when the first two colleges[1] were established, to 1975, when all sixty-eight of them were full-flowered universities.

GRADUAL IMPROVEMENT IN LIVING QUARTERS

The first living quarters were called dormitories or barracks, depending on the emphasis on the military program. During the early period (1855-1890), these structures were quite primitive in nature. They had no indoor plumbing, no running water, no electricity, no automatic heating, no air-conditioning equipment, and no elevators. In fact, the distinguishing features of the first dormitories or barracks were the bathrooms on the ground floor, the open fireplace for the burning of coal in each room, or the pot-bellied stove, also for the burning of coal or wood, on each floor, the kerosene lamps, and the interconnecting stairs between adjacent floors. In sharp contrast, the dormitories or barracks built during the intermediate period (1890-1940) were equipped with electric circuits for furnishing light and operating fans, and with two sets of pipes, one for carrying water for drinking and bathing, and the other for carrying steam from a central coal or oil-fired heating plant to one or more radiators in each room, which in many colleges were thermostatically controlled. In fact, the tall smokestack of the central heating plant on any given campus may be considered a landmark

---

[1]The Agricultural College of the State of Michigan, and Farmers' High School of Pennsylvania.

and a distinguishing feature of the living quarters during this intermediate period. Finally, the dormitories built during the modern period
(1940-1975) were equipped with electricity as the sole source of energy
for furnishing light and for running the thermostatically controlled air-
conditioning and heating equipment. Thus, the inconveniences of the
early and intermediate periods were gradually eliminated, and from the
standpoint of the student the physical environment closely approached
the ideal.[2]

THE GRADUAL CHANGE IN THE WORK ETHIC
*From Compulsory Manual Labor to Voluntary Manual Labor
and the Development of the Laboratory Period*

Constructive work combined with the head and the hands has always
been a prominent phase of student life at the Morrill land-grant colleges
and universities. At first this work was compulsory. In fact, the first
board of trustees of all of the colleges and in one instance the state
legislature (Michigan) required that "each physically able student shall
be engaged in manual labor each work day." In addition, the first
presidents and the first faculties felt that work on the part of the
student would be helpful to his training and education. For example,
General S. D. Lee, the first president of Mississippi A and M College,
in a report to his Board of Trustees in 1883, wrote, "A student here
has many advantages. He not only gets his tuition free from the state,
but he also has opportunity to work and pay from one-half to two-thirds
or more of his board."

Type of Work Projects

In general, two types of work projects were conducted by the students under the general supervision of the faculty: (1) projects having
to do with the landscaping and beautification of the campus and with
the preparation of the college farm for the raising of crops and for
conducting experiments, and (2) projects having to do with ordinary
housekeeping. Projects of the former type varied with the condition of
the original campus and farm. As discussed in chapter 4, the experimental farm at most of the colleges was in poor shape for the con-

---

[2]On some campuses dormitories heated by steam from a central heating plant
with its smokestack exist side by side with dormitories heated solely by electricity.
On other campuses dormitories originally heated by steam from a central heating
plant are now heated solely by electricity and the central heating plant no longer
exists.

ducting of experiments. For example, at Michigan Agricultural College the campus and farm were part of the primeval forest. Consequently, operations in sequence were similar to those used by the Michigan pioneers: felling and hauling the trees into piles for burning, planting seed, usually corn, among the stumps, splitting rails for fences, erecting the fences, and digging ditches for drainage. At Mississippi A and M College the campus and farm consisted of a severely eroded and previously neglected cultivation area. Consequently, operations in sequence were erecting terraces, filling the gullies, cutting and burning the brush, building fences, and digging ditches. A similar situation existed at most of the other Morrill land-grant colleges.

Projects having to do with ordinary housekeeping were practically the same at all of the land-grant colleges. In general, these included taking care of the farm animals, sweeping floors, carrying coal, delivering mail, working in the kitchen and dining rooms, and attending the kerosene lamps.

Number of Hours and Pay

In general, the student was required to work from two to three hours per day for a five-day week. The rate of pay varied from six to ten cents per hour, depending on the institution and the type of work done. Since most of the work involved ordinary housekeeping—milking the cows, feeding the livestock, and cleaning the stables—it was not related to the student's field of interest and it did not provide learning situations for both the students and the teachers. As a result, this type of work caused considerable dissatisfaction on the part of the students and the teachers. To overcome this odious situation the teachers of agriculture and the mechanic arts began to use the work period as a laboratory period for specific courses. For example, Professor Liberty Hyde Bailey, an outstanding teacher and research worker in horticulture, stated that "I adhere to the principle that the primary object of student labor is to instruct the student." For example, he used the work period to instruct the students in various types of grafting, and the teacher of mechanical engineering used the work period to instruct the students in drawing and design. Similar changes took place in other phases of agriculture, engineering, and home economics. Thus, the labor period for specific courses gradually displaced the compulsory labor period. In fact, by the end of the first decade of the twentieth century the compulsory labor program at all of the Morrill land-grant colleges had been abolished and a real beginning had taken place in combining "the head and the hands" or science with practice in the teaching of the science of agriculture, home economics, and the mechanic arts.

THE RELIGIOUS PHASE

From Compulsory Chapel on
a Daily Basis to Student-Faculty Convocations

During the first twenty or thirty years in the life of the Morrill land-grant colleges all students were required to attend chapel exercises every day on weekdays and either chapel or some local church on Sundays. In other words, attendance at chapel was compulsory, and demerits were dispensed for unexcused absences. In general, and for any given college, the president or some member of the faculty was in charge of the program, and the program in turn consisted of reading selections from the Bible, singing selections from a hymnal, and prayer. As the colleges grew not only in number of students and faculty but in diversity of subjects taught and problems investigated, exercises of a religious nature were gradually considered to be the province of denominational groups. Thus, chapel, as originally conceived and conducted, gradually changed from a compulsory to a voluntary basis and from a daily to a two- or three-times-per-week basis, and these meetings in turn changed to a once-per-week or an occasional student-faculty convocation at which a nationally or internationally known person addressed the group on some pertinent problems of the day. Finally, the religious aspects of student life were taken over by the YMCA, the YWCA, and student denominational centers on campus.

THE DEFENSE PHASE

From Compulsory to Voluntary Training
in Military Science and Tactics

Blessed are the peacemakers for they shall be called the children of God.
                                                                —MATTHEW 5:9

In general, the American people have always worked toward the establishment of peace and goodwill throughout the world. Their leader in this respect is the president. Consider, for example, President Wilson and his slogan during World War I, "Let us make the world safe for democracy," and his program immediately after the war, which supplied American food to thousands of people in the war-ravaged countries. As a second example, consider President Roosevelt and his Four Freedoms of World War II: freedom from want, freedom from fear, freedom of religion, and freedom of speech, and his good-neighbor policy toward all nations. As a third example, consider President Truman and his Point Four program—a program of unbounded generosity and technical assistance: (1) to nations who fought with the United States, (2) to nations who fought against the United States, and (3) to underdeveloped countries. In fact, all of the presidents of the United States have advocated the promotion of peace and goodwill to all nations.

The Early Period (1862-1916)

During the early period and at all institutions training in military science and tactics was compulsory during the freshman and sophomore years and elective during the junior and senior years. At first the instructors were officer-veterans of the Civil War or retired officers of the armed forces. Later, the War Department (now part of the Department of Defense) assigned regular officers of the United States Army to that important duty. The students were known as cadets and their daily routine was prescribed by the Board of Trustees or by the presidents of each institution and the faculty. The degree of emphasis on military training varied with the region of the country. In general, cadets of northern and western colleges wore the uniform only during the period of instruction in military science and the period of drill, whereas cadets of the southern colleges wore the uniform at all times except during the laboratory period. In fact, certain Morrill land-grant colleges of the southeast—Clemson Agricultural College, Texas A and M College, and Virginia Polytechnic Institute—acquired the atmosphere of a military post or school, and the daily routine of the students was governed by the military bugle. For example, the Monday-through-Friday schedule of the cadets at Louisiana State in 1870 was as follows: reveille 5:30, chapel 6:00, sick call and inspection 6:30, breakfast 7:00, classes and studies 8:00-1:00, dinner 1:00, classes and studies 2:00-4:00, recreation 4:00, drill 5:00, supper 6:00, call to quarters (study) 7:00, and taps 10:00. A similar schedule was followed at other southern land-grant colleges.

The Middle Period (1916-1944)

During the middle period World War I and World War II took place. During each war marked and significant changes occurred in the military phase. These changes are discussed in chapters 9 and 11.

The Reserve Officers Training Corps (ROTC). The object of ROTC is to develop educated men and women for leadership positions in the armed forces. As stated in chapter 9, this program was established in 1916. At that time all physically fit students enrolled in the Morrill land-grant colleges were required to take the course during the freshman and sophomore years, and they could elect the course during the junior and senior years. In other words, work of the freshman and sophomore years was necessary. However, in 1923, the entire four-year course was placed on an elective basis. In general, this program has turned out to be extremely wise and necessary, particularly during the dark days of World War II. During this war most of the officers of the U.S. Army were graduates of ROTC. So great were their contributions to the success of the armed forces that General George C. Marshall, Chief of Staff of the U.S. Army during World War II, declared, "The most valuable asset we have had in this emergency [World War II] has been the officer product of ROTC."

The Modern Period (1946-1970)

The modern period is characterized by two interrelated events: (1) the agitation to abolish ROTC and (2) the result of a nationwide survey on the relation of ROTC to the American way of life.

The agitation to abolish ROTC occurred during the sixth decade of the twentieth century and varied in intensity from mild to severe. Examples of the former were the picketing against ROTC and against the recruiting of students for positions in war-related industries at many of the land-grant colleges. Examples of the latter were the burning of buildings at the University of Wisconsin and at Colorado State University, the breaking of windows at Michigan State University, and the disruption of normal campus activity at Cornell University and at the University of California-Berkeley. Unfortunately, this agitation disrupted many research, teaching, and extension programs, resulted in the destruction of taxpayer's property, and manifested abrogation of student responsibility.

The survey on the relationship of ROTC to the American way of life by the National Association of State Universities and Land-grant Colleges included the results from 111 institutions in the fifty states. The results show that (1) ROTC promotes rather than violates freedom to learn; (2) the courses in ROTC merit collegiate credit, since, in common with nonmilitary courses, they provide the opportunity for young men and young women to think for themselves and acquire the ability to solve practical problems; (3) courses in ROTC contribute to the broad education of young men and young women for leadership in the American way of life, and (4) the ROTC program as a whole assured that our military officers shall continue to be representative of American society.

Despite the unrest and agitation of the 1960s, enrollment of students in ROTC has remained at a substantial level. In 1969 Army ROTC graduated approximately 16,000, more than 21 times the number graduated from West Point; Air Force ROTC graduated about 5,000, about

35 percent of the total; and Navy ROTC graduated about 1,900, more than half of the total.[3] Thus, ROTC with its various programs in schools, colleges and universities throughout the country may be considered an essential part of the American system of higher education and the American way of life.

THE SOCIAL PHASE
From Boarding Clubs to National Fraternities and Sororities

During the early and intermediate periods the principal factor concerned seems to be the degree of emphasis on military training. As discussed previously, military training in the northern and western institutions was restricted to a definite period of the day, usually to a two-hour period in the afternoon. As a result, the students were free to select any boarding club that was available or form a club of their own. A significant feature of these boarding clubs is that they provided opportunities for students with a common background or interest to eat together, for training in food service management and for securing work. In general, the student manager at each club bought the groceries, kept accounts, and received pay from each individual student boarder and paid the bills, and the student waiters prepared the tables and served the food. In this way many young men either wholly or partially worked their way through school.

These boarding clubs seem to have been the forerunner of local literary societies. For example, the historian of Pennsylvania State College states, "These eating clubs which appear to have been nurseries for fraternities developed loyalties and rivalries which added spice to college life."[4] The bright spot of the local literary societies was the literary program every Friday evening. The president of any given society would preside, turn the meeting over to a program chairman, and he in turn would introduce the speaker(s) and lead the discussion. In this way, the members received excellent training in parliamentary procedure, in debate, and in public speaking.

In sharp contrast, military training and procedures in southern institutions prevailed throughout the entire day. The student body was organized into cadet companies with their complement of freshmen, sophomores, juniors, and seniors. The individual student arose and went to bed by the bugle, and, at the appropriate time for breakfast, dinner,

---

[3]*Reader's Digest*, November, 1969.

[4]Wayland F. Dunaway. 1946. *History of Pennsylvania State College.* Lancaster Press, Lancaster, PA.

and supper, he marched out with his company from the barracks to the mess hall and back from the mess hall to the barracks. The waiting on the tables was usually delegated to the freshmen.

During the modern period the principal factor seems to be the removal of the ban on secret organizations by the Board of Trustees of many of the land-grant colleges. Thus, the local literary societies were free to join national or international fraternities and sororities. As a result, the local literary societies characteristic of the early period gradually disappeared and their place has been taken by a comparatively large number of nationwide fraternities and sororities. In general, these fraternities and sororities compete with each other in scholastic attainment, intramural activities, and student politics. They have become an integral part of student life on campus.

THE INTRASPORTS PHASE
From Interclass Rivalry to Comprehensive Programs of Intramural Athletics

Human beings are always changing potential energy to various forms of kinetic energy. With other factors favorable, the rate of change varies with the age and development of the individual. Children, adolescents, and young adults give off more energy per unit of time than older adults. Consequently, it is imperative that this abundant and seemingly excess energy be directed into useful and beneficial channels. This section deals with the use of this so-called excess energy in organized play or more specifically in intramural athletics. As in many other phases of student life there are three rather specific but overlapping periods: the early, the intermediate, and the modern.

The Early Period (1855-1890)

For the first two decades in the life of the Morrill land-grant colleges there was very little if any interest in playing of games or in athletic contests. As explained in the section on the work ethic, all physically able students were required to work two or three hours during each day of the work week. As a result, the students had little excess energy for indulgence in sports. With the gradual reduction in and final elimination of the compulsory labor requirement, the students began to play games primarily to get rid of the excess energy and to maintain tiptop physical condition. These games began in contests between classes, particularly between the freshman and sophomores in baseball and football. This in turn led to student requests for setting aside definite areas of the campus and equipment for playing games.

For example, at Pennsylvania State, the students petitioned the faculty for the use of a small area back of Old Main (the first dormitory) as an outdoor gym, and for equipment consisting of horizontal and parallel bars, a swing with seats, and one with wings. A similar situation existed at the other Morrill land-grant colleges. Thus, although the presidents and faculties encouraged the students to take an active part in sports, no definite intramural program in sports developed during this period.

The Intermediate Period (1890-1940)

This period is characterized by the concern of the administration and faculty for the well-being of all the students and by the development of the concept "sports for all the students." With reference to the former most colleges examined the freshmen for possible defects. (For example, at Ohio State in 1907 of 1,236 students examined 35 percent had faulty posture, 28 percent had uneven shoulders, and 26 percent had flat chests.) They also required them to take one hour of "gym" each week in order to promote the physical well-being of the students.

With reference to the latter the athletic director and his staff at each of the land-grant colleges developed intramural programs in baseball, football, tennis, swimming, and bowling for the men, and in tennis, swimming, bowling, and hiking for the women. In general, the students have taken part in these intramural games with zeal and enthusiasm. For example, the historian of Cornell University records that, in 1927-1928, 3,945 students at Cornell were engaged in intramural activities in "soccer, touch football, basketball, tennis, hockey, softball, and other sports. In basketball, despite the insufficient gymnasium facilities, there were 600 players in 12 leagues divided into 59 clubs." In fact, by 1940 intramural sports had become an integral part in the life of the students at all of the Morrill land-grant colleges.

The Modern Period (1940-1975)

During this period the intramural athletic program came into full flower. The concept of "sports for all" continued, but, in contrast to the previous period, it was placed entirely on a voluntary basis. Nevertheless, the students continued to show zeal and enthusiasm for this type of program. As a result, the colleges and universities built new or enlarged old gymnasiums, developed additional playing areas and tennis courts, and broadened their programs to include such sports as golf, archery, skiing, table tennis, and billiards. Some of the more affluent institutions developed recreation areas for all of the students. These areas contain swimming pools, tennis courts, playing fields, and clubhouses.

THE SELF-GOVERNMENT PHASE
From No Self-Government to
Full Self- or Autonomous Government

During the early period the rules and regulations governing student life on any given campus were promulgated by the Board of Trustees. These rules and regulations generally failed to provide opportunities for self-discipline on the part of the students. In northern institutions self-discipline began through the need to maintain order in the dormitories. For example, the presidents of Michigan Agricultural College and Iowa Agricultural College arranged students into specific groups or units and asked each group to elect a cadet captain and a cadet lieutenant. At the Michigan College these officers arranged for the trials of disciplinary offenders and served as judges. At the Iowa College the offenders were tried before a student council presided over by the president of the student body, with one student serving as prosecutor and one other representing the accused. However, in southern institutions, the cadets were housed in accordance with the military organization of the cadet corps. In other words, the cadet officers and the cadets of any given company were housed together. This method was particularly advantageous in maintaining order in the barracks, since the cadet officers of any given company were vitally interested in promoting exemplary conduct on the part of their cadets, and in providing a more favorable environment for study.

During the intermediate period self-government expanded to all fields of extracurricular activity. This growth is characterized by the formation of student councils of many types—men's student councils, women's student councils, interfraternity councils, and intersorority councils. The function of any given council was usually to coordinate the work of groups working on the same project. The student councils led to a further expansion of student self-government in the formation of all-men student government associations and all-women student government associations, each of which considered many aspects of the extracurricular affairs of student life.

During the modern period the men's student government associations, the women's student government associations, and the various student councils banded together in the formation of all-student, campuswide self-government associations. For example, at Pennsylvania State University in 1939 the plan of organization and operation was similar to that of the federal government of the United States with its three main branches: the legislative, the executive, and the judiciary. In general, and for any given student body, the legislative usually consists of an all-college cabinet with senators and representatives from specific organizations and groups and has the authority to promote legislation that affects the welfare of the entire student body; the executive consists of an all-university student president and vice-president and they have authority to conduct the day-to-day affairs of the student association; and the judiciary consists of a student tribunal appointed by the president and has authority to serve as a judiciary body. According to Dunaway (the historian of Pennsylvania State College), this plan has worked admirably. Similar organizations have developed at other land-grant colleges and universities.

THE SCHOLARSHIP PHASE
From Local Scholarship Clubs to Nationwide and International Scholastic Organizations

The main business of students of the Morrill land-grant college is study. The student is given an opportunity to acquire a working knowledge of the fundamentals within his chosen field and to develop the ability to apply this knowledge to the solution of practical problems. Many surveys have shown a close positive correlation between success in college, as determined by grades, combined with participation in extracurricular activities, and success after college. For example, the American Telephone and Telegraph Company conducted a comprehensive survey in 1965 with 1,700 of their employees who had graduated from a four-year college. The object of the survey was to determine the relationship of grades in college to financial success in the company. The result showed a very high positive correlation between high grades in college and financial success at AT&T. Almost half the men who graduated within the top third of their college classes were earning salaries within the top third at AT&T. This positive relation of success in college to success after college is well known. In fact, a prospective employer usually examines a student's grades before he makes a decision to employ the student.

As would be expected, the growth and development of scholastic organizations coincided closely with the growth and development of each of the several land-grant colleges. Thus, the first organizations destined to recognize and promote scholarship were in the fields of agriculture, engineering, and home economics. As the colleges expanded to other fields, scholastic organizations within each of these fields developed. At present these organizations are many and varied. Note from table 14-1 that certain societies have chapters in the United States and in one or more other countries; others have chapters in the United States only, and others exist on one university only.

Scholarship Day

Scholarship Day is a very happy occasion at each of the land-grant colleges. On this day a special effort is made to recognize the students of high scholastic attainment, and to stress the relation of high scholarship to the orderly progress of human affairs. Although the program of recognition varies in detail with the college, it usually consists of an all-student-faculty convocation, the printing and distribution of programs containing the names of the scholars, and an address by a nationally or internationally known scholar.

Table 14-1.

EXAMPLES OF HONORARY OR SCHOLASTIC SOCIETIES

*Chapters at Several Universities in the United States
and at One or More Other Countries*

Phi Kappa Phi (general), Sigma Xi (science), Gamma Sigma Delta (agriculture).

Chapters at Several Universities in the United States Only

Alpha Zeta (agriculture), Tau Beta Pi (engineering), Omicron Nu (home economics), Scabbard and Blade (ROTC), Alpha Kappa Psi (business), Omicron Delta Epsilon (economics), Gamma Sigma Epsilon (chemistry), Phi Kappa Pi (education), Phi Delta Epsilon (journalism), Xi Sigma Pi (forestry).

Chapters at One University Only

Lion's Paw (Penn State), Excalibar (Michigan State), Senior Staff for women (North Dakota State).

THE JOURNALISM PHASE
*From a Relatively Small, Infrequently Published Report
of Campus Events Only to a Large Comprehensive Report of Events
on a Campuswide, Nationwide, and International Basis*

As with other activities the growth and development of the student newspapers have corresponded closely to the growth and development of the institutions. Since during the early period all of the land-grant colleges had two schools or departments (agriculture and mechanic arts) and in addition some had departments of veterinary science and home economics, the editors limited themselves to promoting the interests of students enrolled in these fields and to events as they occurred on the campus, with emphasis on intercollegiate football, baseball, tennis, and track, and the activities of social fraternities and sororities. Thus, the first student newspapers were small in size and limited in scope and influence.

With further growth of these institutions, as manifested by the addition of other fields, particularly education, business and industry, and science and the arts, the editors expanded their interests accordingly and with emphasis on the relationship of the alumni and alumnae to the welfare of the institutions. For example, the editors of three student newspapers took a leading role in securing subscriptions to three badly needed buildings: the Memorial Stadium at the University of California-Berkeley, the Student Memorial Union at Michigan State, and the Student Memorial Union at Iowa State. In addition, the editors advocated student rights, student responsibilities, and a more servicewide land-grant university. In this way, the student newspapers increased in size and in scope and influence.

Finally, with the land-grant colleges and universities embracing practically all fields of human endeavor, the editorial staffs of each student newspaper expanded their interests to all fields and to events as they occur on a nationwide and worldwide basis. As a result, the modern student newspaper has become large in size, comprehensive in nature, and published on a twice- or thrice-weekly or daily basis. In fact, the student newspaper of many of the land-grant colleges and universities has the aspects of a large cosmopolitan daily, and the editors do not hesitate to take forthright stands on the educational and political issues of the day. Thus, the student newspapers have become a constructive influence in promoting the welfare of the institutions and the people as a whole. Table 14-2 gives the name of the student newspapers during the early, intermediate, and modern period of each of nine institutions.

STUDENT TRADITIONS AND THE DEMOCRATIC SPIRIT
From Intense Interclass Rivalry
to Interclass Friendship and Cooperation

During the early period, rivalry between adjacent classes was quite pronounced. The sophomores considered themselves the guardians of the freshmen, and the juniors considered themselves the guardians of the sophomores. At most of the colleges, this rivalry was particularly intense between the freshmen and the sophomores. It began with an event known as the class rush, and the program varied somewhat with the college. At Michigan State the members of each class engaged in a football scramble, with the freshmen on one side and the sophomores on the other; in a flag rush, with the sophomores underneath a flag suspended on a line between two poles; and a tug-of-war across the shallow Red Cedar River, with the sophomores on one side and the freshmen on the other. At Ohio State and the University of California-Berkeley the members of the sophomore and freshman classes engaged in physical combat until all of the members of one class were thrown to the ground and securely tied. However, this type of physical activity was frowned on and disapproved by the upper classmen and faculty. By the end of the third decade of the twentieth century the class rush and similar events were dropped.

Table 14-2

TITLES OF STUDENT NEWSPAPERS OF
SELECTED MORRILL LAND-GRANT UNIVERSITIES

Land-Grant University	Early Period	Intermediate Period	Modern Period
Arkansas	*University Weekly*	*Arkansas Traveler*	*Arkansas Traveler*
Illinois	*Student*	*Illini*	*Daily Illini*
Kansas State	*Student Herald*	*Kansas Aggie*	*Kansas State Collegian*
Maryland	*MAC Weekly*	*Diamondback*	*Diamondback*
Massachusetts	*Aggie Life*	*College Signal*	*Massachusetts Collegian*
Michigan State	*Speculum* (Quarterly)	*Holcad* (Weekly)	*Michigan State News* (Daily)
Ohio State	*Lantern* (Weekly)	*Lantern* (Five days/week)	*Lantern* (Daily)
Pennsylvania State	*Free Lance* (Monthly)	*State Collegian* (Weekly)	*Daily Collegian*
Wisconsin	*University Press*	*Aegis* (Weekly)	*Daily Cardinal*

Of greater significance as a tradition is the promotion of goodwill and friendship among all classes and all groups on the campuses of the Morrill land-grant colleges and universities. Examples of this goodwill and friendship are manifested by the upperclassmen assisting the freshmen in orientation and registration, by students and professors greeting each other with a smile as they go from class to class and from building to building, and more particularly by making any stranger on the campus "feel at home." It is not uncommon for a student to direct or personally escort a stranger to the place he wants to go. In other words, everyone does his part in fostering the congenial democratic spirit that prevails at each of the Morrill land-grant colleges and universities.

REFERENCES

Califano, James A., Jr. 1970. *The Student Revolution—A Global Confrontation.* W. W. Norton, New York, NY.

The author presents reasons for the campus unrest of 1960s in the preindustrial and postindustrial nations.

Fisor, J. 1969. "And the Wall Came Tumbling Down," *L.S.U. Alumni News,* 45:4, 8-11.

A reinterpretation of the phrase *"and including military tactics"* in the Morrill Land-grant Act of 1862.

Overcash, Jean P. 1963. "Scholarship in Horticulture," *Proceedings of the Association of Agricultural Workers,* 60:251-52.

The positive relationship of success in college, as measured by grades, to success after college.

Rulon, Philip R. 1973. "Plowboys and Blacksmiths," *Phi Kappa Phi Journal,* 53, No. 4

An interesting account of the development of student life at Oklahoma State University during the early part of the twentieth century.

Tomlinson, K. Y. 1969. "ROTC Under Attack," *Reader's Digest,* November.

An explanation of the role of ROTC, the reasons for its establishment and maintenance, and its relationship to the life and well-being of the nation.

15

PROBLEMS OF THE PRESENT
AND THE IMMEDIATE FUTURE

How can we judge the work of a society? On what basis can we predict how well a nation will survive and prosper? We propose this criterion: the concern of one generation for the next. If the children and the youth of a generation are afforded opportunities to develop their capacities to the fullest; if they are given the knowledge to understand the world, and the wisdom to change it, then the prospects for the future are bright. In contrast, a society which neglects its children, however well it may function in other respects, risks eventual disorganization and demise.
— RUSSELL SAGE FOUNDATION

PLANET EARTH AND ITS UNIQUE POSITION

In our planetary system the sun is the central body, and nine planets revolve around the sun. These planets with increasing distance from the sun are Mercury, Venus, Earth, Mars, Jupiter, Saturn, Uranus, Neptune, and Pluto. Further, these planets not only vary in their distance from the sun but also in the composition of their atmospheres and in temperatures on the surface. Mercury has no atmosphere and its temperature reaches a maximum of 750°F (399°C) on the sun side and a minimum of −400°F (−240°C) on the dark side. Venus has a dense cloud cover of 25 miles (40 kilometers) in depth, consisting mostly of carbon dioxide, and a surface temperature of about 600°F (316°C). Mars has a thin cloud cover consisting of carbon dioxide, traces of water vapor, and no free oxygen, and a surface temperature varying from 80°F (27°C) to −100°F (−73°C). The remaining planets, Jupiter, Saturn, Uranus, Neptune, and Pluto, because of their tremendous distances from the sun are extremely cold. For example, Jupiter and Saturn have surface temperatures varying from −200°F to −400°F (−129°C to −240°C). Thus, with all of the planets, except Planet Earth, the temperatures on the surface of each are either too high or too low to sustain living things as they exist on the surface of Planet Earth. Because the temperatures are unfavorable, other factors, such as the water supply, the light supply, and the essential mineral supply, even if available would also be unfavorable to support life as we know it. For these reasons, Planet Earth occupies a unique and special place in our planetary system.

THE SIGNIFICANCE OF THE CROP-PLANT

Automorphs and Heteromorphs

All living things may be placed in one of two groups: automorphs and heteromorphs. In general, automorphs have the ability to trap or capture their energy directly. These in turn comprise the chemomorphs and the photomorphs. The chemomorphs consist of a few species of bacteria and have the ability to transform the potential energy in certain inorganic compounds containing sulfur, or iron, or nitrogen into chemical energy in foods, whereas photomorphs comprise all living things that contain chlorophyll and have the ability to transform the kinetic energy of light to the potential chemical energy of foods and other manufactured compounds.

In sharp contrast to the automorphs, the heteromorphs do not have the ability to obtain free energy directly from the sun. They obtain their free energy from the foods that automorphs make. Man considers himself the dominant or most important heteromorph. From time immemorial his free energy or food supply has been a serious problem. Over the years he has discovered that certain plants make more foods per unit time or per unit area in terms of quantity or quality than other kinds. He has continually tried to improve the efficiency of these kinds and he has called them agricultural crops and given them special names. These crops are the basic components of agriculture, the *source of most of our wealth,* and the foundation of our present-day civilization.

Basic Biochemical Reactions of Crop-Plants

The basic biochemical reactions are photosynthesis and respiration. Essentially, photosynthesis is an energy-storing or energy-fixation or light-trapping reaction. Within the tissue containing chlorophyll and the presence of light, and specific enzyme systems, carbon dioxide and water combine in the formation of potential energy containing carbohydrates and related substances. In this reaction the kinetic energy of light is transformed or fixed or stored in the potential form. In this way, a supply of energy from the sun is made available for most living things. This fundamental transformation, the change of kinetic energy of light to potential energy of food, is illustrated as follows.

$$\text{kinetic energy of light} + \text{(specific enzyme systems)} \atop \text{chlorophyll} + CO_2 + H_2O \longrightarrow \left\{ \begin{array}{l} \text{manufactured} \\ \text{compounds} + O_2 \\ \text{containing} \\ \text{potential} \\ \text{energy} \end{array} \right.$$

Essentially, respiration is the reverse of photosynthesis. Manufactured foods, usually the soluble sugars, combine with oxygen in the formation of carbon dioxide and water, with the liberation of heat and other forms of kinetic energy. In this way the light energy reserve built up by crop-plants becomes available for all crop-plants, for all crop-animals, and for all mankind. This fundamental transformation, the change of potential energy of foods to kinetic energy, is illustrated as follows:

$$\text{Manufactured compounds containing potential energy} + O_2 \longrightarrow \underset{\text{(specific enzyme systems)}}{CO_2 + H_2O + \text{heat}} + \begin{cases} \text{other forms} \\ \text{of kinetic} \\ \text{energy} \end{cases}$$

In general, these fundamental reactions show that human beings are dependent on the sun for their existence and before they can use the energy from the sun it must be captured or trapped by the all-important chlorophyll-containing crop-plants.

The Relation of Rate of Photosynthesis and Rate of Respiration to Growth and Yield of Crop-Plants. The relative rates of photosynthesis and respiration of crop-plants have a significant bearing upon their marketable yield or ability to produce a supply of potential energy for the human race. As an example, consider the potato, a major food crop. Potatoes are grown for their tubers. The tubers are primarily organs for the storage of starch. Starch is made from glucose, a common sugar, and glucose is made in photosynthesis. Therefore, with other factors favorable, the greater the rate of photosynthesis the greater will be the amount of glucose available for starch and tuber formation. However, glucose is decomposed in respiration. Therefore, the greater the rate of respiration the less will be the amount of glucose for starch and tuber formation. Thus, the difference between the rate of photosynthesis and the rate of respiration will determine the amount of glucose available for starch formation and yield of the tubers.

As a second example, consider the sugarcane or the sugar beet, also major food crops. These crops are grown for their ability to store sucrose. Sucrose is made primarily from glucose and this compound is made in photosynthesis. Therefore, the greater the rate of photosynthesis, the greater will be the amount of glucose for sucrose formation. However, glucose is decomposed in respiration. Thus, the greater the rate of respiration the less will be the amount of glucose for sucrose formation. Thus, the difference between the rate of photosynthesis and the rate of respiration will determine the amount of glucose for sugarcane and sugar beet formation and the yield of the plants.

As a third example consider the cotton plant, a major fiber crop plant.

Cotton is grown for its cellulose fibers. Cellulose is made from glucose and glucose is made by photosynthesis. Therefore the greater the rate of photosynthesis the greater will be the amount of glucose for cotton fiber formation. However, glucose is decomposed in respiration. Therefore the greater the rate of respiration the less will be the amount of glucose for cotton fiber formation. Thus the difference between the rate of photosynthesis and the rate of respiration will determine the amount of glucose available for cotton fiber formation and the yield of the cotton plant.

In general, this relation of the rate of photosynthesis to the rate of respiration exists for all crop-plants. In other words, the greater the rate of photosynthesis, in proportion to the rate of respiration, the greater will be the amount of manufactured compounds available for the growth, development, and yield of any given crop; and if the crop-plant is grown according to approved agricultural practices the greater will be the marketable yield. This statement may be expressed mathematically as follows: $P-R=Y$, where P represents the rate of photosynthesis, R represents the rate of respiration, and Y represents the marketable yield. Thus, if the rate of photosynthesis is high and the rate of respiration is normal, the yields are likely to be high. However, if the rate of photosynthesis is high and the rate of respiration is also high, or if the rate of photosynthesis is low and the rate of respiration is normal, the yields are likely to be low. In general, for satisfactory crop-plant production, the rate of photosynthesis should be at least eight to ten times greater than the rate of respiration.

Total or Gross Photosynthesis vs. Apparent or Net Photosynthesis. The rate of photosynthesis may be determined by using either of these two measures: the rate of gross or total photosynthesis, abbreviated P_G, and the rate of apparent or net photosynthesis, abbreviated P_N. If a measure of gross photosynthesis is necessary the rate of respiration is determined in the dark at exactly the same temperature as that during the light, and the results are added to the rate of photosynthesis during the light period. Thus, $P_G = P_N + R$. Transposing, $P_N = P_G - R$, because, as explained in the preceding paragraph, $P_G - R = Y$, $P_N = Y$. In other words, the rate of net photosynthesis (P_N) may be considered a measure of the marketable yield or the amount of potential energy available for the metabolic requirements of the human race.

This close and direct relation of apparent or net photosynthesis to yield explains why an efficient and strong agriculture is dependent on crop-plants with high rates of apparent photosynthesis, and why crop-plant scientists have been measuring the rates of apparent photosynthesis since the beginning of the Morrill land-grant colleges and universities and their concomitant agricultural experiment stations.

PLANET EARTH AND ITS LIMITATIONS

In general, our perception of Planet Earth depends upon the point of view. For example, a person flying in a helicopter at skyscraper level above a large city gets the impression that the planet is similar to a big anthill, with large numbers of people scurrying from place to place and bustling about from here to there. And the same person flying also in a helicopter over an area consisting of family farms gets the impression that the planet is open, roomy, spacious, and not crowded. However, unlike the man in the helicopter flying over a city or a farming area, the astronauts Neil Armstrong and Buzz Aldrin as they traveled from the moon to the earth saw the planet as a whole and as it exists in space, with its canopy of clouds, its patches of green and its patches of water, and above all its solitude. As Lester Pearson, a former prime minister of Canada, stated, "Our Planet is indeed as the astronauts saw it from the moon—small, fragile, beautiful, alone; above all, alone and one."

Further, Planet Earth is a finite object. As such, everything about it is limited: (1) its carrying capacity for any given unit of time, (2) its living space (3) its food, fiber, and forest products producing capacity, and (4) its energy-supplying capacity. In fact, the only supply of inexhaustible free energy is the light from the sun that bathes Planet Earth, and this supply is limited by man's ingenuity in using it. In general, these limitations have had a direct bearing on the problems of the past, and they challenge man's ability to solve the problems of the present and the immediate future.

PLANET EARTH AND ITS PERTINENT PROBLEMS

Rate of Growth of the Human Race

The rate of growth of the human population refers to the increase in number of individuals per unit area, and per unit time. Usually, population experts use any given country as the unit area and any given year as the unit time. In other words, the rate of growth is measured on a national basis and from the beginning of one year to the beginning of the next.

In general, two factors are involved: (1) the number of births per unit time and (2) the number of deaths for the same unit time. These two values may be compared arithmetically or geometrically. With the arithmetic comparison, the number of deaths is subtracted from the number of births. For example, if the number of births and the number of deaths per unit time and area are equal the rate of population growth is zero. With the geometric comparison, the number of births and the number of deaths are used as a ratio. For example, if the number of births equals the number of deaths per unit time and area the ratio is 1; if the number of births is greater than the number of deaths the ratio is greater than 1, and if the number of births is less than the number of deaths, the ratio is less than 1. In general, population experts use the arithmetic comparison, that is, the rate of increase in births over deaths.

Rate of Increase on Planet Earth as a Whole

Since about 1940 a vast amount of literature has developed on the consequences of rate of growth of the human race. In general, there are two schools of thought: (1) those who refer to the rate of growth of the human race as the population explosion, and (2) those who view the rate of growth with less alarm than the first. Members of the first group claim that Planet Earth is already crowded and advocate immediate zero population growth or a growth index of one, whereas the members of the second group believe that the human race has the ability to stabilize its rate of growth before individuals or groups of individuals begin to fight each other for living space, for food, shelter, fuel, and other factors. Note in figure 15.1 the rate of growth of the human race as a whole. From 40 B.C. to the thirteenth century the rate of growth of the human race was exceedingly low; from the thirteenth to the eighteenth century, it was moderately rapid, and from the eighteenth to and including the twentieth century, it was very rapid and logarithmic in nature. Thus, if this rapid rate of growth continues, food will become scarce and insufficient for all individuals.

Rate of Increase in the United States and Other Developed Countries

Since 1960 the birthrate in the United States has rapidly declined, so much so that a slow rate of population growth has been attained. Clearly, a slow rate of growth is more desirable than a fast rate. A zero or slow rate would ensure an adequate supply of food to all individuals; it would confine the women to a relatively short childbearing period; and it would provide greater opportunities for the continuing education of both parents. In other words, a zero or a slow rate of population would provide for the quality aspects of human life rather than the quantity aspects. See figure 15.2.

Other nations have had a low population growth for some time. Examples are Switzerland, Ireland, Great Britain, West and East Germany, Luxembourg, Italy, Hungary, Sweden, and Japan. In fact, it seems that a strong agriculture, a well-developed group of nonagricul-

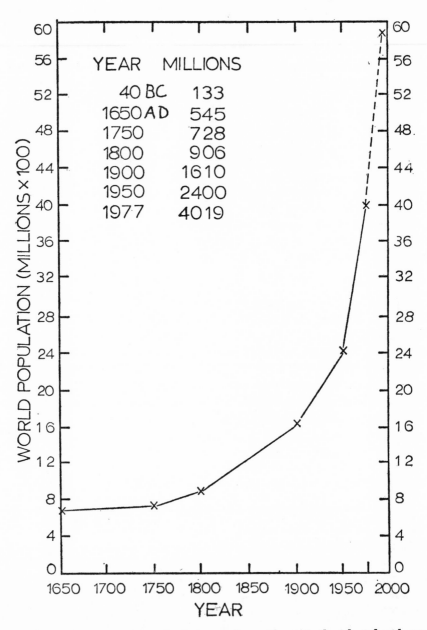

FIGURE 15.1. *Rate of growth of the people on Planet Earth. Adapted with per-mission from E. S. Devey, Jr. "The Human Population,"* Scientific American 203: *September 1960.*

tural industries, and strong research, teaching, and extension programs in all phases of human activity are positively associated with low to zero population growth. Many countries have established research, teaching, and extension programs on population problems. For example, in the United States centers have been established at the Universities of Michigan and North Carolina, and at Harvard, Pittsburgh, and Johns Hopkins Universities.

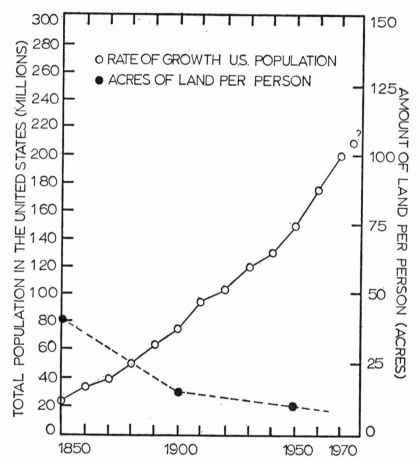

FIGURE 15.2. *Relation of growth of the U.S. population to the amount of land per person. Adapted with permission from graph in* Progressive Farmer, *January 1965.*

The Food Supply

As previously stated, food for humans comprises a wide variety of organic compounds. In general, they may be divided into two great groups: (1) compounds that contain potential energy and supply substances for the making and maintenance of the tissues, and (2) compounds that are necessary for the changing of the potential energy in foods to the various forms of kinetic energy. Examples of the former are the many kinds of carbohydrates, proteins, and fats, and examples of the latter are certain vitamins and hormones.

Basic Requirements

The basic requirements include both the foods and vitamins and hormones. With the foods the requirement is based on their ability to supply kinetic energy. This kinetic energy is measured as number of calories[1] per unit weight. This in turn varies with the nature of the food. For example, one gram of sucrose, a common carbohydrate, contains 4.1 calories, and one gram of fat contains 9.3 calories. In fact, carbohydrates contain lesser quantities of potential energy than fats. With the vitamins and hormones the requirement is based on the needs of the individual. As shown in table 15-1, the daily energy requirement varies with age and sex. Regardless of sex, twenty-five-year-olds require more energy than forty-five or sixty-five-year-olds, and regardless of age, men require more energy than women.

Table 15-1.
DAILY ENERGY REQUIREMENTS
IN TERMS OF CALORIES FOF MEN AND WOMEN
AT THREE DIFFERENT LIFE STAGES.[1]

Desirable Weight (lbs.)	25 Years		45 Years		65 Years	
	Men	Women	Men	Women	Men	Women
110	2500	2050	2350	1950	1950	1600
121	2700	2200	2550	2050	2150	1750
132	2850	2350	2700	2200	2250	1850
143	3000	2500	2800	2350	2350	2000
154	3200	2600	3000	2450	2550	2050
165	3400	2750	3200	2600	2700	2151

[1]From: Calories and Body Weight, U.S. Department of Agriculture Yearbook for 1959, p. 103.

The Hypothesis of Malthus

In 1798 T. R. Malthus, an English economist, postulated that the rate of growth of the population in any given country increased geometrically, e.g., 2, 4, 8, 16, 32, . . . , whereas its rate of food production increased only arithmetically, e.g., 2, 3, 4, 5, 6, ... He concluded that unless the people practice restraint in rate of population growth, the amount of food for any one individual eventually becomes lower than that required for his basic needs. As a result, the

---

[1]A calorie is the amount of heat required to change one gram of water from 14°C to 15°C.

people would starve and become susceptible to various diseases. Thus, inertia, unproductivity, disease, and pestilence would prevail. How do the countries of the world compare with reference to the rate of population growth and the ability to produce food? In general, they may be placed in one of two groups: the developed nations and the underdeveloped nations. Each group has definite characteristics, and these are set forth as follows.

The Developed Nations. Food is plentiful. In fact, the rate of population growth is lower than the rate of food production. Therefore, the hypothesis of Malthus does not hold. The people, as a whole, support extensive programs in research, teaching, and extension work in agriculture, as manifested by the numerous colleges of agriculture with their agricultural experiment stations and agricultural extension services. As a result, there are high yields per plant and per animal. In other words, the people have developed a strong and efficient agriculture, with a large segment of its people employed in fields other than agriculture. The educational level of the people is high, and the standard of living is also high.

The Underdeveloped Nations. In sharp contrast, food is scarce. In fact, the rate of population growth is greater than the rate of food production. Therefore, the hypothesis of Malthus holds. The people, as a whole, do not realize that a strong and efficient agriculture in turn requires intensive programs in research, teaching, and extension in agriculture. As a result, marketable yields per plant and per animal are low, and costs of production are high. Further, a large segment of its people is engaged in the production of food. Because of the scarcity of food, with its accompanying undernutrition and malnutrition, and because the biggest problem of any given family is the next meal, the standard of living is low and there is no joy in living. As pointed out previously, mere survival of any given individual family or group of individuals is not enough.

Fortunately, many underdeveloped countries are now trying to become highly developed. With many of these countries the first requirement seems to be that of land reform—the breaking up of individually owned large tracts of agricultural land into individually owned small tracts. This would place the production of food and fiber in the hands of a relatively large number of growers or farmers, as was practiced in the United States immediately after the passage of the Homestead Act of 1862.

The Farmer's Land

The farmer's land is a mantle or layer of decomposed minerals and organic matter on cultivated fields, timber tracts, forest, and gardens. This mantle is known as soil. As is well known, soils have a significant relation to human welfare. They supply water and essential compounds to beneficial organisms: examples are the nitrogen fixers, the organic matter decomposers, and the nitrifiers,[2] and they supply water and all the essential compounds except carbon dioxide to crop-plants. With the exception of a few instances in which crops are raised hydroponically, that is, by the growing of crops without soil, most crop-plants throughout the world are raised on soil. How do the countries compare with respect to their maintenance of fertility in the soil? Here again, they may be placed in one of two groups: the developed countries and the underdeveloped.

The Situation with Highly Developed Countries. In general, the people of developed countries realize the value of fertile soil to human welfare. In fact, their colleges of agriculture with the research and extension services have established intensive and extensive programs with reference to the maintenance of soil fertility and the reduction in soil erosion. As a result, the productive capacity of the soil is high. However, in these developed countries, there has been and continues to be a constant scramble for the farmer's land for projects other than that of food, fiber, and timber production—a scramble for the building of highways, e.g., the interstate superhighway system in the United States, and for the development of residential areas, supermarkets, industrial parks, and recreational areas. These projects reduce the potential for food, fiber, and timber production. For example, certain authorities have estimated that for every increase of one million of the population of the United States, 100,000 acres of fertile land are lost for the production of food, fiber, and timber. Obviously, this sort of thing cannot go on forever. In fact, the time has come for all individuals to appreciate the relation of fertile soil to the welfare of crop-plants and crop-animals, and of these in turn to the welfare of the human race. Obviously, the time has come for setting aside all fertile areas for the production of the usable products of photosynthesis. Fortunately, some states have already established definite policies with reference to the use of fertile land.

The Situation with Underdeveloped Countries. In sharp contrast, the people of underdeveloped countries have not as yet established intensive research, teaching, and extension programs on pertinent phases of the behavior of the soil. In fact, the relation of soil fertility to human welfare remains to be fully realized. With the rapid rate of population growth there is a corresponding need for land for the development of homes. But because of the low standard of living the amount of land

---

[2]The nitrogen fixers take molecular nitrogen from the air in the formation of their protoplasm, the organic matter decomposers change organic matter to ammonia, and the nitrifiers change ammonia to nitrates.

lost for the production of food is less than that taken out in the developed countries. Nevertheless, as with the developed countries, the people should realize the important relation of the soil to the welfare of the crop-plant and the people as a whole, and the need for a definite policy on the use of fertile land. Here again, it seems that all fertile areas should be reserved for food and fiber production.

POLLUTION OF THE LIVING ENVIRONMENT

Pollution implies contamination—the presence of unwanted or harmful substances in the living environment. This living environment includes the troposphere, the canopy of air that surrounds Planet Earth, and the waters and land on the surface of the earth.

Pollution of the Troposphere

A natural or clean troposphere contains molecular nitrogen about 70 percent, molecular oxygen about 20 percent, carbon dioxide about 0.03 percent, and small quantities of water vapor and particles of dust. The nitrogen is neded by certain beneficial soil organisms and crop-plants for the making of their proteins; the oxygen is needed for the respiration of all living things; and carbon dioxide is needed for photosynthesis.

Unfortunately, the atmosphere of highly developed countries has become contaminated with other substances. These contaminants may be divided into two groups: (1) the tiny particles of solids called particulates and (2) gases. The particulates, usually fly ash and soot, get between the crop-plant and the life-giving sun. This reduces light intensity and is likely to reduce the rate of photosynthesis, growth and yield of crop-plants, and the food and/or fiber supply. The gases usually are sulfur dioxide, carbon monoxide, oxides of nitrogen, and incompletely oxidized hydrocarbons. Those that are the components of smog are particularly injurious. According to the Air Pollution Research Center, Riverside, California, smog injures all kinds of plants—plants both inside and outside the home, plants in commercial gardens and orchards, and trees of the forest. Air pollution has damaged crops in other states also—in Florida, Michigan, New York, New Jersey, Oregon, and Washington. For these reasons, anything that stands in the way of the crop-plant and the life-giving sun should be removed, and the air in the vicinity of crop-plants should be kept continuously clean.

In addition, pollutants in the air are inimical to human health and well-being. They harm health indirectly by reducing the rate of photosynthesis, with a subsequent reduction in the rate of food and oxygen production, and directly by disturbing or interfering with the normal metabolism of the body. In particular, carbon monoxide combines with the hemoglobin of the blood and renders this pigment incapable of absorbing oxygen. Sulfur dioxide combines with water vapor in the air in the formation of sulfuric acid, which irritates the delicate membranes of the nose and lungs. Smog irritates the eyes and throat and reduces the supply of oxygen to the living cells and may even induce death. For example, in the winter of 1952, 40,000 persons in the city of London, England, died as a result of inhaling smog, and in July, 1970, the authorities in smog-choked Tokyo sent more than 80,000 persons for treatment in hospitals. Here again, the atmosphere should be kept continuously clean, not only for the welfare of phytoplankton, beneficial bacteria, crop-plants, and crop-animals, but for the health and well-being of all mankind.

Pollution of the Waters

Clean or nonpolluted water contains relatively low concentrations of nonpoisonous soluble salts and relatively low concentrations of carbon dioxide and oxygen. In general, the salts, carbon dioxide, and oxygen are needed for the growth and development of phytoplankton, and oxygen is needed for the development of all living things in the waters. Here again, as with the air of highly developed countries, the streams have been contaminated. Examples are detergents containing phosphorous, nitrates, oil, hard, relatively insoluble pesticides, and sewage. The detergents and nitrates supply phosphorus and nitrate ions for the growth and development of algae. As a result, the algae grow luxuriantly and the algal mass becomes thicker and thicker until the lower layer receives no light. As a result, photosynthesis in the lower levels stops and decomposition of these layers begins and continues at a rapid rate. Under these conditions the decomposing bacteria use practically all of the oxygen, and the valuable edible fish die.

Oil from tankers is deleterious from two points of view: (1) the oil contains compounds that are toxic or poisonous to plants and fish and (2) the oil reduces the rate of diffusion of oxygen from the atmosphere into the water. This reduction in the diffusion of oxygen is likely to affect disadvantageously the behavior of beneficial organisms, the phytoplankton and edible fish.

The so-called hard pesticides retain their chemical structure for a relatively long time after they have been applied. Thus, the probability that they will injure beneficial organisms is quite high. For example, experiments have shown that DDT (diethyl-dimethyl-trichloro-ethane) as low as 10 parts per billion reduced the rate of photosynthesis of four species of phytoplankton, and a concentration of 100 parts per billion stopped the rate of this basic reaction. Thus, pesticides that reduce the rate of photosynthesis should be handled with the utmost care.

Sewage affects living things in the waters of the earth in much the same way as deep layers of algae, in that it reduces the rate of photosynthesis of phytoplankton and the oxygen supply for fish.

Pollution of the Soil

In general, clean soil consists of finely divided minerals and organic matter in various stages of decomposition, a certain amount of space between the particles and certain species of lower forms of plant life—the friendly bacteria. The decomposed minerals and organic matter supply essential elements for the growth of crop-plants and beneficial soil organisms; the spaces between the particles supply water and oxygen also for the growth of the crop-plants and the beneficial soil organisms; the nitrogen fixers take nitrogen from the air in the making of their protoplasm, the ammonifiers decompose the organic matter to ammonia, and the nitrifiers change the ammonia to nitrates. For the most part, substances that contaminate clean soils are the relatively stable, slowly degradable compounds, the so-called hard pesticides, and excess soluble salts. However, tests have shown that if the hard pesticides are applied at recommended quantities they become part of the soil and are found in streams only when soil itself is carried to the streams. In general, excess salts are removed by leaching with irrigation water.

THE ENERGY SUPPLY

In general, there are two kinds of energy: the energy of position or storage, known as potential energy, and the energy of motion, known as kinetic energy. According to the first law of the universe, energy cannot be created or destroyed. It can only be transformed. Thus, potential energy may be transformed to various forms of kinetic energy, and kinetic energy may be transformed to various forms of potential.

Supplies of Potential Energy

For the world as a whole the principal supplies exist as coal, natural gas, and oil. Millions of years ago the potential energy of these supplies existed as the kinetic energy of sunshine, and the transformation to potential energy was made possible by the basic fundamental biochemical reaction known as photosynthesis. In other words, green plants transformed the kinetic energy of light to the potential energy in coal, natural gas, and oil. The important thing for all citizens to remember is that these sources are definitely limited and exhaustible. As such they cannot last forever. For example, certain authorities state that the planet's supply of crude oil is likely to become scarce by the year 2000—a short period of 23 years—and that our relatively large supplies of coal and lignite will become scarce in about 500 years.

Supplies of Potential Energy within the United States

The lifestyle of the people of the United States requires tremendous quantities of potential energy. Most of this potential energy is derived from crude oil, with about 45 percent from wells within the country with the remaining 55 percent from wells outside the United States. This imported oil is very expensive and essentially results in the transfer of considerable quantities of wealth outside the United States.

The Need to Expend Energy to Get Energy

To become more self-sufficient in its energy requirements, the nation has undertaken Project Independence. However, projects of this type are feasible only if the energy content of the new source is greater than the energy required to discover, transfer, process, and carry the new source to the place of consumption. As a first example, consider the depth of oil wells at present (1977). The first wells in the United States had an average depth of 300 feet, in 1900 they had an average depth of 1,000 feet, and in 1927 and 1957 they had an average depth of 3,000 and 6,000 feet, respectively. Obviously, it takes more energy to bring oil from deep wells than from relatively shallow wells. As a second example, consider the amount of energy required to bring crude oil from the north slope of Alaska to the refineries in any one of the forty-eight contiguous states. As Clark[3] has pointed out, it takes energy to get energy. What is significant is the net energy not the gross energy of any new source. Net energy is that which is left after the new source has been discovered, processed, and transported to the place where it is to be used. In other words, net energy of any given product is equal to the gross energy of that product minus the sum total of the energy required to place the product in the hands of the consumer. Obviously, the gross energy per unit weight should be greater than the net energy.

Energy Expenditure of Important Crops. During World War I the American farmer began to substitute the farm tractor for horses and mules. This substitution has continued until at present (1977) most farmers depend entirely on petroleum products for their power needs. The question arises, Do crops vary in the amount of oil they need for their establishment and growth and development, and for harvesting

---

[3]Wilson Clark. 1975. "It Takes Energy to Get Energy. The law of diminishing returns is in effect," *Smithsonian Magazine*, 84-90.

and processing of the product? Note the data for the vegetable, fruit, and agronomic crops listed in table 15-2. In general, the vegetable crops require relatively high quantities, the citrus fruits, rice, and peanuts require moderate quantities, and the deciduous fruits and agronomic crops require low quantities. Fortunately, many major food crops of the world (e.g., wheat, sugarcane, and rice) require small quantities of energy for their establishment and culture.

Table 15-2.

AMOUNT OF OIL REQUIRED FOR THE PRODUCTION
OF CERTAIN CROPS IN THE UNITED STATES*

Crop	Barrels Oil/Acre/Year	Crop	Barrels Oil/Acre/Year
Tomatoes	18.4	Peaches	3.9
Lettuce	15.0	Apples	3.2
Snap beans	13.4	Grapes	2.7
Potatoes	9.6	Corn	3.6
Lemons	8.4	Sugarcane	1.8
Grapefruit	8.0	Soybeans	2.0
Rice	8.2	Oats	1.6
Peanuts	7.9	Wheat	0.6

*From Figure 1, *Frontiers of Plant Science*, Spring, 1975. Connecticut Agricultural Experiment Station, New Haven, CT.

Plant vs. Animal Products. What is the difference in amount of energy required for the production of plant and animal products? Consider the data in table 15-3. With the production of plant products there is a net gain in energy content. This is due to the light-trapping ability of photosynthesis, whereas in the production of animal products there is a net loss in energy. Nevertheless, the amount of energy required to produce animal products is relatively low. Heichel states, "The production of food on the farms of the United States requires the equivalent of 340 million barrels of oil per year. This is 2.6 percent of the nation's energy budget for the year [1975], one-tenth of the energy burned in all cars, trucks, trains and planes per year, and one-seventh of the energy used in heating buildings each year."[4] Consequently, the amount of oil used by farmers of the United States for the production of crops is much lower than that used by nonfarmers in their various enterprises and activities. Further, the reader should re-

[4]Gary H. Heichel. 1975. "Accounting for Energy Use in Food Production," *Frontiers of Plant Science*, Spring, 1975, Connecticut Agricultural Experiment Station, New Haven, CT.

Table 15-3.

AMOUNT OF OIL REQUIRED TO PRODUCE SUFFICIENT PLANT
AND ANIMAL PRODUCTS FOR ONE PERSON FOR ONE YEAR[*]

Kind of Product	Food Consumption (lbs/person/ year)	Daily Consumption (/person K Cal[a])	Energy Requirement for Production (K Cal[a])	Gain or Loss (K Cal[a])	Energy Requirement for Production (bb[b]/person)
Plant	786	2,010	1,320	690	0.33
Animal	666	1,380	3,630	-1,250	0.91

[*]From Tables 1 and 2, *Frontiers of Plant Science*, Spring, 1975, Connecticut
Agricultural Experiment Station, New Haven, CT.
[a]Kilogram calories.
[b]Barrel.

member that dairy cows and beef cattle are efficient converters of
inedible human foods to the edible form.

The Growing of Crops and Using Organic Waste Directly for Fuel

As previously stated, our planetary supplies of oil, natural gas, and
coal are the result of past net photosynthesis. In other words, the potential energy in these fossil fuels at one time existed as sunshine. Since
these fuels are expensive and exhaustible, the question arises concerning
the feasibility of using present-day sunshine for the growing of crops
and the using of organic wastes directly as fuel. According to Professor
Fred Benson, dean of the College of Engineering, Texas A and M University, the growing of crops, e.g., grain sorghum, for fuel, combined
with the use of organic wastes from agricultural sources as fuel, could
produce sufficient fuel to eliminate the need for the importation of oil
from other countries.[5] Obviously, this suggestion elicits further consideration.

Supplies of Kinetic Energy

The primary source of kinetic energy is the sun. The sun is a slow-
burning hydrogen furnace. Within its center and for every second 564
million tons of hydrogen are changed to 560 million tons of helium,
with the release of 4 million tons of kinetic energy. Not all of the

---

[5]C. G. Scruggs. 1975. "Can Agriculture Find an Answer to the Energy Crisis?"
Progressive Farmer, 21, 22, November.

kinetic energy that is directed toward Planet Earth reaches its surface. Some of the energy is absorbed by layers of ozone, or by carbon dioxide or water vapor in the troposphere. Nevertheless, the amount of kinetic energy that falls on Planet Earth is enormous. According to Wilhelm, "The solar energy which falls on the Arabian Peninsula in one year is twice the amount of oil reserves of the entire Planet." Further, the energy from the sun is clean and unlimited. In other words, its capture and use are restricted only by man's ingenuity in transforming it.

Use of the Sun's Energy Directly. In the past man has used the sun's energy directly in the formation of dams and windmills. In the formation of dams, the sun's energy changes liquid water to the vapor form that rises in the formation of clouds. Because of changes in temperature, the water vapor changes to liquid water, which drops to the surface in the form of rain. The rain in turn collects as streams or rivers on which man has built dams, which in turn drive generators for the production of electricity.

In the use of windmills the sun's energy creates currents of air. These currents in turn rotate the wind machines that run generators for the production of electricity. During the Christmas holiday season of 1939 the author visited a farming area in southwest Missouri. He discovered that each farm had a windmill, that each windmill was equipped with an electric generator, and that the produced energy was stored in a series of Delco batteries, which in turn provided lights for the home and the barn. Here is an excellent example of man's ingenuity in transforming the free and unpolluted energy of the wind to the kinetic energy of light.

The Need for Additional Research. Since the lifestyle of the people of the United States requires tremendous supplies of energy, and since present supplies are becoming scarce and expensive, the people, as a whole, have decided to become independent of outside sources and to undertake research projects that will eventually lead to independence from imported energy. Projects that involve the kinetic energy of the wind are (1) the development of vertical-axis wind towers, (2) the development of wind machines anchored just off the shore of the oceans, and (3) the production of electricity for the hydrolysis of water in the making of hydrocarbon fuel. Projects that involve the kinetic energy of the sun are (1) the use of solar heat collectors for the heating and cooling for homes and other buildings where members of the human race live and work, (2) the development of ocean thermal power stations and solar cells for the production of electricity, and (3) the development of solar satellites to collect and transform photons from the sun to microwaves for transmission to Planet Earth. Thus, if the lifestyle of the people of underdeveloped countries develops along the same lines as that of the people of the United States and other developed countries, the need for potential and kinetic energy for any given unit of time will be tremendous, and opportunities for doing constructive work in solving the energy problems of the planet will be accordingly tremendous.

THE DEGREE OF AFFLUENCE AND LIVING SPACE PER FAMILY

The Degree of Affluence

In general, affluence refers to the acquisition of wealth per family or individual. As is well known, families throughout the United States vary in degree of wealth or affluence. They may be classified as follows:

1. *The extremely affluent.* Examples are the Rockefeller, Kennedy, and Ford (motorcar) families and the families of presidents of large corporations.

2. *The affluent.* Examples are the families of presidents of relatively small corporations or businesses, the editors and publishers of nationwide magazines and newspapers, the presidents and vice-presidents of public universities, and the presidents and vice-presidents of private universities.

3. *The moderately affluent.* Examples are the families of senior scientists of public and private research organizations, the full and associate professors of public and private universities, and the superintendents and shop foremen of food-processing plants, industrial factories, and refining plants.

4. *The slightly affluent.* Examples are the families of assistant professors and instructors of tax-supported universities, public school teachers, blue-collar workers in food-processing plants, industrial factories, and refining plants, salesmen of manufactured products, and retired persons with an income in addition to that from Social Security.

5. *The nonaffluent.* Examples are families with an income slightly above, equal to, or lower than that required to meet the basic needs for food, clothing, and shelter.

For the most part, the proportion of families in each class has always been dynamic, with the changes taking place in the upward direction. In other words, the degree of affluence has always increased rather than decreased.

Living Space per Family

In general, a family may be defined as one, two, or more persons living in a house trailer; one, two, or more persons living in an apartment; or one, two, or more persons living in a house. The amount of living space per family varies more or less directly with the degree of affluence. At one extreme is the extremely rich family, with its large estates, one or more large, well-landscaped residences, and its well-kept, parklike grounds; and at the other extreme is the poor family living in a trailer or a small house situated on a small city lot. In other words, extremely rich families occupy the most space, followed by the affluent, the moderately affluent, slightly affluent, and the nonaffluent, in descending order named. Because living space on Planet Earth is limited, it follows that the number of families the planet can carry for any given unit of time without crowding is in direct relation to the degree of affluence per family; that is, the greater the degree of affluence per family, the less will be the number of families Planet Earth can carry from one year to the next. The question arises, What is the optimum number of families for Planet Earth? To what degree of affluence is each family entitled? In the author's opinion this relation of the degree of affluence to the density of the population is extremely significant in human affairs. Clearly, this relation and its implications should be put before all of the people in order that a planetwide debate can take place on the subject, and a planetwide policy can be developed and established.

INDIVIDUAL FREEDOMS, RIGHTS, AND RESPONSIBILITIES

In 1942, Franklin Delano Roosevelt, president of the United States, and Sir Winston Spencer Churchill, prime minister of Great Britain, promulgated four freedoms or rights to all persons on Planet Earth, regardless of race, color, sex, ethnic origin, or creed. These freedoms are: (1) freedom of speech or expression; that is, everyone has the right to his own opinion; (2) freedom of religion; that is, everyone has the right to worship God in his own way; (3) freedom from want; that is, everyone has the right to an abundant supply of nutritious food and adequate clothing and shelter; and (4) freedom from fear; that is, every person is entitled to live in the absence of physical or mental harassment or aggression. To these four freedoms another freedom or right may be added: (5) the freedom or right of every individual to develop himself to his fullest capacity.[6]

However, to each individual freedom or right there is a corresponding responsibility. With freedom of speech or expression every individual has the responsibility to avoid using false, libelous, or slanderous ex-

---

[6]These freedoms are an outgrowth of England's Magna Charter, 1215, the English Bill of Rights, 1689, the Virginia Declaration of Rights, 1776, the Constitution of the United States, 1791, the Morrill Land-Grant Act, 1862, and the Universal Declaration of Human Rights, 1948.

pressions against his neighbor; with freedom of religion he has the responsibility to permit his neighbor to worship God in his own way; with freedom from want he has the responsibility to help others acquire the basic essentials with respect to food, clothing, and shelter; with freedom from fear, every individual has the responsibility to promote an environment free from harassment or assault, and with freedom of growth and development every individual has the responsibility to help others to develop their potentialities into constructive actualities. The five freedoms or rights and the corresponding responsibility of each are presented in table 15-4.

Table 15-4.

FIVE FREEDOMS AND THEIR CORRESPONDING RESPONSIBILITIES

Freedom or Right	Responsibility
of speech or expression	to avoid slander or libel
of religion	to permit others to worship God in their own way
from want	to assist others to acquire the basic essentials with respect to food, clothing, and shelter
from fear	to remove fear of harassment or aggression
of growth and development	to help others to grow and develop

The Need for Self-Discipline

Self-discipline involves both individual rights and responsibilities. For example, a motorist has the right to use the highway, but he has the responsibility to discipline himself to observe the rules of the road and to drive within the posted speed limits; a student has the right to learn, but he has the responsibility to discipline himself to meet classes and complete assignments; a researcher has the freedom to discover new knowledge, but he has the responsibility to confine his work to the assigned field of investigation; a teacher or extension worker has the right to disseminate new knowledge, but he has the responsibility to limit this knowledge to the field within which he is an authority; a factory worker has the right to a constructive job, but he has the responsibility to discipline himself to give a "full day's work for a full day's pay"; and the farmer has the right of decision in the growing of crops, but he has the responsibility to discipline himself to the growing of crops that will add to the nation's food, fiber, and lumber supply. Many other examples could be cited. In other words, without self-discipline there would be a lack of progress in the solution of problems. This in turn would result in chaos and decay and the dissolution of the beloved country.

THE BASIC BLESSINGS OF AMERICA

The basic blessings of America are (1) the production of an abundant supply of nutritious food at reasonable cost to the consumer, and (2) the opportunity for all of the people to develop themselves to their fullest capacity without injury to others. Certain factors are in harmony with the operation of these blessings, whereas others are not.

Factors in harmony are (1) the geophysiographic position of the United States as discussed in the preceding topic, (2) the division of fertile areas into relatively small tracts, with each tract owned and operated by a farm family[7], (3) the recognition on the part of the people that the first step in the development of the abundant life is a strong and efficient agriculture, (4) the research and extension workers of colleges and universities banding themselves together as interdisciplinary teams to solve pertinent problems in all fields of human endeavor, (5) the right of the farmer and the industrialist to make decisions under our system of enlightened free enterprise, (6) the open borders between adjacent states permitting the free flow of raw materials and manufactured goods from one to the other, (7) the open communication between all persons in all states permitting the free flow of constructive ideas from one to the other, and (8) the positive attitude of the faculty and staff of the Morrill land-grant colleges to the solution of problems.

Factors not in harmony are: (1) the damaging misconceptions with reference to the federal budget, (2) a lack of understanding on the part of the people as a whole that they cannot get "something for nothing," (3) a lack of a nationwide land policy, particularly with reference to the highly productive, fertile crop-plant production areas, (4) the need to educate all of the people that all of the resources of spaceship Earth are definitely limited and finite with the exception of the light energy it receives from the sun,[8] (5) the lack of definite information on the relation of the degree of affluence to the population density, and (6) the relation of population density to human activity.

---

[7]According to the Census of Agriculture for 1969 there were 1,480,565 family farms, 1,221,535 partnership-operated farms, and 21,516 corporation-type farms. Investigations have shown that the family farm is more efficient than the corporation farm.

[8]Even though the light energy from the sun is infinite and unlimited, its use is definitely limited by man's ingenuity in capturing and using it.

*The Unique Problem-Solving Experience of the
Morrill Land-Grant Colleges*

Since their establishment in 1862, the Morrill land-grant colleges have always been engaged in the solution of problems—first problems in the field of agriculture, home economics, and engineering and now (1978) problems in practically all fields. Thus, they have had over a century of experience in the solution of problems and in teaching the people how to apply the results of research to the solution of their problems. Despite certain reports to the contrary,[9] the Morrill land-grant colleges and universities have been highly successful in the solution of problems and in promoting the welfare of the people. With the continued support and encouragement of the people (the taxpayers), combined with the freedom required of all research (the search for truth), and for all teaching (the dissemination of the truth), there is no question that the Morrill land-grant colleges and universities can solve the pertinent problems of the present and the immediate future.

May the basic blessings of America spread to all the people on Planet Earth.

FIGURE 15.3 *Old Glory and the flag of Mississippi on the campus of Mississippi State University. The flags and flagpole were donated to the University by the University Horticulture Club as part of the country's Bicentennial celebration.*

Problems of the Present and the Immediate Future*199*

REFERENCES

Anon. 1974. "The Imperative Need for a U.S. Food and Agriculture Policy," *Progressive Farmer*, 89, No. 12.

An argument that any given area of fertile land should be assessed according to its productivity rather than its real estate value.

Anon. 1942. "The Four Freedoms of the Atlantic Charter." *Congressional Digest*, 21:227-228.

Four universal freedoms as developed and promulgated jointly by Franklin D. Roosevelt and Winston S. Churchill.

Barrons, Keith C. 1975. *The Food in Your Future.* Van Nostrand-Reinhold Co. New York, NY.

An eminent crop-plant scientist presents a forthright discussion on food production problems within the United States and what the citizens must do to assure themselves of a continuous supply of high-quality food at reasonable cost.

Caldwell, John T., and Giles, William L. 1968. "Agriculture, Morality and Freedom," *Progressive Farmer*, January.

Two land-grant university presidents discuss three keys to the future of America: the continuous maintenance of a strong agriculture, the continuous search for truth in all phases of human behavior, and the continuous advancement of freedom to all the people.

Chancellor, W. J., and Goss, J. R. 1976. "Balancing Energy and Food Production," *Science*, 192, No. 4236, April 16.

Two eminent agricultural engineers discuss the relation of population growth to the food supply in both developed and underdeveloped countries.

Coleman, Charles H. 1941. "You and the Bill of Rights," *American Legion Magazine*, 31: No. 6, December.

The individual rights as embodied in the first ten Articles of the Constitution of the United States and their corresponding duties or responsibilities.

Dennis, Landt. 1977. "A New Gust of Yankee Ingenuity," *Country Gentleman*, 127, No. 3, Summer.

A review of research projects on transforming wind power to electricity by the federal government and state agencies and by private corporations and individuals.

Keller, George C. 1968. "The Biggest Gamble in History: Our Investment in People," *Reader's Digest*, 93, December.

The relation of education of the individual to the prosperity of the nation.

Reuther, Walter. 1963. "As Horticulture Enters Its Second Century," *Proceedings of the American Society of Horticultural Science*, 83:855-861.

An eminent horticultural scientist discusses the changes that took place in American agriculture from 1900 to 1960 and assesses some of the problems of the present and the immediate future.

---

[9]Jim Hightower. 1973. *Hard Tomatoes Hard Times: A Report of the Accountability Project on the Failure of America's Land-Grant College Complex.* Schenkman Publishing Company, Cambridge, MA.

Von Habsburg, Otto. 1977. "The World Food Shortage," *Country Gentleman,*
     Winter, pp. 24, 26, 27.
          The author presents the hypothesis that the operation of the Marxist
     Leninist economic system is primarily responsible for the low food produc-
     tion in the Soviet Union, mainland China, and India.
Wilhelm, John L. 1976. "Solar Energy: The Ultimate Power House," *National
     Geographic,* 149, No. 3, March.
          The author points out that in the past the people of the United States
     have for the most part relied on a single source of energy, first with wood
     (1776-1800), later with coal (1800-1950), and now with natural gas and
     oil (1950-1975.) He states further that by 2020 with adequate research
     and development, six sources, the sun, oil, natural gas, coal, dams, and
     wind may collectively meet the nation's needs.
Young, G., and Blair, J. P. 1970. "Pollution, Threat to Man's Only Home,"
     National Geographic, 138, No. 6, 735-780.
          A forceful and well-illustrated account of the effects of polluted air and
     polluted water on the behavior of living things and of man's progress in
     cleaning the air and the waters.

INDEX*

Affluence, 194-95
  degree, 194
  living space for family, 194-95
Agriculture
  colonial, 3
  curricula, 60
  fields, 58
  lack of science, 29-30
  meaning, 17
  North American Indian, 3
  resident teaching, 59
  status of 1862-1870, 23
  trains, 23
Agriculture Adjustment Act, 128
Agriculture College of the State of Michigan, 7-8, 59-60
Agriculture Experiment Stations, 38-53
  accomplishments, 52-53
  federal, 50-52
  funds, 44
  reasons for, 38
  state, 39-49
Agriculture Extension Service, 38-83
  directors, 81-82
  first county agents, 76-77
  publications, 94
  relation to other organizations, 95
  specialists, 81
Air pollution research center, 187
Alaska purchase, 5
Alumni Organizations, 148
America
  basic blessings, 197-98
    factors in harmony, 197
    factors not in harmony, 197
American Association of Agricultural Teachers, 61
American dream, 104
American Telephone and Telegraph Company, 171

Ames Ambulance Unit, 118
Appropriations, reductions in, 124-25
Armistice, effect of, 119-20
Army Special Training Program (ASTP), 135
Attachment difficulties, 32-37
Automorphs, 117

Bailey, Liberty Hyde, 162
Bankhead-Jones Act, 129
Black Morrill Land-Grant Colleges, 63-65, t. 63
Blitzkreig, 131
Board of Trustees, 8, 9, 11, 12, 13, 60, 130, 144, 162, 165
Borlaug, Norman E., 154

Calvert, C. B., 10
Carbon monoxide, 187-88
Cary, Freeman G., 22
Change in name, 112-14, t. 113
Charter, nature of, 15
Chemistry, 134
Chicago and North Western, 104
Chlorophyll, 88, 156, 177
Civil War, 12, 18, 25, 185
  effect of, 26
Classical colleges, attitude of, 29
Clemson, Thomas Green, 20
Clemson Agricultural College, 165
Climatic regions, 102, t. 103
Colonial agriculture, 3-4
Continuation education, 145-47
  facilities for, 147
  organization, 146-47
  type of work, 147
  reasons for, 146
Corn, 3
Cornell, Ezra, 145
Cornell University, 169

---

*Page references preceded by *t* indicate tables.

201